I am dead

when I'm dead

of earth

d the skin

ai and blue eyes

d than at birth

howling in

~~kstattig~~ came in the w
~~ckld the skies~~

By the same author
A Strong Song Tows Us: The Life of Basil Bunting

SIMPLIFY ME

THE LIFE OF KEITH DOUGLAS

Richard Burton

infiniteideas

Copyright © Richard Burton, 2020

The right of Richard Burton to be identified as the author of this book has been asserted in
accordance with the Copyright, Designs and Patents Act 1988.
First published in 2020 by
Infinite Ideas Limited
www.infideas.com

A CIP catalogue record for this book is available from the British Library
ISBN 978–1–913022–24–2

Front cover: Keith Douglas in the desert
Endpapers image courtesy of the British Library

Printed in Great Britain

CONTENTS

To Aileen, born in the same decade as Keith Douglas

INTRODUCTION

On 8 June 1944, two days after D-Day, Keith Douglas's regiment, the Sherwood Rangers, pushed on south of Bayeux in northern France, crossing the N13 road, and according to the historian of the Normandy landings, James Holland, they made a right hook towards the village of Audrieu and took up positions on a ridge overlooking the villages of Saint-Pierre, Tilly-sur-Seulles and Fontenay-le-Pesnel. Along the top of the ridge a track ran, lined by beech trees, with woods beyond. Beyond Tilly lay the next ridge, which gave a commanding position with clear views to the long ridge that barred the route south. Moving his tanks forward of the track, Major Stanley Christopherson, the regiment's commanding officer, ordered them into positions in the trees beyond, directly overlooking Saint-Pierre. It seemed quiet in the village but he sent Douglas, his second-in-command, and one of his troop commanders, Lieutenant John Bethell-Fox, down in their Sherman tanks to reconnoitre. In the village they discovered most of the civilians hiding in their cellars, but eventually they persuaded one old man to come out and he told them Germans were already in the village and had tanks in Tilly. Douglas and Bethell-Fox went back towards their waiting tanks only to walk straight into a German patrol. Both parties were so surprised that they each turned and fled, Douglas firing his revolver wildly as he ran.[1]

Christopherson wrote in his diary that on the following morning:

Keith Douglas, my second-in-command, was hit in the head by a piece of mortar shell as he was running along a ditch towards his tank, and was killed instantly … When he joined the Regiment he appeared to have a grudge against the world in general and particularly his fellow Yeomanry officers, of whom there were quite a few at that time, who had been with the Regiment before the war and consisted of the wealthy landed gentry: these he regarded as complete snobs and accused of being utterly intolerant of anyone unable to 'talk horses' or who had not been educated at an English public school. He was a complete individualist, intolerant of military convention and discipline,

1

which made life for him and his superior officers difficult. His artistic talents were clearly illustrated by his many drawings and the poetry that he wrote very much in the modern strain, and, had he lived, I am convinced that he would have made a name for himself in the world of art. I recall so many times at various conferences and order groups having to upbraid him for drawing on his map instead of paying attention.

In action he had undaunted courage and always showed initiative and complete disregard for his own personal safety. At times he appeared even to be somewhat foolhardy – maybe on account of his short-sightedness, which compelled him to wear large, thick-lensed glasses. I regret that he was not spared to know that he was mentioned-in-despatches for outstanding service.[2]

Douglas wrote a book, *Alamein to Zem Zem*, about the Regiment and the desert campaign in North Africa, which he asked Christopherson to read and write a foreword to. Douglas disguised all the regiment's personalities with fictitious names and included some unkind and unjustified allusions to certain officers who had been killed. Christopherson insisted he omit these for the sake of next-of-kin who would find such references hurtful.

Christopherson continued: 'In the original text he described my dancing as being "deplorable", to which I objected, pointing out that he had never seen my efforts on the dance floor and that I considered myself well above the average, and as a result of my protest he agreed to alter the text.' Holland comments that Douglas

> ... was as good as his word, and by the time *Alamein to Zem Zem* was published, Stanley's dancing had been upgraded to 'competent' in the 'restrained English style'. It says much about Stanley, however, that what he objected to was the description of his dancing when some of the other comments Douglas made about him might, on the face of it, have seemed more hurtful ... Padre Leslie Skinner claimed that Douglas had had premonitions of his death, although John Semken remembers him talking about wanting to be part of the invasion so that he could then write about it. 'He wasn't proposing to write about it hereafter, was he?' says John. Stuart Hills, a new troop commander in C Squadron who had been befriended by Douglas, thinks it was inevitable that, after several years of war, those who had survived until then would harbour fears of approaching death.'[3]

As Vernon Scannell says, 'I do not think there can be much doubt that Keith Douglas was haunted by a strong premonition of his own death in action. It might be objected that every man in a fighting unit at that quite early stage of the war would suffer a similar feeling of his impending and violent end, but the truth is that the majority of fighting men, while rationally conscious of the chances of their being killed in action, did not really believe that they would be chosen. They feared death, were uneasily aware that his choice of victim was random, but this is a vastly different condition from Douglas's amazingly brave, clear-sighted and unhistrionic contemplation of the inevitable.'[4]

Douglas wasn't the first soldier poet to have had something like a death wish. Alan Seeger, who was killed in action in 1916, wrote:

I have a rendezvous with Death
At some disputed barricade,
When Spring comes back with rustling shade
And apple-blossoms fill the air –
I have a rendezvous with Death
When Spring brings back blue days and fair.'[5]

But Douglas had a strange premonition of death. In 1940 another poet, John Waller, in the second part of his essay, 'Oxford poetry and disillusionment', in *Poetry Review* wrote: 'Keith Douglas is one of the keenest, most musical, and careful poets Oxford has produced. He subjects all his work to a searching critical analysis and is rarely contented with inferior workmanship … Recently Douglas has become obsessed with the question of death.'[6]

Raymond Pennock, his friend and rugby-playing colleague at Merton, recalled that Douglas was sure that he would join a good cavalry regiment and that he would 'bloody well make my mark in this war. For I will not come back.' Pennock also remembered him saying that his name would be on the next one as they passed a First World War memorial.[7]

We think of Keith Douglas, if we think of him at all, as a war poet; perhaps the most important poet of the Second World War. But the merest glance at the complete poems show that over 75 per cent were written before Douglas had any direct experience of war.[8] Ted Hughes wrote in 1964 that 'now, twenty years after his death, it is becoming clear that he offers more than just a few poems about war, and that every poem he wrote, whether about war or not, has some special value.'[9]

Hughes reflected on the evolution of the poetry of Keith Douglas's short career:

Leaving his virtuoso juvenilia, his poetry passed through two roughly distinguishable phases, and began to clarify into a third. The literary influences on this progress seem to have been few. To begin with, perhaps he takes Auden's language over pretty whole, but he empties it of its intellectual concerns, turns it into the practical experience of life, and lets a few minor colours of the late 1930s poetry schools creep in. But his temperament is so utterly modern he seems to have no difficulty with the terrible, suffocating, maternal octopus of ancient English poetic tradition.

The first phase of his growth shows itself in the poem titled 'Forgotten the Red Leaves'. He has lost nothing since 'Encounter with a God', but gained a new range of imagination, a new ease of transition from image to image. Yet in this particular poem the fairyland images are being remembered by one still partly under their spell, indulging the dream, and this mode of immaturity is the mark of this first phase, which lasts until he leaves Oxford in 1940.

Before he leaves, a poem titled 'The Deceased' heralds the next stage. Here, the picturesque or merely decorative side of his imagery disappears; his descriptive powers sharpen to realism. The impression is of a sudden mobilizing of the poet's will, a clearing of his vision, as if from sitting considering possibilities and impossibilities he had stood up to act. Pictures of things no longer interest him much: he wants their substance, their nature, and their consequences in life. At once, and quite suddenly, his mind is whole, as if united by action, and he produces poetry that is both original and adult. Already, in … 'The Deceased', we can see what is most important of all about Douglas. He has not simply added poems to poetry, or evolved a sophistication. He is a renovator of language. It is not that he uses words in jolting combinations, or with titanic extravagance, or curious precision. His triumph lies in the way he renews the simplicity of ordinary talk, and he does this by infusing every word with a burning exploratory freshness of mind – partly impatience, partly exhilaration at speaking the forbidden thing, partly sheer casual ease of penetration. The music that goes along with this, the unresting variety of intonation and movement within his patterns, is the natural path of such confident, candid thinking.

There is nothing studied about this new language. Its air of improvisation is a vital part of its purity. It has the trenchancy of an inspired jotting, yet leaves no doubt about the completeness and subtlety of his impressions, or the thoroughness of his artistic conscience. The poem titled 'Egypt', for instance, could be a diary note, yet how could it be improved as a poem?

The war brought his gift to maturity, or to a first maturity...[Douglas] showed in his poetry no concern for man in society. The murderous skeleton in the body of a girl, the dead men being eaten by dogs on the moonlit desert, the dead man behind the mirror, these items of circumstantial evidence are steadily out-arguing all his high spirits and hopefulness.

Technically, each of the poems of this second phase rests on some single objective core, a scene or event or thing. But one or two of them, and one in particular, start something different: the poems are 'On a Return from Egypt' and 'Simplify me when I'm Dead'. Their inner form is characterized not by a single object of attraction, but a constellation of statements. In the second of these poems, more liberated than the first, Douglas consummates his promise. Here he has identified a style that seems able to deal poetically with whatever it comes up against. It is not an exalted verbal activity to be attained for short periods, through abstinence, or a submerged dream treasure to be fished up when the everyday brain is half-drugged. It is a language for the whole mind, at its most wakeful, and in all situations. A utility general-purpose style, as, for instance, Shakespeare's was, that combines a colloquial prose readiness with poetic breadth, a ritual intensity and music of an exceedingly high order with clear direct feeling, and yet in the end is nothing but casual speech. This is an achievement for which we can be grateful.[10]

I have quoted Hughes at length because he seems to have been the first well-known poet to have appreciated Douglas's work, although Robin Fedden wrote that the Cairo poets considered Douglas's 'war poems [as] near the top of the small body of presentable English poetry that the war has thrown off.'[11]

It is pointless to speculate on what Keith Douglas would have become had he not been killed in action in 1944 but, as Declan Ryan wrote in the *Times Literary Supplement*, when he died he 'had arrived at a poetic maturity and accomplishment that almost defied belief.'[12] G. S. Fraser did speculate, however, in his 1956 Chatterton Lecture to the British Academy: 'if he had been spared … he might well be, today, the dominating figure of his generation and a wholesome and inspiring influence on younger men. He had courage, passion and generosity. These are three qualities that our age generally needs.'[13]

If Douglas was a 'war poet' the obvious comparison is with the famous poets of the First World War, Owen, Sassoon, Graves, Brooke, Thomas and Rosenberg. Douglas was scathing about the quality of the poetry of the Second World War, but what was the difference? Douglas himself was sure that it was because the poets of the Second World War had nothing new to say. In an article written in May 1943 but not published until April 1971 he wrote that 'hell cannot be let loose twice: it was let loose in the Great War and it is the same old hell now. The hardships, pain and boredom; the behaviour of the living, and the appearance of the dead, were so accurately described by the poets of the Great War that everyday on the battlefields of the western desert – and no doubt on the Russian battlefields as well – their poems are illustrated. Almost all that a modern poet on active service is inspired to write, would be tautological.' The other reason for the difference is the one innovation of modern warfare that Douglas saw, the relative mobility of war, which 'does not give the same opportunities for writing as the long routines of trench warfare.'[14] This is more plausible than it perhaps may seem. Poets are ingenious and they will write about something else if the obvious subject is taken away. They could not be 'war' poets in the tradition of Wilfred Owen and Siegfried Sassoon. The sheer pointlessness of all this fighting had been captured perfectly in Owen's sonnet 'Futility', and we are perhaps less shocked by the crowd of flies around the German corpse in Douglas's 'Vergissmeinnicht' if we have encountered Rosenberg's queer, sardonic rat in 'Break of day in the trenches'. We are shocked by the laconic delivery not the subject of Douglas's poem. Its matter-of-fact tone stresses the universality of death in war. As Henri Barbusse famously wrote: 'Two armies fighting is one great army that kills itself.' We should not be surprised by the condition of any corpse, regardless of its nationality. As Lorrie Goldensohn said, 'little remained for the soldier-poets of World War II to do but reiterate, or amplify, the witness given in 1914–18.'[15]

The inhumanity and violence unleashed before and during the Second World War was so great that it seemed to be beyond poetry. It is unlikely that Theodor Adorno was alone in thinking that 'to write a poem after Auschwitz is barbaric'.[16] Douglas's view was later endorsed by Vernon Scannell, another poet who saw action in the north African desert: 'The authentic British poetry of the Second World War was not a poetry of protest, still less was it a poetry inspired by patriotic enthusiasm … The serviceman of 1939–45 could not be disillusioned because he held no illusions to start with.'[17] Scannell also saw the point of the relative mobility of the Second World War: 'The Second World War had no fixed habitation. It was a mobile war. Soldiers were not long enough in one place for a single warscape to establish itself in the imagination and memory. Even in the Western Desert, where one might have expected a sameness of surroundings, progress was fast and changes of physical detail fairly frequent. It is true that a dug-out in No-Man's Land would hardly prove the ideal place for meditation and the composition of poetry, but at least there would be quite lengthy periods of inactivity when it would be possible, however difficult, to put words down on paper.'[18]

There is also the assumption that the first war was particularly meaningless, essentially about the exploitation of overseas territories by European countries, whereas there was a necessary outcome of the second war, the eradication of totalitarianism. Douglas himself was sure that Hitler had to be stopped (as he made clear to his old Merton College tutor, the First World War poet Edmund Blunden, in his letter of April/May 1944[19]). Basil Bunting, one of the greatest British poets of the twentieth century, made the same point. Bunting had been a conscientious objector in the first war. 'During the First World War,' he said, 'it was possible to believe, I did believe, that it was a totally unnecessary war fought for purely selfish ends, to get hold of markets and things like that. You couldn't believe that, in the second one at all. It was perfectly obvious for years beforehand that nothing short of war and violence would ever stop Hitler and his appalling career.'[20] As Robert Graves said: 'it is extremely unlikely that [the poet of the Second World War] will feel any qualms about the justice of the British cause or about the necessity of the war's continuance; so that, even if he has experienced the terrors of an air raid, he will not feel obliged to write horrifically about it, to draw attention to the evils of war.'[21]

We now think of the poetry of the First World War as overwhelmingly critical of political and military leaders' strategy and tactics, articulating a sense of hopeless valour in the teeth of insuperable horror, but this is largely because the poetry that has survived (because it is the best) was written by poets who subscribed to the view that it was the futility and horror that needed to be in a perverse sense celebrated. In fact, of the 2,225 poets who published during the years of the war hardly any expressed the views that have for generations of students defined its poetry.[22] Jon Stallworthy wrote that 'the poems of the Second World War have had less impact – not because they were less good, but because the reading public has become increasingly attuned to prose, and because the Word (prose as well as verse) has increasingly lost ground to the Image.'[23] As Worth Howard, the acting Dean of the Faculty of Arts and Science at the American University at Cairo, put it in his preface to *Oasis*, the original anthology of Middle East forces, in 1943: 'Newsreels and daily broadcasts have kept the public far better informed of the progress of the forces than has been possible in any previous war. An untold number of photographs have been taken, showing men in action and recording the aftermath of battle. Cartoonists and artists have employed their skill to portray scenes on the battlefield and life away from the front.'[24] Howard went on to praise the cultural life of the forces: 'thousands of men have searched for beauty in a variety of forms. With what evident joy have they flocked to concert halls to hear a Beethoven sonata, a Brahms concerto, a Schubert symphony. Men have crowded the cathedral courtyard to listen to a Handel oratorio. They have sought hungrily for the privilege of good books. Men and officers have gathered to share their love of poetry – others have read and acted plays together ... Let no man say that all those in uniform have become simply cogs in a machine – that military discipline has made of them mere automatons.'[25] The poets of the Second World War were not silenced by their lack of culture. Lawrence Durrell recalled that in desperation at the lack of reading material one officer had erected a plyboard panel with a few hastily assembled poems and satires and asked for more contributions. Within a day the board was covered with poems and the officer was obliged to increase the size of the notice board.[26]

But if the war's futility and horror had been taken from the Second World War poets as a subject what did they write about? The answer is that they wrote about the war, but in a different way. Scannell again: 'If the poet in uniform was going to register in his work the changes that occurred in the *Zeitgeist* since 1914, and he could scarcely do otherwise, it ought to have been obvious that, in 1939 or 1940, he would not be writing the same sort of poetry as the young soldier-poets were producing at the outbreak of the First World War.'[27] As John Cromer put it in his essay, 'Poetry To-Day', in *Oasis*: 'The emotions produced by war are subjects for poetry and in all wars poets have been quick to appreciate this and capture their stress in their words.'[28] The poets of the Second World War were no different.

Douglas's mother wrote of her son: 'He was happy by nature, but the futile suffering of the world and the inability of such a large proportion to appreciate beauty in any form depressed him heavily at times. He did not have a conventional artistic temperament because he understood and appreciated the ordinary man too well. But he had the extreme sensitivity of the artist and I think there was no sensation of fear, pity, misery, hate, pain, love, and exhilaration which he had not felt to the full. He seemed able to achieve a complete absorption in his full pursuit of any given moment to the exclusion of all else; and he had the faculty of looking on himself from a distance, as it were – seeing his faults and assets as though he were judging another person.'[29] G. S. Fraser, the poet and critic who knew Douglas in Cairo, assessed Douglas's character in his Chatterton Lecture:

> Douglas's attitude to war was, though humane and deeply compassionate, a heroic attitude. It had nothing in common with the humanitarian, pacifist attitudes of contemporaries of his like Nicholas Moore or Alex Comfort or Douglas's friend, John Hall. He was a good soldier, and in a sense he enjoyed his war. He enjoyed, at least, the exercise of the will in action. He was an officer, and an efficient officer, who enjoyed the company of his fellow officers, and accepted and enjoyed the responsibility that went with his rank … he was a very intelligent man, as these aphorisms ['On the Nature of Poetry' in *Augury*] on poetry prove, but not a man, I think, who had much use for intellectual chatter. The two or three times I personally met him, I do not remember our exchanging a word on any abstract topic. Whatever else he may have pined for during the war years, it will not have been evening parties in Chelsea … He was an aloof, gay, and passionate man. He loved risk. The state of the world, and perhaps the nature of man, and perhaps his own nature in its depths, filled him with profound sadness; nevertheless, for him the sadness of human existence was a kind of destiny that had to be bravely and lovingly embraced. He was as far as can be from a nagging or carping attitude to life.'[30]

After Douglas's death his mother wrote to Maurice Wollman: 'His last completed poem ('On a Return from Egypt') reflects, I think, his doubts and urges – his longing to carry out the things he once planned and looked forward to – all the writings, illustrations, back-cloths … all the travel. And through all, the sense that if he did not face and share in every experience that came his way neither could he write any more. So for him there was no other choice despite his fear. So he went. He might have stayed in a safer spot. But I understand he couldn't. He always loathed the "safety first" idea, holding that one might as well be dead as afraid to move. He believed in venturing and having – or losing if need be. If he had lived to be a thousand I think he would still have gone on trying to weave his gathered experiences and knowledge into some comprehensible pattern of words and shapes – or sounds.'[31]

Unmaternal commentators weren't so generous. R. J. Sapsford wrote an essay in *The Blue* (the official magazine of Christ's Hospital school) of January 1966 comparing Douglas and Blunden. He describes Douglas at school, saying 'this strange mixture of the aesthete and the athlete, as a contemporary called him, was always something of an enigma, respected but not liked by his contemporaries, treasured by a handful of masters, condemned by the majority for his insolence. "He was very loyal to his friends," Mr. Hornsby [his housemaster at Christ's] writes, "but a great hater of injustice and of those whom he did not like"; apparently the latter were in the majority. A contemporary at Oxford describes him as an unattractive person, unimpressive at first meeting, with small eyes hidden behind glasses set high on a large, fleshy nose. He also claims to have detected in him a marked tendency to latch on to people, to demand their company without giving much in return; this judgement may well be a fair one, for he knew what he wanted and was not slow to ask for it …'[32]

One of Douglas's contemporaries, C. T. Hatten, reacted angrily to this characterization of Douglas in *The Blue*, pointing out that he was 'a member of the Blackberries, a school concert party that flourished in the thirties. You were elected to it by the other members … and you had to be amiable and amusing and prepared to make a fool of yourself. If you look at the photograph if the 1st XV, 1937–38, you will see Douglas with a great grin on his face which was as often there as not.'[33]

Sapsford rejected Hatten's criticism in the same issue[34] but Hatten was supported by the Director General of the National Book League, J. E. Morpugo, who, though he wasn't a particular friend of Douglas, was in the unusual position of knowing him both at school and in the army. Morpugo told a story about rugby when he and Douglas had been on a training course in Sarafand in Palestine: 'We … found ourselves playing rugger for a very scratch side against an even more scratch side. We were ordered to play centre-threequarter, something that neither of us had ever done before. Keith let it be known to our opponents that I was wearing a Richmond jersey (it was in fact my old House jersey) because my modesty would not allow me to wear my England colours. He emphasized the subterfuge without words by himself wearing a plain blue jersey and white shorts and insisting that Douglas was a good Scots name, and once on the field we did nothing fast except talk, to the entire confusion of the opposition who were lured into belief in our skill to the tune of some 30 or 40 points.'[35]

Blunden himself probably had it right in his 1966 introduction to Douglas's *Collected Poems*: 'Keith's character was … complex in the manner of many artists. Against his generosity and zest for life must be placed, if the portrait is to be (as he would have wished it to be) true to life, certain less endearing qualities – an impulsive and obstinate streak which was sometimes the despair of even his closest friends.'[36]

The rest of this book explores the enigmatic character of Keith Douglas and the dispassionate poetry he produced. As with Henry James's Roderick Hudson it appears that Douglas's friends and family had to tolerate a great deal of erratic behaviour in the process of enjoying his genius. Douglas was not always easy to like but he had a boarding school upbringing from the age of 6, before he went up to Oxford (then a largely male domain) and then joined the army, not an ideal preparation for social success.

I

CHILDHOOD

THE ARRIVAL OF A MILITARIST

The First World War changed everything. By January 1920 Britain was shell-shocked.[1] The armistice that had ended the bloodiest war in history had been signed only in November 1918. Those lucky enough to return from the war found that Blighty had changed utterly. The news might have been dominated by the post-war settlement that culminated in the Treaty of Versailles, but outside Fleet Street the rest of society was adjusting rapidly to the new realities of post-war life. As A. J. P. Taylor put it, 'freedom burst out overnight.'[2]

Young men, who in normal circumstances might never have left the places where they had been born, had suddenly had the opportunity to see foreign countries and brought home their exotic experiences. Older men had forsaken retirement and returned to farms to increase food supplies. Women had enjoyed the freedom and high pay available in munitions factories, sometimes after years of domestic service.

The Labour movement was emerging from murky beginnings in the trades unions and the intellectual rigour of Fabianism to become a fully-fledged political party that was able to form governments, albeit minority ones. The Liberal Prime Minister David Lloyd George had promised a country that was 'fit for heroes' returning from the war, but demobilized soldiers found it increasingly difficult to get work. Deprivation was widespread and industrial relations deteriorated. The number of days lost to strikes reached 26 million in 1920, rising to 85 million the following year, when miners withdrew their labour. The Communist Party of Great Britain was formed in 1920 as the British economy stumbled. Britain had ended the war with some £8 billion of debt and servicing that accounted for a quarter of government expenditure in 1920.

The 1918 Representation of the People Act had enfranchised all men over the age of 21, and propertied women over 30. The electorate increased to 21 million, of which 8 million were women. Although it excluded working class women, who mostly failed the property qualification, the case for full women's suffrage was becoming more compelling by the minute. In December 1919 Nancy Astor became the first woman to sit in the Houses of Parliament. American-born Astor was not the first woman to be elected to the British parliament but she was the first to take her seat.[3] Also in December 1919 the Sex Disqualification (Removal) Act made it illegal for women to be excluded from most jobs and allowed them to hold judicial office and enter the professions. Women could now become magistrates, solicitors and barristers and Lincoln's Inn admitted its first female bar student. In 1920 women at Oxford University were for the first time allowed to receive degrees.

As church attendance collapsed many sought solace in alternatives to mainstream Christianity like Second Adventism and Spiritualism. The official war statistics claimed that about three-quarters of a million British lives were lost but, as Martin Pugh points out, since many men died in peacetime from wounds or injuries received during the war that figure is clearly understated. Another 230,000 British people died during the flu pandemic that hit Britain in the winter of 1918–1919. With so many families grieving it isn't a great surprise that people turned to Spiritualism to communicate with their dead friends and relatives. At the start of the war there had been 145 societies associated with the Spiritualists' National Union. By 1920 there were over 300. Apart from the opportunity to communicate with the dead, Spiritualism spoke to the egalitarian mood of the inter-war years. It had never had much to do with hierarchies.

Europe too was reeling, and the seeds of a new disaster were being sown. Mussolini had helped form the Italian Fascist party in 1919. The German Worker's Party, also founded in 1919, was renamed the National Socialist German Worker's Party, the Nazi Party, in 1920. The conservative revolution that swept Europe was not simply political. It had great intellectual support. The philosopher Martin Heidegger had links to the Nazi Party. One of the most influential books of the twentieth century, Oswald Spengler's *Decline of the West*, was used as a blueprint for fascism. It had influential supporters in the arts. The three primary modernist poets, T. S. Eliot, W. B. Yeats and Ezra Pound, were demonstrably reactionary. But it wasn't simply the forces of reaction that changed the face of post-war society. Popular cultural revolutions that were apolitical, or pro-democratic, like jazz, pioneered by black musicians who were welcomed in European cities but restricted to segregated venues in the US, challenged prevailing norms as they had never been challenged before. As historian Philipp Blom says: 'The Jazz Age with its flappers in the United States, the Bright Young Things in Britain, and the androgynous, fun-loving girls and boys in the bars of Berlin and the cellar joints of Paris was a spontaneous protest against an era that was growing too serious, a time that seemed either devoid of hope or inflated with utopian dreams of the partisans of left and right.'[4] People were desperately searching for meaning. The war had held back growing social fissures, there were no certainties, no truth, no universally accepted moral code.

This seething world was changing rapidly when Keith Castellain Douglas was born into it at the Garden Road Nursing Home in Tunbridge Wells on 24 January 1920.[5] He was relatively lucky to have been born during a period when levels of infant mortality (deaths within the first twelve months of birth) were dropping significantly.[6] Douglas was born in typical January weather. The wind was moderate or fresh, occasionally strong, and there was a great deal of low cloud as well as some rain or drizzle. The day was overcast with poor visibility and the temperature hovered between three and seven degrees.[7] The birth of Keith Douglas was announced in the weekly *Tunbridge Wells Advertiser*: 'DOUGLAS – On January 24th, at Tunbridge Wells, to Marie Joséphine (nee Castellain) and Keith S. Douglas, M.C., late Captain R. E., a son.' The advertisement cost 2 shillings.[8]

Douglas's mother had been born Marie Joséphine Castellain in Guildford in June 1887. Jo (as she was usually called), the daughter of Charles Castellain and Amy Gertrude Towse, was brought up near Cranbrook in Kent. Jo came from a relatively aristocratic family. Her father's grandfather was a French aristocrat from Lille who had fled the Revolution, and Charles had spent his entire life supported by private means. His mother, Maria, was the daughter of Frederick Huth, the so-called 'Napoleon of the City', a German-born British merchant and banker who established the London bank Frederick Huth & Co in 1809. Charles had been a cotton broker in Liverpool and a merchant banker in Egypt, but he had no need to work and lived on his capital.[9] Jo had a sister, Marguerite, who was born in 1892, and two brothers, Charles, born in 1886, and Ernest, born in 1888. Her father had children, two daughters and a son, by his previous marriage to Catherine Florence Wollace, who died in 1876. Jo was not herself wealthy. She married Keith Sholto Douglas on 5 February 1915 at Holy Trinity Church at Brompton in Kent.[10] She was 27 years old and he was 32.

Douglas's father, Keith Sholto Douglas, had volunteered in the first month of the First World War and joined the Royal Engineers two months later. He served in the Near East and embarked for Gallipoli in 1915 with the 71st Field Company, and thence to Mesopotamia where he contracted malaria and sandfly fever and was wounded. He earned the Military Cross and when he was discharged he was a captain with 'initiative and resource'. His behaviour at the front was described as 'quite fearless', much as his son's would be in the Second World War.[11]

Douglas's paternal grandfather, Dr William Douglas, died at the age of 84. He was the son of Alexander Douglas of Belfast, where he had been born in 1845. He was educated at Queen's College, Belfast and at the University of Edinburgh, graduating in medicine in 1869. He practised at Leamington and specialized in mental illness. A member of the Royal Medico-Psychological Association and of the Society for the Study of Inebriety, he travelled extensively, and lived in Madeira for a time. He was also a surgeon on the Cunard Line. For fifty years he played a very active part in the British Medical Association, which had been formed in 1832, and was a strong believer in the democratization of the association. He was at one time President of the Kent branch, and retired to Staines.

* * *

Douglas was baptized on 14 April 1920 according to a Christ's Hospital questionnaire Jo completed in March 1931. His early years were spent some 44 miles west of Tunbridge Wells in Cranleigh, a medieval village (the parish church of St Nicolas dates from about 1170) although some claim it has been a human settlement since the Stone Age.[12] Cranleigh is 38 miles from London, tucked away in the south-west corner of Surrey, on the edge of the Fold country. It lies on the southern slope of the Hurtwood sandhills and so enjoys the shelter of the North Downs. Cranleigh's war memorial was unveiled and dedicated in December 1920. Today the war memorial shows where one name has been erased. A returning soldier called Stedman was surprised to see his brother's name on the memorial and reported to the authorities that he was alive and well and sitting at home.[13]

Douglas's parents had rented Curfew Cottage, near Cranleigh's village green, since the previous year. According to Graham it was a 'large Tudor cottage ... [with] its own small orchard to one side, herbaceous borders lining a brick path which led to the front gate, and wisteria covering the weathered red brick of the front wall.'[14] There is a photograph of Curfew

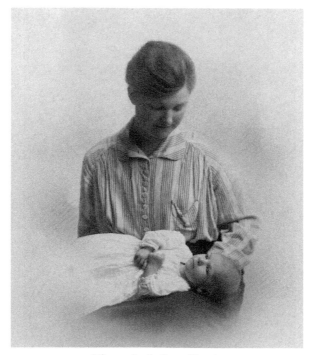

The arrival of a militarist

Cottage taken when Douglas was still a baby and it's easy to see why Douglas's parents loved it.

When Douglas was three the family moved to Dalkeith, in Avenue Road, Cranleigh, part of the Woodlands estate which had been laid out in 1894. Dalkeith was 'a plain stuccoed house … [which came with] two and half acres of land', which Douglas's father converted into a chicken farm.[15] Douglas's father had been unhappy since being demobilized. Although he had trained as an engineer he struggled to find work. He had found a job with a building firm in Hemel Hempstead in October 1920 but it was temporary; Jo stayed at Curfew Cottage working as a secretary to an artist. The outbreak of civil war in Ireland gave Douglas senior the opportunity to resume his military career with the Royal Engineers, but he returned to Cranleigh in June 1922, still looking for work. Dalkeith gave the Douglas family a chance of financial security. Douglas senior built hen houses to accommodate 150 laying hens and designed his own system to run water to each of them. He also built brooder houses for raising chicks and installed incubators.

Keith Douglas with his mother

Douglas had a complex relationship with his father, whose return from Ireland when the boy was two and a half shattered the bucolic life he had been living at Curfew Cottage with his mother and maternal grandfather. As a young child Douglas clearly idolized his father's military bearing and carried the military style throughout his short life, but he didn't speak or write to him again after Douglas senior left home in 1928 with Olwen (also known as Phoebe), the girl who the family had employed as a help.[16] When his father, 'a hearty playmate whom he secretly feared and wholeheartedly admired', he wrote in a school exercise book, 'disappeared and Olwen too, he wept as much as his mother'.[17] His mother was a considerable feature of his life. He wrote to her in the year before his death:

> … you seem to imagine that after the war I shall be buzzing about the world without you. Well, get that idea out of your head. Whoever is in my life & whether I marry or not I shall always want you. I don't know how you manage to be like you are when I think of the atmosphere in which you grew up & Granny & Grandpa & the people who surrounded you. But the fact remains I have

never met anyone like you for quick fair & complete understanding & summing up of things, even the ones with which you completely disagree. You always seemed to know beforehand the difficult things I wanted to tell you (nothing is difficult now) & you have many times been the anchor which prevented me going off the deep end. Things which loomed impossibly large & difficult to face somehow shrunk to normal proportions when I mentioned them to you.[18]

In a letter to John Waller and G. S. Fraser she wrote after his death: 'Keith was always a great one for making future plans – the unlikelihood of fulfilling them was no deterrent. On his first voyage to the Middle East he wrote that he would go and work in South African mines to earn some money and then buy a South Sea Island where we could live most of the time and he would write. The latest he made, I think, were to return to Oxford for two years, then take a British Council job in the Middle East and take me on a North African trip to meet his various friends in Sousse, Cairo, Tel-a-viv, and Alexandria.'[19]

Douglas as a fierce toddler

The chicken farm at Dalkeith was short-lived but relatively successful. Graham reports Jo telling him that the farm:

found good markets. Cranleigh School provided a steady customer for the eggs and any surplus could be sold in Guildford market: Mac Fisheries in Guilford took all the table birds they could offer. For such deliveries and the collection of chicks and foodstuffs the Douglases bought a pony and cart, but supplying their customers still took plenty of time. In addition Olwen and Mrs Douglas had to collect, clean and pack the eggs, pluck and prepare the table birds. Such activities were not the concern of Captain Douglas: new schemes for watering, improved runs and houses, and over-all expansion absorbed him. They also absorbed most of the income. Mrs Douglas, in charge of accounts, found that despite their good markets a diminishing amount of money was available for the day-to-day expenses of running the farm, paying food bills, and buying new stock.'[20]

Douglas's earliest surviving letter was written at Dalkeith and is dated July 6th [1925]. Written to his grandfather, Charles Castellain, to thank him for his card it has a note on the reverse, written probably by Keith's mother to her father: 'This was his quite unaided effort spelling & all. No one else but Robin [a local friend who Douglas sent his love to in a letter to his mother written in 1927][21] in the room. But he was told yesterday how to spell "Grandpapa".'[22] Sure enough the next letter, written from 6 Albert Road in Bexhill, to his grandmother spells 'Grandpapa' perfectly.[23] We have only seven letters, all written to his maternal grandparents, before he left for Edgeborough School on Thursday 23 September 1926. The letters are typically dutiful, telling them about his new tooth, the woodpeckers in the garden and his river trip with Aunty Elyon, visits to 'fate' and fair, where he bought a gun for four pennies, rode on the swingboats and merry-go-rounds and had throws at the 'cocoanuts' (he hit one but doesn't say if it was disturbed from its stand) and thanking them for their letters and small gifts.

Douglas was clearly a precocious child. According to his mother he

… showed interest in form and sound at an incredibly early age. Learnt to read by recognising the entire shapes of even long words quite apart from spelling.

Weilded [sic] a pencil from the age of 18 months & at 2 years attempted to draw a large variety of objects. As a child could be led but never driven. Had a logical & enquiring mind & wished to get at the reason for all behaviour of grown ups.

Keith Douglas dressed as a king

He resented being told lies on [crossed out: account of his age] the assumption that he would not understand the truth &, taking things very literally he sometimes lost his temper under the impression he had been deliberately deceived – as when, at the age of 3½ having seen a picture of a mammoth & being told they were found in ice, he rushed out and smashed every puddle in the road & came back livid to say it was a lie – he couldn't find even a tusk.[24]

A story, written in 1932, the year after Douglas left Edgeborough School, is autobiographical:

As a child, he was a militarist, and like many of his warlike elders, built up heroic opinions upon little information, some scrappy war stories of his father. Most of the time he was down in the field, busy, with an absurdly purposeful look on his round face, about a tent made of an old sheet, and signposted with a board saying 'sergeants' mess'. He was quite at home there for hours, while he was four and five, telling himself stories as he ran about, and sometimes stopping a moment to contemplate the calf who shared that field, a normally quiet animal, but given to jumping five-barred gates. As you would expect, he played with lead soldiers, and toy artillery, and was most fond of the cavalry and the highlanders

… His father did not spend very much time with him, but would speak to him of war and boxing and shew the boy his great muscles, for here at least he could shew them off to unbounded admiration. He teased his son, and pinched and tormented him at times, but Keir [i.e. Douglas] liked his father better than his mother, who fondled him a deal too much and cried sometimes …'[25]

His mother wrote of this story: 'I found this attempt at the story of Keith's own life as a small child … He never mentioned it to me or spoke about his father after he 10 [sic] years old, when since he asked me point blank I had to tell him, we were left on our own. I suppose he just wrote it & forgot it, & perhaps it helped him in some way at the time. People have remarked to me about his letters at that date that his hand writing was very "formed" for his age. I think so too.'[26]

He was confident and self-sufficient. His mother recorded that 'an only child & often having to amuse himself alone for hours he never seemed to find time hanging heavily. He invented games, talking unceasingly to himself & imaginary companions or toys. He was by nature gregarious & never missed an opportunity of collecting other children to play with him & share anything he possessed. On one occasion at 4 years old, having been given a toy motor car he collected half the village infant school & spent the morning giving them rides, finally inviting the whole boiling to lunch in a lordly manner, without so much as a reference to any parent.'[27] Certainly he was curious about words and how they could be used from a very early age. Douglas's mother recalls him buying a sixpenny book of synonyms from Woolworth's at the age of six 'so as not to use the same word too often.'[28]

Douglas's mother became ill towards the end of 1924. It is likely that the stress of the chicken farm was a contributory factor. Jo seems to have been treated well. Other women were not so fortunate. As Martin Pugh says, at this time, as far as women were concerned, 'the medical profession relied on a modicum of science generously tempered by prejudice and ignorance.'[29] His mother's breakdown had a lasting effect on Douglas. He described her sudden collapse in his autobiographical story:

… it occurred to him that people were about in the house and his mother's and father's beds were empty. He went and peered out, and saw through the bannisters a group of people standing in the hall, about his mother, who lay asleep on a stretcher … He realised almost at once that his mother was ill and ran downstairs on his bare feet asking what was the matter with her, as they took her away out of the front door. Someone he had never seen took him back to his bed with some unsatisfying explanation, and locked the door on him. He began immediately to scream and beat upon it, but they had all gone and he was alone, locked in. He became frantic, fell on the floor and shouted curses he had heard 'Curse damn bother darn bloody' in a string as long as he could put together, until he got up from the floor and hit his head on the door knob. It hurt and with some idea of punishing the door knob he hit his head on it five or six times more, very hard, and then subsided on the bed sobbing. In a few minutes his grandfather came up and succeeded in calming him, explaining that his mother had an illness, called Sleepy Sickness, but she would be well soon, when she had gone to the Hospital and had a rest.[30]

He was content with his grandfather's explanation 'for the moment'.

'Sleepy Sickness' was encephalitis lethargica, a disease which attacks the brain and leaves some victims speechless and motionless. 'Sleepy Sickness' barely exists now but a global epidemic from 1915 to 1926 affected about 5 million people, a third of whom died. Many survivors didn't recover fully. Douglas's father was told by a specialist that if his wife did survive she would probably be mentally ill for the rest of her life, and although she did recover she suffered from lack of concentration, amnesia and headaches.[31]

In 1926, Douglas's father left home in search of work and Douglas went to school.

NAUGHT DOES HIS CHARGING AVAIL

Keith Douglas's first day at Edgeborough School was 23 September 1926. He was six years old and a boarder. According to his mother there was no local day school for him to attend.[32] He was enrolled in Form I with three other boys, Donald Cecil Claude Taylor, who had been born in October 1918, Joseph Henry Creigh (November 1916) and Ernest Heath Reid (March 1919).[33] For some time Douglas was the youngest boy in the school.

Meanwhile the post-war world continued its long, uncontrolled suicide mission. Hitler attempted to increase his control of the Nazi Party at Bamberg in February and in November Joseph Goebbels was appointed Nazi Gauleiter of Berlin. In the UK the Trades Union Congress (TUC) had called a general strike in support of coal miners in May 1926, briefly bringing transport to a halt before the workers called the strike off after just over a week. The miners had been treated as mere profit fodder by the mine owners but the government of the day had been expecting nationwide industrial action and was well prepared. The strikers didn't have a chance. Francisco Franco was promoted to Brigadier General in February, making him the youngest general in Spain (and perhaps the youngest in Europe). Benito Mussolini survived assassination attempts in April, September and October 1926, and there were military coups in Poland and Portugal in May. Europe hadn't reached boiling point in 1926 but the signs were there.

Edgeborough School moved to its current site near Farnham in 1939. In Douglas's time it was in Guildford. Established in 1906 as a small, privately owned boarding school for boys by 1926 it had grown to a community of 12 teaching staff and 81 boys, including Douglas. The teaching staff was entirely Oxbridge educated, apart from a Miss Topham who taught drawing, a Miss Lamborn (dancing) and one H. J. Underwood ('carpentering'). These three appear to have had no education worth mentioning and appear in the records below a line that is as unconsciously segregationist and as much of its time as the infamous Cutteslowe Walls in Oxford and the Gentleman Player distinction in English cricket. Douglas and his mother had a good relationship with Edgeborough School. As their names were written in the book presented to Mr and Mrs A. H. James, the headmaster and his wife, on their retirement on 28 July 1934, we can infer that they took part in the celebrations.[34]

He wrote, apparently happily, to his mother two days after arriving. He was seemingly already enjoying himself: 'the little boy I sleep with is sometimes nice and sometimes rather boring.'[35] He wrote to his father the same day, a Saturday, to report that there were six boys in his form (although the official school record shows only four) and that at first the teachers thought he couldn't read but that when they 'tryed to find out' they discovered that he could.[36] In fact at that stage, according to John Waller, who co-edited the first published collection of Douglas's poetry, he could 'read and write fluently. He enjoyed maths, fairy tales, historical anecdotes, and an old *History of the Boer War*. He also showed an early interest in model-making and drawing, arts in which he later acquired a considerable proficiency.'[37] Certainly the early drawings which accompany some of his letters to his mother are astonishingly precocious.

A few days later he wrote cheerfully to his maternal grandparents. He was still enjoying life at Edgeborough, he had three friends and was playing rounders and football.[38] At around the same time he gave a fuller account to 'peobe' (Phoebe). He had half an hour's break in the morning lesson, he was starting Latin and French, and he played football every afternoon except Sundays.[39] This is his only extant letter to Phoebe (Olwen) although

Keith Douglas in his Edgeborough uniform

he does refer to her occasionally for the next 18 months or so, until, that is, she ran away with Douglas's father. During the rest of the Christmas term Douglas wrote to his father and his paternal grandfather as well as his mother, Phoebe and maternal grandparents. He appears to have made good progress. According to a letter of 20 November to his mother 'I got top marks for Arithmetic and the other day I had a page of nothing but ticks and Rs by the side of sums and in the middle 10 out of 10 which was full marks I am on Ex. 17 in Latin Exercise and a boy called Creigh is on Ex. 10 and Donald is on Ex. 7 and Reid is on Exercise 3 Creigh is 10 years old and Donald [Taylor] is 8 years old and Reid is 7 years old. Miss Streeter says she hopes I shall go up in to the Second form next term when I am 7. Reid does not know amavi yet and I know what Victoria and Belgae mean and what Cotta means. Tell Dadda I got on quite well at boxing.'[40] His mother remembered a more heroic boxing performance: 'Here in his first term he entered himself for the fly weight boxing – knowing nothing whatever about it. Needless to say he did not win on points but he gave a good account of himself & knocked his opponent out.'[41] One suspects that if he had indeed knocked his opponent out he would have won the bout. Douglas's mother had a tendency to overplay his successes.

By 11 December he wrote to his parents that he was becoming very excited by the fact that term was nearly over.[42] He had made a 'splendid beginning' in Latin[43] and generally seems to have had a good first term at Edgeborough but how much of that was a combination of 1920s English behaviour and his father's military stiff upper lip we will never know. He seems to have been genuinely resilient. He wrote to his mother on 27 November 1926: 'I pulled my tooth out myself so I did not have any thing to make a fuss about. I just pushed it for ward and I heard it snap and then pulled and it came out.'[44] Phoebe sent a children's newspaper every week and his mother (and others) visited him on some Sundays, but by the standards of Britain one hundred years later it seems a tough environment for a six-year-old, however well-meaning the adults involved were. Douglas's first report was encouraging. James wrote, 'An excellent start. His work is promising.'[45]

The following term started badly for Edgeborough School. The headmaster, writing in the April 1927 edition of the school magazine, reported that 'Influenza in various forms prevented a full gathering of our numbers on January 21st. It was not until early February that every one had returned. There was little hope we should escape the epidemic. The first case occurred on the first Sunday of term – the introducer shall be nameless – and for three weeks or so we were in the thick of it. It came in a very mild form. All the victims, some thirty of them, recovered quickly, and the rest of the term has been remarkably free from even minor ailments, with one exception. We had our first case of appendicitis in 21 years.'[46]

Douglas, now in Form II, didn't even mention this dramatic episode in his letters home. He was more preoccupied by the school's rugby performances and the weekly form marks (he was third from bottom of Form II at the end of January[47]). It's difficult to know if admiration or pity prompted 'every Body' to look at him 'this morning when the Marks were put on the Black Board.' He had just turned seven years old and was still the youngest boy in Form II, which now consisted of 11 boys.[48] The boxing report in the April edition of the school magazine announced that Taylor had beaten Douglas on points in the first series of fly-weight bouts.[49] It was around then that Douglas's grandfather Castellain died, during term so he missed the funeral.

Four of Douglas's letters from the summer term survive, all written to his mother (although we know that he wrote separately to Phoebe).[50] The first is postmarked 15 May and shows an enthusiasm for cricket – 'I generally

Keith Douglas, aged about seven, looking less fierce

start by hiting [sic] Boundrys' – but underlying the sporting bravado is a small boy who wants visits from his family. Anyway, his mother recalled that he was 'too dreamy' for cricket.[51] 'Can you come next Sat. or Sun … please come next Saturday and watch me play Cricket … could Granny come with you,' he beseeched Jo.[52] There are three extant letters written in June. In the first he reports being 'wacked', not by the headmaster this time, 'thank goodness', but by Mr West. Douglas doesn't disclose the reason for the corporal punishment but since it happened in the changing room we may reasonably infer that it had something to do with some sports-related misdemeanour.[53] The longing for visits continued in June[54] but the long summer vacation was beckoning: 'The Term seems to have Gone very Quickly It seems that I have only Been Here about a month and The a [there are] only about five weeks Left not that now But not four yet, Still they won't take Long Will They at Least one thing is they won't seem Long.'[55] Encouragingly his scholarly performance had taken a turn for the better. Having been second from bottom of the class in January, he was second from top by June, and in July he won his first prize, for which he received Dickens's *A Tale of Two Cities*, which he enjoyed, though his behaviour left something to be desired: 'He is passing though the difficult stage when he does not quite realize how far he can go with impunity! It will dawn upon him before long, in work as in other ways.'[56]

The rest of 1927 seems to have passed quietly. Some time in the second half of the year Douglas's father left Surrey for a job in Wales. His parents had managed to sell the chicken farm and had moved to Shere. Only one of Douglas's letters survives from the autumn term, though he clearly wrote many more.[57] He enjoyed a visit from his mother on Saturday 1 October, and in the evening a lecture on the Isle of Man inspired a sketch of ships a mile from Douglas harbour that he sent to his mother the following day. After four terms Douglas was now the fourth youngest boy in the school and his academic work had improved. James wrote on his report that he had had 'a very satisfactory term's work'.[58]

Douglas turned eight in January 1928. Life at Edgeborough School continued much as before; Douglas was now in Form III. He continued to make progress academically, and he still begged his mother for visits, but we don't have much to go on apart from three letters to his mother and an entertaining interchange with 'Edward Sharp & Sons Ltd/Makers of the celebrated Super-Kreem toffee' over the summer. Douglas wrote to them to tell them that 'many of my friends and I have decided that no other Toffee-makers can hold a candle to your firm for quantity, quality and Flavour', for which compliment he received a sample of Sharp's new Toffy-choc.[59] James wrote in Douglas's report in summer 1928 that he was doing very well.[60] As we have seen, his outlook was militaristic and his literary tastes mirrored his outlook. He enjoyed D[orothy] K[athleen] Broster's 1925 novel, *The Flight of the Heron*, the first in 'The Jacobite Trilogy', which tells the story of two men on opposing sides of the 1745 Jacobite uprising under Bonnie Prince Charlie.[61] His Form II prize, *A Tale of Two Cities*, is set in England and revolutionary France, relying heavily on Thomas Carlyle's *The French Revolution: A History*.

He met lifelong friend Tony Rudd in the Easter holidays of 1929. Rudd was four years younger than Douglas and he was impressed by the older boy's imagination and leadership. Rudd recalled that Douglas 'built a dirt track for racing cars in the front drive of the house at Boarshead, in Sussex, and a mountain railway over the rock garden, and played elaborate and inventive games with toy soldiers. Rudd remembers him as 'seeming an heroically tough leader whose endless fund of imaginative schemes never disappointed'.[62] By the Christmas term Douglas was in Form IV but much was to change during the following year. Douglas refers to his father in an undated letter of 1929[63] but Douglas's father asked his wife for a divorce at Easter. Olwen had followed him to Wales and eventually became his second wife. Keith Sholto Douglas had not played a great part in his son's first eight years; he played no part thereafter. When his son left secondary school Douglas senior wrote to his son to suggest a meeting. Douglas characteristically didn't take up this invitation. James wrote kindly to Douglas's mother on 12 December 1928, offering to keep Douglas at the school at no cost: 'We shall be only too glad to keep Billie on here until the time comes for him to enter his Public School, either as a scholar, or, if it should be necessary, under some endowment fund.'[64] James was positive on Douglas's Christmas 1928 report. Although he had to work harder at Mathematics he was doing really well, considering his age[65] (he was nearly three years younger than the average age of his form).

Douglas had been promoted to Form V and life at Edgeborough School carried on much as normal, although the summer term was challenging for pupils and teachers alike. Edgeborough was attacked by scarlet fever early in the term and then by chickenpox: 'Then we knew we were in for it,' James wrote in the school magazine. 'Very few boys had had it ... so, unless a miracle happened, it was certain to drag its miserable, tantalising course throughout the rest of the term, if not longer. We have reached the last week. There are only five boys left who have not had it.'[66] Perhaps the general illness helped Douglas to win the one-length competition at the annual swimming gala,[67] although he won it again in the autumn when the scarlet fever and chickenpox epidemics had subsided.[68] As with the first boxing match, his mother recalled a more glorious occasion than that recorded by the school magazine: 'At 7 he entered for a swimming race in the miniature school swimming bath, never having learnt – or tried – to swim. He was much jeered at by older boys for this but undeterred he plunged in & by some kind of dog stroke not only kept up but beat the others by a head. When it was chalked up that "one length" had been won by Douglas he was filled with joy. I think he must have made so much splashing that the other swimmers, all expecting him to drown, were demoralized.'[69]

By the end of 1929 there were only 11 staff and 64 boys.[70] James explained this blithely in the school magazine: 'At the moment we are experiencing a slight drop in our numbers. This is partly due to the fact that an unusually large number have left for their Public Schools or Dartmouth this year, but chiefly to the fact that we have given up having even quite young day-boys, and have decided to have only boarders in future. This will right itself before long.'[71] Douglas's school performance continued to improve. An undated letter of early 1929 to his mother reported that he was top of the class for the week just passed and that he was 'getting on much better at rugger now.'[72] By the summer term he was playing cricket again and 'getting on fairly alright in work'[73] as well as growing his stamp collection. James stated in Douglas's summer 1929 report that he was 'very satisfied with his work, and general development.'[74] In early December 1929 he was playing football and told his mother that he was told 'by about 5 people that [one of his shots at goal] was one of the best shots of the game, which is saying rather a lot, because the match in 3rd we won 18–0!'[75] He continued to perform well during 1930, in March writing to his mother that he was '4th in the week's order, with 341, it was awfully close this week, and the top only got 358, but the bottom got 147.'[76] A few days later he told her that he was 'second in the Algebra paper and second in the work we did today in Algebra.'[77] That letter (of 5 March 1930) records Douglas's first poem. His class had been tasked in English with writing a poem on any subject in history, and Douglas, perhaps predictably, chose Waterloo:

> 1.
> Napoleon is charging our squares,
> with his cavalry he is attacking:
> let the enemy do what he dares,
> our soldiers in braveness aren't lacking.

I forgot bravery for the moment, so I used Poet's license and put 'braveness'.

This is the second verse:

> 2.
> But naught does his charging avail,
> he cannot do anything more;
> for not one heart does fail
> e'en when tis at death's door.

And this is the third:

> 3.
> 'I have you!' Napoloen cries!
> but he has a great mistake made;

for every French soldier flies,
and is caught by a fierce cannonade.

And this is the last:

4.
Napoleon is charging our squares,
but only in memory now;
we remember his charging mares;
and we always will, I trow.[78]

Desmond Graham claims too much for this poem: '[Douglas's] shift from direct narrative to the event as remembered shows subtlety, and his enthusiasm catches the dramatic irony of Napoleon's mistaken shout.'[79] In reality 'Waterloo' has little to suggest that its author would become one of the most celebrated war poets of the twentieth century, but he was only ten years old.

Douglas's mother filed a petition for divorce on 22 January 1930, and the court minutes show that a decree nisi was granted on 6 June 1930 (the final decree being dated 9 March 1931). Jo's petition was that she had been lawfully married to Keith Sholto Douglas on 5 February 1915 at Holy Trinity Church at Brompton and had lived with him at various addresses in Surrey but that he was now residing at 160 Inverness Place in Cardiff and had 'frequently committed adultery with a woman called Phoebe Lawson Wood'. It was stated that on 7 and 8 December 1929 Douglas committed adultery with Phoebe at the Bush Hotel in Wokingham. Phoebe (of 154 High Street, Guildford) and Douglas were given eight days to object to the petition. Jo signed an affidavit swearing that there had been 'no collusion or connivance' between her and her husband and that was it.[80] Douglas's father did not appear at the hearing before the Honourable Sir Alexander Dingwall Bateson but the petitioner had sufficiently proved the contents of her petition and the judge decreed that the marriage was dissolved because Keith Sholto Douglas had been guilty of adultery. Jo was granted custody of her son and Douglas's father was ordered to pay £40 12 shillings and 7 pence in addition to the sum of £30 already paid to cover her costs. Douglas did not see his father again.

By the end of his time at Edgeborough Douglas was exploring more quasi-military themes. He wrote to his mother that 'Street, I, & some others, including Taylor, are going to Act a play, which Strasse, pronounced Straaza,

(Street), & I, wrote. It is about 3 German spies who murder Professor W. Cooper, who has discovered some poison gas, & they are all killed by the poison gas. And then the police come, & first of all, when lot the animals screams [sic], constable 'arris hears it rushes in, & then after some fruitless efforts, he at last makes the telephone work, but can only stutter out that there is a murder at 77, Park Lane, before he, too becomes a victim to the gas.'[81] Douglas played one of the German spies.[82] James congratulated Douglas on an excellent report at Easter 1930 and noted in the summer report that Douglas's work was 'distinctly good'.[83]

There exists, in the Brotherton Library in Leeds, a commentary on Douglas's letters that indicates that he was at least four years ahead of his time. It is written by 'Norman' to his friend 'John' (presumably Waller) in the late 1960s. Norman appears to have been an expert on handwriting and a note on the manuscript reads, 'At first glance my friend suggested early "teens", but as Norman notes Douglas was only nine at the time. He was 'full of compassion for a little boy clearly not violently happy to be away from home!', and his comments are thoughtful:

> from 'internal' evidence, that he is nine years old. He would now, therefore, be nearly fifty.

> from vocabulary, that his background is very articulate, that he uses words he has heard and not read, that he knows the social vocabulary extensively but not perfectly: all of which suggests an upper age of ten. e.g. note his formal initialled signature.

> from spelling, that his spelling age is about 12 and a half, but this is often unreliable and far in advance of chronological age. e.g. "quiet" but "abserlutely".

> from syntax, that he has had a long contact with adult speech and writing habits, and his punctilious expression, varied with the 'in-group' colloquialism ("bates", etc.) is just that of a 9/10 year old.

> from orthography, that he is of this age; typical experimentation with different styles of cursive, becoming often nearly illegible when he is excited by what he is writing. Also he is clearly trying hard to write running cursive.'[84]

There is no doubt that Douglas was a precocious child.

In the summer issue of the Edgeborough School magazine James reported that the Reverend E. D. Deane was leaving for a chaplaincy at Christ's Hospital in Horsham.[85] One wonders if Deane played any part in Douglas's acquiescence to his mother's decision to go himself to Christ's Hospital. In any event he sat the exam and passed into Christ's Hospital in September 1931. Douglas's mother recalled to Desmond Graham that there were no fees to pay at Christ's Hospital, and no costs attached to uniforms or equipment. The departure of her husband left mother and son in real financial difficulties, and it was only through the intervention of the headmaster that Douglas was able to continue at Edgeborough for his final year. Jo paid no fees and was told by James, who remained true to his earlier promise, that she could pay when she felt able to do so.[86]

James noted on Douglas's Christmas 1930 report that 'it is a pity that he assumes such a defiant, almost truculent air at times. It does not help him & often creates a false impression.'[87] By Easter 1931, though, he noticed an improvement: 'Less bumptious and argumentative – in short, much pleasanter to deal with.'[88] By his final Edgeworth report James was guardedly optimistic: 'His work is much above the average for his age, but he cannot afford to be careless. He will find himself gradually losing ground if he is. I hope we shall have good news.'[89]

2

HAPPINESS SEEMS JUST TO HAVE STARTED[1]

At the age of 11, Keith Douglas was already proving truculent. John Waller quoted Douglas's mother in the brief biographical introduction to the poet in his, with G. S. Fraser, 1951 edition of Douglas's poems. As he joined Christ's Hospital at the age of eleven 'he had', according to Jo, 'too much individuality to be popular with many of the Powers – but there were those who appreciated him despite the headaches he sometimes caused.'[2] In other words, as Jasper Milvain says of his writer friend, Edwin Reardon, in George Gissing's *New Grub Street*, 'he hasn't the tact requisite for acquiring popularity'.[3]

Jo continued:

He was impatient of most people's opinions till he had tested them personally. He loved an argument and would cheerfully argue against his own opinions and (theoretically) prove them wrong, rather than have no basis of argument. He did this so convincingly that people who did not know him well sometimes believed his views to be the exact opposite to what they were.

He was accused by the Headmaster of being constitutionally lazy. The truth was he had unbounded energy and perseverance in anything he considered really worth while. He was keen on Rugger and Swimming, on Riding, on Dancing and Acting. He was intensely interested in people and the reasons for their behaviour.

As a boy he was violent over things and people he disliked; bitter and sarcastic in his criticisms but, even when onesided, often with a degree of truth not easy to refute. That naturally did not help his popularity at school. Later he could be just as trenchant, but with a humour that tempered the bitterness.

Few people knew of the difficulties he had to contend with in his private life as a boy and the final characteristics which triumphed were largely due to H. R. Hornsby, David Roberts, and Sir Reginald Spence, all of whom he valued as friends. I think early recognition of his literary ability was due to Mr. Stokoe of Edgeborough, now dead. Keith had a great capacity for making – and keeping – friends.

Waller pointed out that the family's financial difficulties were occasionally so acute that 'every possession of value had to be sold; and but for the generosity of his Headmaster, who gave him free schooling, Douglas would have been obliged to leave his preparatory school. From the age of eleven, however, when Keith Douglas entered Christ's Hospital on the Nomination Exam, he won all his own education by scholarships; as he grew older he earned what he could to contribute towards his holidays. He rarely had any place he could call home. Ironically – as his mother comments – his death provided her with the home she could never quite achieve for him.'[4]

A friend at Christ's Hospital, Norman Ilett, wrote some ten years after Douglas's death that:

> … his contemporaries at school will remember an early air of maturity, physical as well as intellectual. He was not an easy person to know. I think many people knew a part of him, as much as he cared to show them or thought would occupy or amuse them. He was interested in a number of things which do not usually go together. This brought him a wide acquaintance who formed not one large but a number of small circles, in each of which he could feel at home without permanently residing in any. His many-sidedness was not due to forethought, so that he consciously changed his coat to match a neighbour's, since he had a number of talents apart from the obvious promise of his writing and drawing … the terms on which he made friends remained exacting and he was sensitive, perhaps through being much alone in earlier days, to any falling off in the required standard. But he loved company and gave most generously to it. He was romantic and adventurous and there was no more stimulating and amusing companion, no better mimic and spinner of favourite yarns. He had violent and jolting views on most subjects, taking nothing on trust, eager for talk and argument. You might quarrel with him, but you picked up a share of his enthusiasm, and if you would come to terms with so sharply-cornered a character it was to your advantage in the long run. Authority found him a problem and he was lucky at school and elsewhere to find its representatives so tolerant. No subject interested him from the purely academic point of view and he lacked the orthodox sort of feeling of responsibility. He had a great sense of style, poetic flair and a good

deal of shrewdness, but little patience for the hard work which sweats at an uncongenial task.[5]

His reputation for prickliness lasted a long time. As late as 1993, at the Christ's Hospital Founder's Day dinner, former deputy head teacher Elizabeth Cairncross recalled that Douglas 'was clearly not an easy or easily-likeable boy to teach or care for – nor, I imagine, to befriend.' She quoted a Lamb A (Douglas's house) monitor by way of illustration. Douglas was 'more able to cope with authority when he believed himself in the right' than most of his contemporaries. Cairncross added that, 'Authority did not like being "coped with", particularly when belief that he was in the right led to a more than casual attitude to other people's property. [He took] two of the Art Master's water-colours from the Art School with the somewhat spurious rationalisation: "Theft is when you deprive a person of something he values and old Rigby didn't even know he possessed these".' [6]

Christ's Hospital was, and is, a charitable boarding foundation especially for children of families in social, financial or other need. Founded in the 1550s it is still primarily an independent school for London's poor, providing food, clothing, lodging and academic rigour. An eye to the future ensured that the children were prepared for future careers to take them out of the poverty that had necessitated charity in the first place. Christ's Hospital still provides bursaries for 80 per cent of the children who attend.

The petition for a place at Christ's Hospital for Douglas was made by his mother and he was presented by the donation governor, Sir Andrew Taylor, one of many benefactors of the school.

Douglas was admitted to Christ's Hospital on 18 September 1931, initially in the boarding house Lamb A (housing about 50 boys aged between 11 and 18).[7] But getting in wasn't made easy for him. The process started in early February 1931 when the headmaster of Edgeborough School, A. H. James, wrote to Christ's Hospital to try to secure a scholarship there for Douglas. James's essential kindness shines through the formality: 'His Mother divorced his Father last year under flagrant circumstances, & she is left with a mere pittance to live upon. The Father owes me a considerable sum in fees, which I do not expect to recover, but I shall keep the boy here until an opening can be found for him. He is just 11 years old & has already reached our top form, just holding his own with boys of 13 in Classics. I think he would stand a very fair chance in the examination. He is a sound boy, with a distinct character of his own. He should do well.'[8]

On 11 March, Taylor sent a completed 'Nomination to Compete' form with a covering letter: 'This is a sad case, in which I believe the mother is in no way to blame. The boy is a very bright boy.' All parties stressed Jo's blamelessness in the divorce case and Douglas's own intellectual promise. Taylor's nomination allowed Douglas to sit the examination on the 4th and 5th of June. Taylor certified that Douglas was educated to the standard required by Christ's Hospital in the compulsory subjects, English (composition and paraphrasing), Arithmetic and Practical Mensuration, and History and Geography, and that in addition he would offer two optional subjects, Latin and French.[9] Jo received a card acknowledging receipt of Taylor's nomination[10] but heard nothing more until the end of April, when James sent her a letter he had received from the school asking if he had a nomination for Douglas. James wrote directly to the school as well, regretting the long delay in answering the school's last letter and explaining that he had been away since Easter and that letters had not been reaching him. In reply to the clerk's specific questions James wrote that Douglas: 'was promoted to our top form last term & came out equal with another boy … His age is 11.2. The average age of the form is 12.9.'[11] Douglas's mother was bemused and pointed out to the clerk that the card she had received indicated that 'the matter will be submitted for consideration at the end of April & a further communication sent, so I cannot understand why a letter was sent to Mr. James asking if the boy had a nomination. I have received no further communication up to date. Please will you let me know if there is anything further I should do and whether practicalities of when & where the exam takes place will be sent to Mr. James … or to myself.' She signs off in a masterpiece of passive-aggressiveness, 'With apologies for troubling you.'[12]

The clerk wrote the following day to Douglas's mother to explain the situation: 'Early this year we received a letter from Mr. A. H. James stating that he was anxious to obtain a nomination for one of his pupils, but he did not give the name of the particular pupil in whom he was interested.' This was true. At no point in James's letter of 3 February which started the whole process does he mention Douglas by name.

Douglas sat the examination in early June but hadn't had any further news by the end of the month. His mother wrote again, this time rather plaintively, to the clerk:

> I should be very grateful if you could let me know the earliest date it is possible to know the result of the Christ's Hospital exam? & whether in the event of a boy

failing, he is allowed to sit again if he gets another nomination & is within the age limit? I am in the position of having to leave these rooms by the middle of August. I do not want to sell my furniture which is my only asset. I cannot afford to warehouse it or take furnished rooms. If I have to sell up it means the end of any kind of home for my boy. I have to make a final decision very soon because it is not easy to find cheap rooms quickly. If I could know my boy has passed I should be much less limited as to district. If on the other hand I know he has failed I must try to go near some endowed school where he might try for a day boy scholarship or some good secondary school. If, in the event of his failure, you are able to give me any information or advice on the subject of education I should very much appreciate it, as I have no one to turn to for either.[13]

This anguished plea prompted a rather terse reply from the clerk. He seems to have had enough of this pushy mum: 'In reply to your letter, I have to inform you that although nothing is as yet definitive, it is probable that on the result of the recent examination, the Committee will recommend to the Council of Almoners on 29th July, that a Presentation be granted to your son.'[14] Progress then, but no promises. There were more hurdles to jump over.

Back in March 1931 Jo had completed a questionnaire designed to assess her financial status. She gave the reason for her unemployment as 'unable so far to obtain a post owing to age & lack of any training. A slight disabiliy [sic], the result of sleepy sickness, adds to the difficulty, but this is getting less.' Jo declared that she wasn't related to any governor of Christ's Hospital, that her child had no separate maintenance, that she rented a flat for £4.10 per month and that her total annual income was £130. To the question about her average annual income for the previous three years she replied: 'No income, but keep in Father-in-laws house after home sold up until his death in 1929. Since then under £100 p.a. till the last 3 months.' To a question about whether she or her child were entitled to any property in reversion she answered: 'Neither I nor the child are entitled to any & I believe the father has nothing either.' As far as special or additional circumstances are concerned she declared that 'the father is no longer in any way legally responsible for the child. His present earnings only allow of the £2.10 fixed as maintenance allowance. This may be raised or lowered as trade varies & in case of his death would cease.' It is a bleak picture. On 2 August she completed the same questionnaire but nothing had changed.[15] Meanwhile a still-confused Jo wrote to the clerk at Christ's Hospital on 5 August. The Presentation Form in support of her son's admission to the school was sent under separate cover but she still wasn't certain of his status. 'I do not quite understand from your covering letter received with the presentation whether the boy is now definitely received into Christ's Hospital or whether he still has to pass another exam before entering? If it is not against any regulation may I have an answer to this question?'[16] That answer has not survived. It is fairly clear that the petition was something of a formality given that it is headed 'in consequence of the boy named herein having been successful in a Competitive Examination of ALMONERS' NOMINEES'.[17] The clerk was doubtless fairly exasperated by this time. In any event Keith Castellain Douglas was finally admitted to Christ's Hospital on 18 September 1931. He'd had a thorough medical in August, including a visit to the dentist and optician and a revaccination. Douglas 'occasionally appears to have a violent cold in the head for an hour or two',[18] which was diagnosed as asthma, but he appeared to be outgrowing it and Jo certified him as now in good health and fit for ordinary school life and work. He'd had whooping cough and rubella in March and August of 1930 respectively, chickenpox in July 1929, and had his tonsils and adenoids removed in 1927.[19]

Douglas in his Christ's Hospital costume

Douglas started at Christ's Hospital on 19 September 1931, a Saturday, and wrote to his mother that afternoon. He had already had a lesson (in carpentry) but had finished work for that day.[20] He wrote again to her the following day, after he had been foraging for nuts with the other new boys ('Out of about 30 only 6 were good!'[21]). He was a seasoned boarder but was nevertheless suffering the classic symptoms of being new in any environment. On the Saturday he reported, not surprisingly, that he had 'not nearly settled down yet', but by the following day he reflected that: 'The term seems to go terribly slowly … I do get rather teased, and have made no friends yet, but still, I can't hope to on the second day! I see quite a lot of the boys in other houses; they seem much nicer than the boys in Lamb A. And Blake who, by the way is a bit of a friend of mine, (but I can't call anyone actually a friend after two days, if you know what I mean), and several others, (new boys), from other houses, all say they don't get teased a bit.' But the teasing had stopped, or he told his mother it had, by later in September and he felt 'quite settled down'.[22] By 4 October he told her that 'there is not a single person in the house who is not jolly nice now'.[23] Most importantly he was showing more signs of a talent that he was to make much of during his short life, drawing. 'Everyone here makes an awful fuss about my drawing,' he wrote on 27 September. 'The art master say[s] I draw well, and everyone else says I shall be an art Grec[ian]!'[24] By October he was doing well academically, even in Greek, which he started badly at, and was getting used to the minor eccentricities of life at Christ's Hospital, notably the uniform (some might say the costume, see p.40) and the culture: 'In the dormitory we have to blow our noses solidly for about a minute, night and morning.'[25] All in all Douglas's first term at Christ's Hospital was a success. He had settled in socially and academically, was playing rugby for his house, and sounded happy: 'I have lost count of how many weeks we've been here, but I think it is eight weeks last Friday, is it not?'[26]

The following year he continued to draw and make models. His letters to his mother contained drawings of an archer, some Tudor waiters, a horse and rider, yachts and a seaplane, as well as requests for glue, 'or better still a new tube of seccotine' and his drawing pads.[27] In October he wrote to his mother that he was 'doing some painting in my sketch work and am going to try my hand at embroidery in art', and asked for coarse and fine sandpaper, 'some dead matches, and – if possible – some white paint.'[28] He started a model-making firm with some friends, 'so please if there is any Durofix or Seccotine in the house, send it.' Douglas had made a Dutch yacht, a fishing boat and a 'Lyons cake box with racing Yacht on sea of crumpled paper painted green flecked with white'.[29] One holiday he made a model of the Trafalgar and fixed its rigging by using his mother's hair.[30]

DOUGLAS'S BÊTE NOIRE

It was at about this time, if we are to take the fragments for and notes on a poem of 1944 called 'Bête Noire' at face value, that Douglas began to suffer acute bouts of depression. The repeatedly failed poem is one of the last things that he wrote and the fragments are reproduced in *Complete Poems*. A few quotations from the fragments make the context clear:

> Yes, I too have a particular monster
> a toad or worm curled in the belly
> …
> This is my particular monster. I know him:
> he walks about inside me: I'm his house
> and his landlord
> …
> The Beast is a jailer
> allows me out on parole
> brings me back by telepathy
> is inside my mind
> …
> I have been trying to get help for about eleven years.
> Three times I got help.
> If this is a game, it's past half time and the beast is winning
> …
> I sit at my table and nobody knows
> I've got a beast on my back.[31]

The notes on the poem are particularly moving: 'Bête Noire is the name of the poem I can't write … it is the poem I begin to write in a lot of other poems … The beast, which I have drawn as black care sitting behind the horseman, is indefinable: sitting down to try and describe it, I have sensations of physical combat, and after five hours of writing last night, which resulted in failure, all my muscles were tired. But if he is not caught, at least I can see his tracks (anyone may see them), in some of the other poems. My failure is that I know so little about him, beyond his existence and the infinite patience and extent of his malignity … I am afraid that I know nothing about this beast at all: he is so amorphous and powerful that he could be a deity. Only he is implacable; no use sacrificing to him, he takes what he wants.'[32] The psychologist R. J. Sapsford later wrote about Douglas's depression: 'He was estranged from people and normal pleasures. He felt inferior because of his self-conscious inability just to be himself and enjoy himself as he imagined other people could, without regthough he were walled in behind glass; nothing was immediate for him, and thus nothing was real.'[33]

Douglas wrote the note at the age of 24 but, from the evidence in the poem, the beast first appeared when he was 13. It is impossible not to feel for him as he confronted this demon for the first time while coping with a new school, isolated from his family and childhood friends. His sense of being alone with it, in spite of getting help three times, explains, perhaps, some of his subsequent behaviour. We should at least keep it in mind. At the age of 19 he explained his aversion to parties in a letter to his fiancée Toni Beckett: 'I have lived for all the time since I was about eleven without the chance of going to any parties at all. We never had any money to give them and mother never had any time to call on people: so no one noticed us, and I had no one of my own age to go about with until I was fifteen and then only one person from Housey, whom I wasn't particularly in line with. I don't expect you to understand the state of mind that sort of thing produces. You can't be expected to imagine what it's like to live on the charity of one or two rich and condescending old people and never to see anyone young except people I don't know going about together and enjoying themselves.'[34] Here he seems to be blaming the environment in which he grew up but in early 1940 he assessed his own personality for the benefit of Toni's parents:

> I spent a fairly stormy career at school and most of my holidays were alone with the result that I came up here (Oxford) a very defiant and rude person with vulnerable but concealed feelings and the wrong attitude towards most people. I shall never get over the idea of the world in general as a powerful force working for my hurt: nor would I wish to, for this conception of things saves me many disappointments. I am over critical of everyone – luckily of myself too, though I do my self-criticism in private. I work rather in spurts and am often plunged into helpless despair ... I alternate between extreme conceit, and an extreme inferiority complex. During intermediate periods I am however normal and tolerable.[35]

In other words, a paranoid depressive. The poet G. S. Fraser later wrote that Douglas 'found it excessively difficult to come to terms with his Shadow

[Bête Noire] just because he was an unusually good man. He had high principles, and he always acted on his principles ... His personal interests he had concentrated on high and wholesome things, on love, and poetry, and comradeship, and adventure. So it seemed to him inexplicable, I suppose, that he should have these black despairing moods. What had he done to deserve them? He had certainly never shirked any duty or danger, he was incapable of a mean act, and yet his black beast was liable to pounce upon him at the most unexpected moments, like the sense of guilt of a very bad, or the sense of inadequacy of a very weak, man.'[36]

CHRIST'S HOSPITAL

Douglas contributed poems, stories, essays and linocuts to *The Outlook*, Christ's Hospital's main vehicle for artistic work, from the March 1932 edition. His linocuts show real verve, with an uncanny ability to portray movement. His galleon in full sail, racehorse with jockey and particularly a medieval knight on his warhorse all show a fine eye for drama. The heavily-armoured knight sits upright and forward on his deep-chested horse, a long sword tucked neatly behind him. Both horse and rider look fully prepared for battle.[37] His linocut of an almost naked African warrior about to launch his spear, whether at game or enemy isn't indicated, appeared in the December 1934 issue and by April 1935 Douglas was extending beyond narrative. His abstract depictions of a wild animal, perhaps an elephant, and an 'alchymist' at work are precocious studies in ferocity and intent.[38]

Desmond Graham's life of Douglas was written while Douglas's mother and some of his Christ's Hospital friends and teachers were still alive, and his biography is informed by their reminiscences. While this is helpful it carries its own problems. The protagonists have a tendency to put themselves centre-stage. Douglas spent the many school holidays at the home of family friends, the Rudds, in Painswick. Tony Rudd was four (six according to Rudd) years younger than Douglas, who had been on holiday to France with Tony and Mrs Rudd in 1931.[39] In Painswick they cycled around the Cotswolds countryside and took art lessons from a First World War veteran. As Rudd recalled, the two boys 'sat one Saturday morning in a field near Painswick painting in sepia the view before us. We were taught by a local artist, a Mr Kennedy, a veteran invalided out of the Royal Flying Corps in 1917 ... I later found that the episode was enshrined in one of his poems in which he had perceived the essence of our crippled teacher in Kennedy's insistence that

Linocuts from The Outlook

we paint in sepia, not colour.'[40] The poem is 'Love and Gorizia', untitled in
the original manuscript:

> And now in the South the swallows
> swirling precisely among the dazzled trees
> are not known, not at this season, among these
> small streets and posters which the lamplight shews:
> but are among the white dusted avenues,
> and where the ruined palace faces the green
> river, and barbers chatter, the sky is clean.
>
> Mr Kennedy, speaking in Painswick among slate,
> insisted on shadows' value, thought
> colour of merely secondary import;
> characteristically, being himself incomplete,
> wound-drained, among these places, where thus late
> the unsatisfied put out their heads, take pleasure
> in reproducing roof tops on rough paper.
>
> This my compassion of where I found you
> with south, redolent of wingtips, suddenly gold.
> You small with your red-brown hair how could I mould,
> so inconsistent, how could I take you? So renew
> desires, Birdlife for Aquileia, different view
> forswearing swallows. Spinsters on their stools
> more valuable than monks until desire cools. [41]

Douglas wrote a school exercise about Painswick in January 1936. 'By half-
past seven we rattled into Painswick and left our taxi, steaming woefully, to
find our way, (round two or three corners), to my hostess's sixteenth century
cottage. Corners, indeed, were my first & last impressions of Painswick.
Painswick is all round the corner. Wherever you stand you are walled in.
Mysterious corners tantalise you, yet you stand in a small, complete world of
your own. Whoever built Painswick – and I am not sure that it did not grow
by some elfin scheme, rather than by design of a human architect – whoever
built it, I think, must have realised that a little of such beauty at a time is
enough for most men, and that to see the entirety of it would be too much
for most.'[42] The same essay contains a thinly-disguised portrait of Kennedy
as 'Mr. Mackenzie'. Douglas describes his appearance and his personality:
'His large glasses, long, thin body, and kindly, humourous [sic] face remind

me of some long-legged wise old bird; probably a stork, though his desire for self-effacement is second only to that of the ostrich ... Although the most noticeable part of him is his unobtrusiveness, I remember him more because, although he is shy, I was always completely at ease with him because of his friendliness. Not the large, expansive friendliness of a playful Alsatian, but the quiet friendliness of known woodland in the afternoon sunshine.'[43]

Graham thinks the girl described in 'Love and Gorizia' was a real person whom Douglas met while he was in Gorizia, but there's no corroborating evidence.[44] Douglas appears to be writing about love itself, rather than a real person, and it's worth noting that the poem is about love *and* Gorizia rather than love *in* Gorizia; similarly, one of his poems to Liz Brodie was more about love itself than the object of that love.[45] It is more of a technical exercise than a poem, a position that Douglas himself seems to have acknowledged when he discarded it apart from a version of the first stanza which appears as 'Bexhill' in *Complete Poems*.[46]

Before they moved to the Cotswolds the Rudds had lived in Boarshead near Crowborough in East Sussex, where Jo rented the flat next door, above Boarshead Post Office. While Jo's mental health was deteriorating Douglas seemed robust. In Rudd's words Douglas was 'a very powerful character, physically strong and rather ruthless. When we played cowboys and Indians, I was always the Indian and he the cowboy and when he shot me clean between the eyes with his airgun, he made me explain to his grandmother that I'd scratched my forehead with a thorn.' Later they played 'long-drawn-out war games with model soldiers, incorporating train movements. We made a mountain railway through the rockery. We constructed a replica of Brooklands out of the drive on which we raced our Alfa Romeo models. Billy became a great modeller, particularly of sailing ships which he made entirely out of his own raw materials. From there he moved into lino cuts, drawing and painting ... Even as a child, I knew that I was being exposed to raw talent of an exceptional kind. It wasn't a comfortable experience but it was certainly stimulating.'[47]

Douglas's mother's situation wasn't improving. She lost her only secure income when her mother died in 1932 and by the end of that year she was close to breakdown. She was saved from destitution by a woman she hardly knew, the local rector's wife, Mrs Miles, who had two sons at Christ's Hospital and who Jo met at Tunbridge Wells station at the beginning and end of school terms. Mrs Miles invited Jo to stay at the rectory until her health improved, and she stayed there for about six months before finding an unfurnished flat to rent in Bexhill. She rented out the flat when she could, intending to find cheaper rooms for herself and her son during the school holidays, but Douglas often had no home to come to. He stayed with the Miles or Rudd families and at least once with Sir Reginald Spence in Blackboys. Spence, by now retired, was an alumnus of Douglas's school and often had Christ's Hospital boys to stay during holiday times. Douglas stayed with his mother in Bexhill sometimes but saw little of her as she was almost permanently occupied as the companion of a demanding older woman.

Unfortunately few of Douglas's letters from Christ's Hospital survive. We know that he settled into the school fairly quickly and that some of the early institutional tensions eased. A postscript in his letter of 16 October 1932 reports that life was 'much nicer this term, with all the snobs gone up into the senior dorm and only one beastly monitor instead of about 4.' He continued to play rugby and performed well academically (although in an undated letter of 1932 or 1933 he told his mother that he had come bottom of the form in maths because he lost a paper). He won the School Certificate, Great Erasmus, in 1933 and in 1934 he played Theseus in *A Midsummer Night's Dream* and represented the school at swimming. Douglas was big for his age, a rugby player, and he was a seasoned boarder so one can imagine that he found the rules and idiosyncrasies of a new school relatively easy to accommodate. Noel Burdett, a contemporary at Christ's Hospital, remembered that 'even in his early teens he was a distinctive figure'; he had a 'certain charisma which ensured him a following.'[48] As his close school friend, Norman Ilett, said: 'he was not a popular figure, but the people (boys and masters) … who knew him well were very fond of him, and his talents were everywhere respected and admired. The stumbling blocks were his tongue, which hurt at times, his manners, which could be appalling, and his snobbery, which he tried to justify by arguing that grace and beauty belonged to the upper classes.'[49] Keith Douglas was already easier to admire than to like. It is a theme that runs through his short life.

We have few letters from Christ's Hospital but his contributions to *The Outlook* were relentless, and not just as Keith Douglas. We know that he used the pseudonyms Billy (his family nickname, taken from the then popular Billiken figure), Raps, Flip and K at the time and many of his poems and linocuts that were published in *The Outlook* appear over these names, presumably to diminish the impression that Keith Douglas was dominating the magazine.[50] His first contribution was 'Reculver' by 'K', published in issue 33 (March 1932), an essay on the early Roman fort and medieval church at Reculver in Kent. The towers impose themselves on Herne Bay and are navigation guides for ships. Douglas's short essay is masterful for a 12-year-old. 'Meet them on a June morning,' it begins confidently, 'when sea and sky mingle in a shimmering haze, and the oyster yawls and cement barges with their brown sails, seem to float suspended in mid-air.'[51] There are two poems by 'Billy' in the December 1934 issue, neither collected by Desmond Graham in his edition of the complete poems, but unmistakably by Douglas. 'Pan' and 'Ave atque vale' appear to be his first published poems:

Pan

Tall trees are standing in a twilit hollow,
Leaves on the bushes hanging silent as the night;
Only the rustle of a hurrying rabbit,
Scuttling in the bushes, in and out of sight.

Softly on the silence breaks a thin, shrill piping,
Animals are hurrying, scurring to hear;
Following the music, maddening, magical,
Falling soft and sweet upon the evening air.[52]

It isn't a great poem, marred by the repetition of 'hurrying' and fairly conventional in tone, but the other poem by 'Billy' in the same issue shows more promise:

Ave atque vale

Your laughter brought the sun to me again,
You came and stole my heart, a willing prey,
Now all the world is dark once more, for then,
Laughing you fled away.[53]

These are Douglas's earliest published poems and they are largely derivative, although they were good enough, according to Graham, for fellow Christ's Hospital student Noel Burdett to 'tear up some of his own efforts in shame'.[54] As William Scammell said, 'The early poems are best seen as a series of skirmishes and try-outs in which he [Douglas] exercises and explores his talent.'[55] Douglas quickly developed a strong and original voice, as though he realized that he didn't have much time for throat-clearing. The following issue of *The Outlook* contained an essay and a poem by 'Billy' and two linocuts, a fine modernist band of musicians (by 'K.C.D.')

as well as an abstract drawing (by 'K.C. Douglas'). The essay, 'On Fishing as an Art', again starts confidently: 'The man who gathers together his fishing tackle, and deliberately sets out to sit in rain and profane silence for a whole afternoon, nay, even possibly for a whole day, deserves only to be laughed at.' It is valuable, however, as a glimpse into how the 15-year-old Douglas spent some of his time, for it has a ring of authenticity:

> O skilful blunderer, when you go for an afternoon's fishing, tramp away over the fields and along the winding shady lanes to some little lake where overhanging trees shut you off from the passing busyness of the farm folk. Row out a little way from the edge, if there is a boat to be had, and lie drifting in the deeper water, when the world is peaceful and there is no sound save the 'plop' of roach jumping for the insects which hum and buzz above them, and no movement save when a kingfisher, perched in the overhanging boughs at the water's edge, darts suddenly downwards and is gone, leaving your eyes still dazzled by his swift brilliance.
>
> There you may hang your rod, propped with a lazy foot, over the edge of your boat, and gaze dreamily up at the unchanging blue above you, till you can feel the movement of the earth, and, growing somewhat dizzy, raise your head to see the green float bobbing suggestively.'[56]

The poem, 'Xaipe', is still derivative but it has a languid charm:

> Down we are going to the clammy dark,
> But vainly closes listless silence round
> Our justling path. Fast follows happiness
> And gay we go, light on our lips the strains
> Of half-forgotten songs, and old brave deeds,
> Like shadows slipping through a sunlit hedge,
> Throng in and out our memories. Though Spring
> No more shall know us, down the heather'd hills
> Like distant pan-pipes in the evening, comes
> The echo of our laughter on the wind.'[57]

The image of 'shadows slipping through a sunlit hedge' anticipates the eye for detail and transitoriness that is such a feature of poems written a few years later. The central theme of these early poems is a landscape in which pagan notes are never far away. They are poems of celebration rather than regret. It is not nostalgia that colours these early poems, but a sense of imminence.

They are liminal; Douglas already loved the interstice between reality and a not-quite-lost Paganism. Pan is close, and ready to return. Indeed, it is noticeable how little a Christian God appears in Douglas's poetry, all the more striking as the collections he was familiar with at school are full of it.

The July 1935 issue carried 'A Simple Story' by 'Billy' and a wretched poem by 'Raps'. As the story appears not to have been published since 1935 it is worth quoting in full. It shows a keen eye for cultural differences:

War was imminent. Manchuria was mobilizing. Russia was re-mobilizing. France was furious. Even England was agitated. In short, things looked Pretty Grim.

And in Geneva the Venerable College of Astrologers and astronomers were asleep round their table. At least, they were not all asleep: one of them was doing calculations on the table with a piece of chalk. Suddenly he leapt to his feet and staggered from the room, dragging with him the bottom waistcoat-button of his neighbour which had, in the course of the years, become entangled in his beard.

In half-an-hour the message of the Astronomer flashed out to the world. 'A large planet' (said the Astronomer), 'is moving rapidly towards Earth, and will strike it some time within the next six months.' The earth was staggered. The entire population of France went mad, and murdered all Paris taxi-drivers under the age of fifty. The entire population of Russia went sane, and murdered M. Litvinoff. A Sanitary Inspector named Herbert Philbottle bit Mr. Lloyd George. Mr. Ghandi broke his eighteen-year fast and ate his loincloth. And Hitler shaved his moustache.

On the 14th day another message was broadcast: 'I regret to announce' (said the Astronomer), 'that I made an error, due to a trifling miscalculation, in my broadcast. The planet will strike Earth, not, as previously stated, within six months, but within 6,666,666 months.'

So the world calmed down again, and there was no more war, because all the Dictators had been killed.

But the Astronomer was unaware of this, for, as he was turning from the Broadcasting House, he tripped over his beard and broke his neck.

Poor fellow.[58]

'A Simple Story' was written some four years before the war in which Douglas died broke out. Though written in a flippant way it feels premonitory. The poem in the same issue is probably best overlooked. It is about rabbits and a 'great lout of a flower-picking housemaid'.[59]

Douglas had been preoccupied by astrology. On 2 June 1933 a London astrologer reported on his horoscope. 'You do not readily communicate your thoughts to others', it said, accurately enough, 'and you are undoubtedly a person to be trusted with a secret, for not under any circumstances would you abuse a confidence or trust.' It goes on to say:

> Honest, amiable and sincere you are greatly liked by those about you; the nature is upright, humane and prudent, and when trained and cultured a love of investigation, analysis and research is active.

> You are fond of music and possess an appreciation of the refinements of life generally, also any form of intellectual expression. The sublime and beautiful in all things appeals to you greatly, and you should have an excellent conception of colour and skill in art ...

> You possess good mental and intellectual abilities, and a ready understanding of character and motive. The intuitive and critical faculties are developed, making you a good judge of human nature. Your first impressions are often the correct ones, and when in doubt you would do well to rely, to a very great extent, upon these, and ask yourself what your first impressions were.

> There is indicated continuity and strength of will, and you are not easily swayed from your course when once your mind is made up concerning it. Your natural abilities fit you to hold any position of trust, where honour and integrity are called for: you possess a sense of responsibility, and an appreciation of what is required of you ...

> You may at times give the impression of being rather reserved, with a tendency to keep somewhat in the background, although this is often brought about by a reluctance to push your aims and interests to the disadvantage of others. It is indicated that you are very loyal in friendship, and stand by your friends in times of adversity or trouble; also that you are reliable and trustworthy, and can keep your own counsel when any matter of confidence is involved ...

> A quality which you should strive to cultivate by every possible means is optimism. I suspect some tendency to look rather at the dark side of things at

times, to give way to occasional fits of depression, and to imagine that your efforts are not appreciated ...

Again you are lacking in adaptability; in you this most essential quality to success is by no means prominent, and although you undoubtedly possess marked ambition and desire for progress, it is likely that along with this there is a certain conservatism of thought, which, unless modified, may be responsible for your allowing many opportunities to pass unnoticed ...

It is likely that you would succeed in some profession concerned with literature or art, or in professions which combine both.[60]

We can't know, of course, how much Douglas told the astrologer of his personality and behaviour but this is a remarkably astute assessment.

By the end of 1935 Douglas was dominating *The Outlook*. The December issue carried two poems by 'Raps', a poem and a linocut by 'Billy' and a linocut by K. C. Douglas. The poems attributed to 'Raps' are 'Song' ('You asked me for a song to sing'), and 'The Alchymist'. 'Song' is as far from the modernist revolution in poetry as one can imagine[61] but, taken on its own terms, it is a delight:

> You asked me for a song to sing
> and this shall be for you
> a many-music'd, joyous thing
> sung to the flower'd dew
> that comes before sun is up,
> When the stars are pale and few.
>
> Open your lips; awhile forget
> old Time's sand-dropping glass;
> put off your shoes, your feet are wet,
> the dew is on the grass,
> behind each cob-webb'd trunk you'll see
> the old Arcadians pass.
>
> Dryads who make the poets glad
> Dance on the forest floor,
> Swing to the wild asclepiad;
> Sweet Orpheus sings once more.

Old Pan, brown-horned and bushy-legg'd ...
Listens with rustic awe.[62]

In view of what was going on in the world these verses seem particularly disengaged. They deal with a remote, legendary, fairy universe and seem wilfully to ignore the growing ugliness of mindset in Europe and beyond. They speak of hope in a world where hope was dying and in this sense they can seem irrelevant. But I think that we can see beyond the subject matter to a poet learning his craft. There is a sense of rhythmic certainty and the ABABCB rhyme scheme is disciplined, the subtle internal rhymes and half-rhymes (the dew 'that comes before the sun is up'), the alliteration and the imagery (the dryads who 'swing to the wild asclepiad' seem to come from the world of jazz, recalling the linocut of the lithe band in the April issue).

Desmond Graham hears Ezra Pound's 'The Alchemist', first published in 1920 but probably written some eight years previously, behind Douglas's 'The Alchymist'[63] but Douglas's alchemist seems to me to inhabit a different universe:

These are my simples ...
toad's blood in tall beakers,
and in the darkness at the cave's end
rows of skulls like after-dinner speakers,
grinning their dead, fixed laughter;
and the mice scrape on each rafter.
Four days I fasted
(si quis mala viderit pabula terrae) ...
And my prayer lasted
from midnight till midnight.
Now I am ready; now
Asmoday is coming;
he is planing, he is swinging,
breathing foulness he is winging;
swift and wrathful at my calling
he is falling
mighty-wing'd through cloud and vapours,
till he capers
bound in my circle.
His wrath is obscene;
livid green his three heads glitter
prison'd in my circle;

on his anguineal tail,
pale, each scale
glares
and the dragon, his familiar,
crouches sibilant,
lewd and vigilant ...
Show me the secret,
secretum secretorum,
the secret of secrets,
tu operans sis secretus horum,
thou that work'st be secret in them
El, Abiel, Anathiel Sedonel,
Heli, Tolimi, by the names of Jahroch,
Tell, Tell, Tell
thy secrets.[64]

I doubt very much that Douglas had ever encountered Pound's alchemist. If the imagery is derived from anywhere it's from Milton's 'Paradise Lost' and it is more likely that the subject itself is drawn from Merejkowski's *The Romance of Leonardo da Vinci* than from Pound.[65]

The combination of drawing and poem is continued in the same issue by 'Billy'. A linocut depicting a fisherman appears with the poem 'Song of the Fisherman'. The fisherman in the linocut is oriental. A turban on his head and a scimitar in his belt, Douglas's fisherman sits under a palm tree with a blazing sun behind him, apparently with no more equipment than a line and a large wicker basket.[66] The fisherman in the poem is also oriental:

The pot is greenish gold, sea wrought
by squamous monsters in their salty caverns
patterned in alchemistic sort,
such as the Tyrian raiders brought
for Suliman or Saba;
and there is
a djinni.
that is what
is in the pot:
he has ten thousand names,
Mustapha ben Ammi Kobail, Radinni ...
his eyes are flames:
Eblis gave him

his blackness; and his height
a thousand times the water's depth
where lay his pot ten aeons sunk in night
caved in the sand, where swim
the ghoul-fish dim ...
bright was my hook,
look,
the rust from the red handle of the pot
clings with the entrails of a weed –
and here a lot
of dragons, red-tailed,
are on the pot's edge,
here the ships that sailed
with Tiglath's treasures
oil-filled measures ...
he oozed out of his jar
twelve cubits high
curling
black in the sky
treacly, but I
caught him again, quick whirling
the lid upon him,
bubbling in his jar,
aha.[67]

We have come a long way from the bucolic delights of 'On Fishing as an Art'.

1935 proved to be a significant year for Douglas besides his 11 contributions to *The Outlook*. His acting prowess was noted in the school's official magazine, *The Blue*.[68] During the summer he went on holiday to Italy and spent two weeks in Gorizia (in Italy but on the border with Slovenia) with his mother's half-sister who was a companion to Douglas's great aunt, Countess Calice. Gorizia had long been part of the Austrian empire but it changed hands during the First World War and ended up, virtually destroyed, as part of Italy. It had, according to the historian of the front between Italy and the Austro-Hungarians, Mark Thompson, been known as 'the Austrian Nice, the city of roses or violets. Blessed by a mild climate in winter, with hills behind and the turquoise Isonzo in front, it flourished under the Habsburgs. Long avenues were lined with handsome villas. The public gardens were exceptionally pretty, the medieval castle on the hill was picturesque. The hospitals and convalescent homes were patronised by wealthy Viennese and Bavarians, who formed a German crust on top of the mixed Italian and Slovene population.'[69] Gorizia became officially part of Italy only in 1920, and during Mussolini's regime Slovene organizations were dissolved and the Slovene language was prohibited. By the time Douglas visited, some 20 years after the fighting came to the city's outskirts, Gorizia had been rebuilt by the local architect Max Fabiani. Several rationalist buildings were erected during this period, and Fabiani needed no excuse to celebrate in fascist architecture the strength, pride and power that the nationalist regime had brought to Italy. He planned the reconstruction of Gorizia, and he was still at work there (designing the Chiesa del Sacro Cuore) the year before Douglas's visit.

There is a strong autobiographical element in the story, 'A Half-bottle of Wine', that Douglas wrote in September 1935. It begins with the remains of a picnic: 'Felix watched Aquileia jolt into view surrounded by the remains of a 10-lira lunch-basket which he had bought at Monfalcone an hour before. Most of the journey had been occupied deliciously in disclosing the unending content of this basket. There had been … veal, and spaghetti, a roll and some cheese, and some gold-coloured cake made of honey; and there was a half-bottle of wine, long-necked, with straw plaited into a sort of jacket round the base of it. The wine, dull red through the coarse green glass, gave him a comfortable feeling of anticipation as he wrestled with the unaccustomed coils of the spaghetti.'[70]

Douglas had a great deal of freedom in Gorizia. He had been able to drink wine and soak up the sounds and sights of a historical city. Returning from that freedom to his impoverished and mentally fragile mother and to the regimentation of school life can't have been easy. He was fifteen but looked seventeen; he still wasn't old enough to have conferred on him the relative freedoms of the Grecians. Gorizia and the surrounding landscape had a profound effect on Douglas's poetry and we hear echoes of the two weeks he spent there in poetry he wrote long after his stay ended.

At around this time an event shook his world at Christ's Hospital. He wrote to the headmaster in December 1935 a long letter (seven pages) of which three pages survive. Douglas had been threatened with expulsion from the school after 'borrowing' a rifle from the school armoury. The pages that survive are a model of righteous indignation, and mature for a fifteen-year-old:

... hunger first made Preece trades-monitor, and then broke open the cupboard. Someone told Mr. Edwards [Lamb A's housemaster] that I had kept the key in order to have the biscuits to myself. He believed it joyfully.

He then had me in, and, with tears in his eyes (this is no sarcasm, but truth) told me how rottenly I had treated him ever since I had been in the house, adding that he would accept no apology, as he knew I should not mean it. I did apologise, whereupon he growled that he preferred deeds to words.

So I am a thief – driven out of all self-control by what I fancied to be injustice: a liar – to a man who could believe anything untrue against me. But you have behaved squarely to me in all things save one, and I have told you no lies. I have nothing against Major Hodgson [leader of the school's Cadet Corps], who sets spies and expects lies. But to Mr Edwards who expects loyalty & gives none, I cannot be loyal. If I were a monitor I would be loyal to the house – and tell him fewer lies than any other monitor – bar Nash.

But that would not be hard.

Now (if you have read thus far) you have my own point of view.

Everything I have set down is true.

I shall expect punishment. But you cannot give anything worse than insults you heaped on me before Major Hodgson. If you could have refrained from laughing, when you were discussing whether to make or break a boy's career, I would not mind so much – As it is you cannot punish me more. This letter is for you and I ask you not to show it to anyone but Mr Edwards. He shall see that it is the truth, though scilicet he will say he knew nothing of some of it.

Perhaps he could have guessed, had he not been so ready to believe things against me. If you remember that in addition to these things I have had boils, work, extra work, games and extra Certificate A parades to think of perhaps you will think less hardly of me.

Yours sincerely
Keith Douglas

P.S. If I have been rude, I must apologise. It is hard to write coolly of something about which I feel so strongly.[71]

Douglas had removed to his home a rifle from the Armoury. He had asked permission from Major Hodgson to take the old rifle home and repair it during the Christmas holiday, but Hodgson had refused so Douglas broke into the Armoury and took the gun. The War Office carried out its four-yearly check during that holiday and Douglas's shocked mother found two policemen at her front-door enquiring about the theft of the rifle, which they found in pieces in her son's bedroom, each piece cleaned and oiled. Douglas was interviewed by his housemaster, a War Office major and the headmaster of the school, Oswald (H. L. O.) Flecker. Before becoming a teacher Flecker, universally known as 'the oil',[72] had been a Lieutenant in the 7th Battalion of the Gloucestershire Regiment, serving in Mesopotamia.[73] He tried to find a diplomatic solution to Douglas's misdemeanour, no doubt touched by the boy's apparently honest indignation. Douglas was not expelled but he was moved from Lamb A house to Middleton B and instructed to have nothing to do with his former housemates, an instruction that he refused to accommodate on the grounds of impracticality. Flecker's diplomacy earned him Douglas's contempt. He told his mother that he didn't trust Flecker:

> I now find that he has taken careful precaution that I shall not be house-captain and probably not get a study. He never told me as I suppose he imagines I will go on behaving myself better if I think I may be house-captain.

> Whereas the only reason I shall behave myself is that I have no doubt he would get rid of me at the slightest excuse rather than admit a mistake. He himself is not fit to be a house-monitor with such a sense of justice, let alone a head-master. His whole character is shown in his behaviour to people under him. He treats the masters very obviously as inferiors, and when he was taking us in the library and a small boy was sent in by another master, to get a chair our polite head master bit his head off and kept up a solid fire of abuse until he was out of the room, as if it was the boy's fault. It's disgusting that such a man should earn money. However I still smile politely at him and laugh at his jokes.[74]

One can imagine Douglas adding that last caveat for the sake of his naturally worried mother. She would have been aware of the family's good fortune in getting Douglas into Christ's Hospital in the first place. She wouldn't have wanted to contemplate the possibility of his losing his place there through rebellion, however principled.

Douglas's world might have been rocked but he continued to dominate *The Outlook*. He made four contributions as 'Raps' and one as 'D' in the April 1936 edition. The first was a poem called 'Countryside':

Why are your songs of other years;
Are all the Little people passed?
Have your paean'd heroes broke their spears
Those once immortal overcast?

Or, sphereless and sempivolent,
Do the gods range the void unseen?
Have they left no equivalent,
Those ones of whom your tale hath been?

Earth is grown old: are all her seed
Unlovely souls, an breed uncouth,
With whom truck not the older breed,
The storied offspring of her youth?

Nay, time will see them come again
To walk earth in their ancient pride,
It cannot be that gods are slain
Or elves and leprechauns have died.

The shaggy god shall tune his pipe,
And all the burrow'd ticket dance,
Where they lie stretched, the time is ripe,
The sleepers take each one his lance
And stand up, ranked for chivalry,
Serried for what may chance.[75]

'Countryside' is another celebration of an old, pagan world which is quietly dominated by a Pan who is simply biding his time. The repetition of 'breed' jars a little, and neologisms like 'sempivolent' (presumably 'always wanting') don't help, but the poem shows a young poet coming to terms with his art.[76] In 'Strange Gardener', which does appear in Graham's edition of Douglas's *Complete Poems*, we can hear the poet finding his real voice:

Over the meadows,
framed in the quiet osiers, dreams the pond;
region of summer gnat-busyness

and, in the afternoon's blue drowsiness,
plops among the water-shadows:
and the cool trees wait beyond.

A young man dwelt there
with a swift, sad face, and full of phantasy,
repeating, as he heard it,
the alliterative speech of the water-spirit;
smoothing his pale hair
with automatic ecstasy.

This was his garden,
uncultivated (order hated him);
whence, in a winter-madness
(whose scourge filled him with recklessness,
Seeing the frost harden),
the water-spirit translated him.[77]

He wrote 'Strange Gardener' in a school exercise book on his sixteenth birthday. The exercise book exists in the British Library and the poem is followed by a lengthy explanation, which is 'intended to shew that although the main idea of the poem was spontaneous, and the poem itself is short, the scheme behind it is lengthily and carefully thought out. The lapses in metre are put in purposely, in an attempt to make it less stereotyped & more interesting.'[78] Douglas's 'explanation' is thorough and professional. He first points out that he doesn't keep 'very strictly' to a metre but that it roughly has a shape, and secondly that the rhyming scheme is A B C C A B, with only the last syllables corresponding in the C rhyme. But it is in the 'meaning' that Douglas's explanation is fascinating:

Over the meadows …	The first line is intended to take the reader well away from his surroundings immediately
framed …	you are a rook flying over the pond, & looking down at it.
the quiet osiers …	you know they are there, like a frame, but their rustling is inaudible, you are not distracted from the important thing, the pond.

gnat-busyness …	this is not, of course, a spelling mistake, but quite a different word from business
fish plop among the	you have flown over the meadows as a bird
water-shadows …	Now you are a water-being, hanging over the pond in the summer.
trees *wait* beyond …	these did not distract you from your contemplation of the pond, but they are there for you, when you are ready, to look at ['them' added by teacher]
a swift, sad face … *the main idea of this verse* *is taken from the chief* *character of 'The Star-born'*	the swiftness of his face is in the lines of it, his high cheek-bones and the curved hang of his hair. It is his eyes that are sad, because his thoughts are more beautiful than reality.
repeating … the alliterative speech … *this idea also from SB* alliterative	he repeats it, struck with its beauty, as a child will repeat what is said to it. the speech of water is an interminable cavalcade of similar sounds.
automatic ecstasy …	he is not aware of his action, but the feel of
his pale hair … C. Day Lewis in *'From Feathers to Iron' speaks of 'tow-* *headed poets'*	his hair, soft and smooth under his hand, gives him pleasure. cf. T. S. Eliot 'she smooths her hair with automatic hand'.
a winter madness … seeing	the sight of the beauty of summer dying all about him caused him such acute misery that he was temporarily mad.
the frost harden … *this has some connection with 'The* *Tempest' 'doth suffer a sea-change' cf.* *'translated'*	
the water-spirit translated him …	i.e. he drowned himself in the throes of his despondent insanity. For the water-spirit cf. Henry Williamson, 'The Star-born'.[79]

I can't think of any other poet who tells us so explicitly how to read his work. The knowledge that Williamson's cryptic novel provides so much of the background to 'Strange Gardener' loads the poem with an occult profundity. As Scammell says, this Narcissus 'doesn't mean to go altogether quietly'.[80]

'Narcissus' from The Outlook

The linocut that accompanies the poem is Douglas's (it is signed 'D'). Without being technically proficient the drawing suggests that the youth is in possession of the landscape, that it was indeed 'his garden'. The slim, pale, naked boy it depicts is not very far from the wood engraving of Starr by C. F. Tunnicliffe in the first edition of Williamson's *The Star-Born*.[81] The two other poems (by 'Raps'), '.303' and 'Youth' also appear in *Complete Poems* with minor changes. '.303' shows his preoccupation with military matters. The .303 was a rimmed rifle cartridge that saw about 70 years as the standard ammunition for British rifles. Douglas's poem is relentless and unsentimental, as most of his poetry is from this point. His poetic stance is not neutral but dispassionate. The first stanza reflects a world in which man's delight in the natural world is at least possible:

I have looked through the pine-trees
Cooling their sun-warmed
needles in the night,

I saw the moon's face white
Beautiful as the breeze.

The cartridge, however, sees a different scene:

Yet you have seen the boughs sway with the night's breath,
Wave like dead arms, repudiating the stars
And the moon, circular and useless, pass
Pock-marked with death.

The cartridge teaches the poet a utilitarian lesson:

Through a machine-gun's sights
I saw men curse, weep, cough, sprawl in their entrails;
You did not know the gardener in the vales,
Only efficiency delights you.[82]

In *Complete Poems* 'the gardener' is 'The Gardener', a more explicit reference to Christ's appearance to Mary Magdalene after the crucifixion, and in the second line of the final stanza we get more than a whiff of the anti-war poetry of the First World War. It recalls the listing technique of Wilfred Owen's 'Dulce et decorum est': 'In all my dreams, before my helpless sight,/He plunges at me, guttering, choking, drowning.'[83]

In its detached, observational tone though, it recalls Isaac Rosenberg rather than Owen. '.303' was written at about the time of Douglas's scrape with the school and War Office authorities over the missing rifle. The contretemps doesn't seem to have dimmed his enthusiasm for matters military. His commitment to the Officer Training Corps (OTC) was remembered by a contemporary as 'fanatical'[84] and he was especially devoted to drilling. Drilling enables a leader to move a unit of men in an orderly way and to instil habits of precision and obedience; unlikely disciplines in a boy who responded to authority with contempt. This seems to be the central conflict of Douglas's adolescence. On the one hand he was attracted to military tackle, to order and to tradition; on the other the military life was dependent on hierarchy, on blind devotion to duty, on authority figures who in many cases knew less than the men they were leading, the sort of unearned authority that Douglas despised. A school friend recalled that Douglas showed a keen 'reverence' for the privates who visited the OTC, but not for the regular officers.[85] The poem '.303' captures the ambivalence. Pan is unable to overcome the reality that is exposed by the cartridge, but the poet is attracted to both. In the summer term of 1937 he led his platoon to victory in the school competition in drill, turnout, map-reading, weapons training and tactics, and was rewarded with the task of choosing the squad for the inter-schools guard-mounting competition in August. 'No. 5 Platoon,' reported *The Blue*, was 'commanded by Serjeant Douglas, who is to be congratulated on thoroughly deserving his success, as he has shown a great keenness and efficiency throughout the year.'[86] Noel Burdett, who was one of the chosen, recalled his surprise at discovering that Douglas was not confident of success in most areas of his life.[87]

Douglas's final contribution to the April 1936 edition of *The Outlook* was a poem 'Youth', by Raps, that has more than a little Kipling in it:

Your sword is brilliant: through the auburn leaves
The sun patches your tunic of smooth-woven green,
Each fold a thousand aery shimmers leaves,
Dazzling as leaping fish a moment seen.

The road curls down below you. In its spell
Pass glebe and woodland, where a hundred ways
Twist, some to fairyland, and some to Hell;
But there are better things beyond the maze.

When you have heard the whirl and song of strife,
When use scratches and rusts your weapons' gleam,
And age has marred the youngness of your life
With dreams, you will come back again and dream.[88]

Desmond Graham thinks the early poetry has a pre-Raphaelite texture, and he traces this to the influence of the Frank Brangwyn murals in the school chapel.[89] This calls to mind the Rider–Waite tarot pack in the description of the landscape and the youth's tunic, and in Douglas's adolescent poetry generally. The popular tarot pack was designed by the mystic A. E. Waite and published by William Rider & Sons in 1910. The illustrations, by Pamela Colman Smith ('Pixie'), are essentially Arthurian. We know that Douglas had been attracted by astrology and the tarot cards evoke a pre-Christian world that is ideally suited to a Pan figure.

Douglas was becoming aware of contemporary writers.[90] He was already familiar with Edith Sitwell, W. H. Auden and two of the giants of modernism, Pound and Eliot. In the summer of 1936 he chose for prizes

Michael Roberts's *Poems* and Ian Parsons's anthology of modern poems, *The Progress of Poetry*, which emphasized the poets of the First World War and was quick to promote Isaac Rosenberg. He also discovered, with history teacher David Roberts's encouragement, Helen Waddell's *The Wandering Scholars* and Dmitri Merejkowski's *The Romance of Leonardo da Vinci* which, as we shall see, formed the backbone of one of his early poems (although he was critical of it in his 'Book Diary'[91]). Douglas also read Geoffrey Grigson's magazine *New Verse*. Ilett recalled coming across Douglas at a school billiard table where Douglas was tap-dancing with a copy of *New Verse* beside him. 'Anyone can write like the stuff in here,' said Douglas. 'Go on then, try: and I bet you can't!' Ilett replied.[92] So Douglas submitted two poems to Grigson in the summer of 1936. Needless to say, Grigson rejected them. What tempted Douglas to send 'Poem' and 'Menippus in Sussex' to *New Verse* is difficult to say. Douglas must have known that his Arcadia wouldn't appeal to Grigson. As Blunden later said: 'His [Douglas's] mythology was energetic, for he had not noticed that the classical world had been sent to Coventry. He was a young man who often did not notice such things.'[93] Grigson's rejection letters are fairly restrained, but to the point: '"Poem" is better than "Menippus in Sussex" – maybe it is less well written, but it shows off a good deal less. It is all right knowing e.g. about trachiotomy [sic] but there isn't as a rule much point about using words which mean nothing to most readers. It smells of Ezra Pound and imitators of all that is less pleasant about Eliot.'[94] And after a further submission: 'This address [the Connaught Hospital in Walthamstow] is why I've not answered your note or returned yr. poem; which is much better ... But it's slighter than anything I want to publish.'[95]

The reasons for rejection may have puzzled Douglas. The editions of *New Verse* that summer are preoccupied by surrealism (there was a surrealist exhibition in London in June 1936) and carry essays and reviews by W. H. Auden, translations by David Gascoyne, a bizarre short essay by Grigson himself and blunt evaluations (often written by Grigson himself as he admitted later when he appeared as Roy Plomley's guest on the BBC's *Desert Island Discs*) of, among others, T. S. Eliot, Edmund Blunden, Michael Roberts's edition of *The Faber Book of Modern Verse* as well as Parsons's *The Progress of Poetry* and *Poetry* (Chicago). It's hard to warm to *New Verse* and Douglas was setting himself up for disappointment if he seriously thought Grigson would be interested in anything that touched on Pan, unless it was to ridicule him. Douglas wrote a fantasy (entitled 'Misunderstanding') which wasn't published until 1980 in *The Outlook* in which he caricatured Grigson. Cedric Kennedy (presumably based on the First World War survivor who taught Douglas and Tony Rudd painting) 'used to send his poems to the editor of a very modern magazine, but none of them had ever been accepted. Cedric still hoped that one day he would think out a poem which would baffle even this hardened man, who, he was sure, never printed poems unless he could not make head or tail of them.'[96]

Douglas contributed two items to the July 1936 edition of *The Outlook*, a poem and the accompanying linocut. The poem, 'Japanese song', described by Scammell as an 'astonishing thing',[97] is collected by Graham as 'Encounter with a God' but is otherwise hardly changed except for the punctuation and spelling.[98] This is the poem as it appeared in *The Outlook*:

Japanese Song

Ono-no-komache, the poetess,
sat on the ground among her flowers,
sat in her intricate patterned dress
thinking of the rowers,
thinking of the god Daikoku.

Thinking of the rock pool
and carp in the waterfall at night.
"Daikoku in accordance with the rule
is beautiful", she said, "with a slight
tendency to angles."

And Daikoku came
who had been drinking all night
with the greenish gods of chance and fame,
he was rotund standing in the moonlight
with a round, white paunch,

who said
I am not beautiful,
I do not wish to be wonderfully made,
I am intoxicated, dutiful daughter,
and I will not be in a poem.

But the poetess sat still
holding her head and making verses,
"How intricate and peculiarly well
arranged the symmetrical belly-purses
Of lord Daikoku."[99]

Ted Hughes wrote in 1964 that 'it is not enough to say that the language is utterly simple, the musical inflection of it particularly honest and charming, the technique flawless. The language is extremely forceful; or rather, it reposes at a point it could only have reached, this very moment, by a feat of great strength. And the inflexion of the voice has a bluntness that might be challenging if it were not so frank, and so clearly the advance of an unusually aware mind. As for the technique, insofar as it can be considered separately, there is nothing dead or asleep in it, nothing tactless, and such subtlety of movement, such economy of means, such composition of cadences, would do credit to any living poet. And behind that, ordering its directions, the essentially practical cast of his energy, his impatient, razor energy.'[100] Hughes is discussing 'Encounter with a God' but he could be talking about the whole of Douglas's work.

As Scammell says, 'Douglas's habitual irony sits well with the tonal limpidity of the Japanese mode, and this says much for his poetic tact.'[101] He illustrates this with an examination of the curious ninth and tenth lines. The 'slight/tendency to angles' refers to Daikoku, the rule and the poetess, not to the carp, the god's paunch or the waterfall: 'so perhaps they refer punningly to the poet. There is an angle to be found on everything, including the gross conduct of the gods themselves. In the lightest possible way, the poem is an affectionate little treatise on art and life, each with its own rules and unruly contingencies.' Scammell's perceptive reading of this poem shows how rapidly Douglas was developing. Scammell isn't alone in thinking this poem a minor masterpiece. Ted Hughes wrote that 'it is quite limited in scope ... but it accomplishes its job, not an easy one, as brilliantly and surely as anything Douglas ever did. And the qualities that create and distinguish his most important later work are already there.'[102]

Douglas made three further contributions, as Raps, to the December 1936 edition, two poems and an essay. The first poem is 'Distraction from classics', only twelve lines but sharp with the authenticity of real observation:

Now my mind's off again. No tears
Of Catullus move me. Though I know, in turn
We, too, will praise these years
Of watching clouds through windows, fluttering pages,
Usefully sometimes, though the beckoning scents
Rise always, wafted from summer grass.
Hearing the loud bees mumble at the glass
And sound of sunlight behind the scratching pens,
We crouch to read the speech of other ages.

Many were here, some cursed, loved some. All these
Alike pass; after a space return,
Loud-voiced, mocking the older memories.[103]

This poem ends after the word 'pens' in *Complete Poems* (where it is titled 'Distraction')[104] but the last four lines, aside from making the poem grammatically correct, supply a context that is otherwise missing. Many of us have mused during apparently irrelevant classes, while the sounds and smells of summer rise outside as the 'sound of sunlight' distracts us, knowing the lesson to be less irrelevant than it appears. Douglas seems to have had a problem concentrating in classics lessons. He wrote in a short story, 'The Siren', that

> Work on these summer mornings was always hard, particularly at the end of the morning, when the bees were about among the flowers in the Headmaster's garden. This garden was just outside the windows of Mr. Dandy's form-room, and occasionally a bee would come away from the sunshine to mumble at one of the dirty panes for a moment. And while he whizzed his little face up and down the glass opposite twenty-five copies of Merk's Roman Reader, or whatever book might lie on that window-ledge, covered with dust and dead flies, concentration departed entirely from the silent inmates of the room. Their hearts leaped away, even from Homer, (which meant something to some of them), to pursue the summer noise of that bee back to his business among the flowers.[105]

The gentle humour of the breeze that flutters the students' pages 'usefully sometimes' is a new note in Douglas's developing voice, one that we will hear more frequently as his poetry matures. The other poem, 'Mummers – a Christmas Poem' has a well-maintained AABCCB rhyme structure (although 'tapestry' and 'artistry' is a bit of a stretch[106]) that shows the apprentice poet learning his technique. The surprising oxymoron of the mummers' 'hands snow-red' is artfully handled: snow may be white but hands that are on the point of freezing are red. The first two stanzas set the wintry scene:

> Put by your stitching. Spread the table
> With winking cups and wines. That sable
> Doff for your brighter silks: are all
> Your glints of pearly laughter shuttered?
> See where the outdoor snows, wind fluttered,
> Through the arched window fall.
>
> See where the deep night's blast has straddled
> The ancient gargoyle, weather-addled
> And barred with melted tapestry
> Of snow; his evil face well-carven
> By Brother Anselm, lean and starven,
> Cell-fasting, rich in artistry.

The final stanza introduces the actors:

> Soon come the quaint masked mummers, knocking
> With hands snow-red; the door's unlocking
> Answers the stars with indoor light.
> Now to the drum-tap, with snow-crusted
> Cardboard steed, and blade time-rusted
> The fabled Saint and Dragon fight.[107]

There are a number of variations in this poem as it was amended by Douglas. Some are minor changes of punctuation but, more importantly, Douglas changed Anselm to Ambrose (presumably for reasons of verbal flow) and 'the fabled Saint and Dragon' to 'Saint and Turk' (presumably a gesture at historical accuracy as the dragon rarely appeared in mummers' plays). According to Graham the poem is meant to evoke the world of Keats's 'Eve of St. Agnes', and there is a half-echo of the mummers' 'hands snow-red' in the 'rose-bloom' on Madeline's hands in Keats's poem.[108] As Scammell says, Douglas's technical assurance is 'startling'.[109] Scammell points out the use of polarities: 'The poem seems to work by the juxtaposition of imagistic blocks of words, rather than by tracing any continuous emotion or thought. The woman at her embroidery and the mummers are as anonymous and thinglike as the gargoyle and its creator … Inside and outside, sable and pearl, starlight and lamplight, mask and stone, saint and Turk: there is a visual and emotional synaesthesia at work in the polarities ("glints of pearly laughter shuttered") which offers parallels between the exterior and interior life.'[110] We might quibble with some of Scammell's 'polarities' (mask and stone?) but his general point, that there is a balancing of images that contributes significantly to the poem's power, is well made. As Vernon Scannell said: 'The whole thing is almost entirely decorative and of course it lacks the substance of informing experience, but the quality of the writing would not disgrace anyone and from a boy of sixteen it is not much short of amazing.'[111] In the month that 'Mummers' appeared in *The Outlook* he wrote to his mother that 'Song' hadn't been printed in the December issue of *Sussex County Magazine* and that he would have to wait until January 1937.[112] The poem duly appeared as 'Pan in Sussex' in January. It was his first poem published outside Christ's Hospital.

The essay in the December 1936 issue of *The Outlook*, 'November' (originally 'November Days'[113]), is a curious piece. Its elegiac (rather Yeatsian) tone is more suited to a middle-aged person than a teenage boy: 'I must think more and more of past summers, chance friends who were very pleasant companions on those sunny days; and who are now passed, with such summers, into oblivion, whence only memory recalls them.' There follows a dream-like passage in the woods near St Martha's church at Guildford. There are reflections on the dream, and the essay ends with an impenetrable paragraph about a Browningesque England in the spring and an odd comparison with Italian 'straw-jacketed wine-bottles' and the clear depths of the waters of the south seas that he had never visited. 'November' has all the hallmarks of a rushed job. Perhaps he was indeed the editor and needed to fill some space (see page 229, note 137).

The Outlook wasn't, of course, Douglas's only focus of attention. He played the brutish Prussian bully, Putz, in Middleton B's production of the Ben Travers farce, *Rookery Nook*, 'a really good show', according to *The Blue*, in which Douglas played a difficult part 'very convincingly'.[114] In March 1937 he acted in J. B. Priestley's 1933 suburban comedy of greed and dishonesty, *Laburnum Grove*, and again earned a positive notice in *The Blue*: 'Although this is not a play that usually goes down well at a house concert, owing to its lack of action … the dialogue was inclined to drag in parts, but Douglas was invariably at hand to liven things up with his excellent performance of Mr. Baxley.'[115] He was congratulated in *The Blue* of June 1938 for his performance as the headmaster in Ian Hay's comedy, *Housemaster*.[116]

He listened to a great deal of jazz, continued to play rugby and did well academically, winning James Stephens's short story collection *Etched in Moonlight* as a prize, but by 1935 he was beginning to put some distance between himself and his mother. They spoke less than before, she recalled, and he replied 'I don't agree' so frequently that she suggested he make a record of the expression, though how much of it was due to her own deteriorating mental health is impossible to judge.[117] He was always combative but in his mid-teens he became more aggressive. The story 'The Siren' is a barely fictionalized self-portrait. Douglas, as John Chadburn, is addressed by the odious Mr Dandy in singularly uncomplimentary terms:

> 'You, Chadburn,' he whispered, 'might be supposed to have even less excuse for idleness than your loafing friend in the corner. At least he is wasting only his father's good money; but your father, Chadburn, does not pay for your lordly existence here. Yet – here – you – sit, leading a serene and workless life UNDERMYVERYNOSE! You have the insolence, the intolerable effrontery, to insult me, and the other people who are unfortunate enough to have to work with you, by lounging in your seat and performing your toilet', (John had been unconsciously playing with a comb), 'while you gaze out of the window. Your supreme and quite unfounded self-satisfaction, I must confess, quite staggers me. Forgive my presumption, Chadburn, if I call you a CONCEITEDPUPPY!'[118]

This self-portrait of the lazy schoolboy is, of course, fiction but it is rooted in fact. Douglas's father made no financial contribution and at times Douglas's self-image was weak. 'I have the face of a parrot,' he told Burdett, 'and a Jewish-looking parrot at that.' Norman Ilett recalled that Douglas 'was always on about his face – contemplating plastic surgery on his nose: pimples: *muscles* – generally rather body conscious.'[119] As luck would have it his school English and History exercise books from 1935 to 1937 have survived. They show signs of distraction it is true, with doodles and drawings of faces, Roman warriors, bagpipers, horses, buglers, monks, drummers. On the back page of one exercise book (dated December 1935) is a series of reddish blobs with 'written in blood' by them in small letters, but there are also copious notes on the Roman empire, on Theodoric and Clovis, on H. A. L. Fisher's *A History of Europe*, on Tiberius as a soldier, on Gaius, Claudius and Nero and other emperors, on the physical education of the Roman boy, on the Dacian wars, on Charlemagne, on political theory, on the individual and society, on sovereignty. There are long, impressive essays on order in Henry II's England, the church in England from the Norman conquest to 1189, on Christ's Hospital, on the Saxon invasions, feudalism, the rule of William I and the importance of the Norman conquest, Magna Carta, Edward I's relationship with Scotland, Edward I's legal reforms, the 100 Years' War, the development of English parliament, on the Roman conquest of Britain, the religion of Odin and Thor, the Vikings, on the Greeks as a chosen people, on the rivalry of Charles V and Francis I. The essay on Christ's Hospital has a peculiar trace of then-fashionable anti-Semitism and Führer-worship: '[Christ's Hospital students] have been brought up with wide interests, and as a result every boy has a great admiration for German methods & for the FUEHRER in particular ... The youth organisations are many, and the few Jews who, by underhand methods, worm their way into the school, are rigidly banned from them. In this way Christ's Hospital carries on fitly the tradition of progress & broadmindedness so dear to the heart of every Nordic youth.'[120] Douglas was 17 when he wrote this, and apparently unaware of the irony of the final sentence. The exercise books contain maps of Roman Germany, Roman Britain, Dacia, Europe. There is a brilliant and coruscating review of Warren Ault's *Europe in the Middle Ages*. There are short stories like the one that starts with a quotation from Frederic Prokosch's poem, 'The Baltic Shore', published in *New Verse* in the February–March 1936 issue. There is a story about Alexander the Great for which he got full marks (35/35) and a commendation from his English teacher: 'Very good – you have an excellent power of expression.'[121] There are drafts of poems. It is not the record of a lazy teenager.[122] One exercise book has a page with just three words on it, the gnomic 'died of overwork' seeming to refer to nobody in particular. Perhaps it was his autobiography.

In one exercise book of 1936 he takes his teacher to task. On his essay on Vikings the teacher wrote 'This is not effective because you simply have not sat down and considered the question as a whole before starting.' Douglas's reply is withering: 'Oh yes I have. I wrote pages of notes. After disposing of your criticisms I shall give a synopsis of points ... I have written nothing which is not giving an example of a general statement ... I could have written them after 1 day's preparation in reading Ault. If they were all you wanted why make us spend a fortnight over reading other books? I have nothing at the back of my mind except the headings which you are unable to supply.' It's not a dialogue that would endear him to his teacher.

The references to Hitler and to the role of Jews at Christ's Hospital is the most venomous display of reaction in Douglas's work, but it is not an isolated example. His reading was leading him in a conservative direction. Yeats, Eliot and Pound were not exactly political progressives and his reading of Waddell, Merejkowski and Henry Williamson (who was a fascist) provided the backbone of a view of art, and to some extent of life, that was frankly reactionary. A poem of August 1937, written in his copy of Michael Roberts's *Poems* but uncollected, expresses an unnerving hostility to democracy:

Commission

Be single like the seagull, who has come
Slanting on windy levels down the gnat's stratosphere
Who seeks worm citizen ploughed out of house and home
thinks in his stomach once and furrows there.

Not you nor Moses hurling ten written stones
To stand astraddle silhouetted places.
Lip flute or trumpet; music, never megaphones;
This way they turn more interested faces.

Love is the King's English; lust its cockney accent,
Now leap and learn it, no need to decry then
The present age, when aitches are so lacking.
Speak to them splendidly; do not deny them

The sun, point him out ere the clouds climbs him.
Not their muck shew. You must demonstrate
Not stones but what's beneath. Set them amiming
The gods, each friend with friend and satiate.[123]

So, the role of the poet is to make the sun accessible to common people before it is taken from them by clouds. It is not the poet's job to reflect the 'muck' they know. It's difficult to read this poem without Eliot's distaste for the demotic in mind.[124] The notes on poetry ideas in Douglas's 'Book Diary' show that he was preoccupied with the resurrection of old gods.[125]

The post-Gorizia Douglas was rebellious and it wasn't just his mother who felt it. At school he was combative and obdurate. His conflicts with the major in charge of the OTC and with the art master, H. A. Rigby, were not isolated incidents. He was successful at swimming and rugby[126] but not well-liked by the adults who trained the teams. He was a significant contributor to Lamb A house events but fell out with the housemaster, the universally popular A. C. W. Edwards. As we have seen, Douglas was moved from Lamb A to Middleton B after the stolen rifle incident, and he tried to prove himself to his new housemaster, D. S. Macnutt. Macnutt reassured Douglas's mother that Douglas settled into his new house quickly but he remained high-spirited, and his new housemates 'learnt that his capacity for making trouble could be a source of attraction and amusement. Douglas, standing up in the dining hall, his plate held out and a spoonful of mince pointed towards the distant back of the Lady Superintendent, was a figure whose boldness had to be admired. His scurrilous songs about the staff gave words to the others' discontent, and his excellent mimicry provided frequent entertainment.'[127] He was popular at Middleton B, but clearly regarded with some nervousness by his fellows. The March 1937 issue of *The Blue* noted that 'several people box, and we had a very enjoyable match with Mid. A juniors, enjoyable that is from the spectator's point of view. The effect of this was unexpected and almost disastrous. Newey, inflamed by the sight of blood, went berserk and attacked Douglas, who was only rescued with difficulty.' The same issue also warned visitors to be 'careful when entering our dayroom, lest you be struck by a flying piling-swivel. Douglas has been teaching us American (?) arms drill. And if plaster falls from the ceiling, do not worry, for it is only Douglas' tap dancing class having a lesson upstairs.'[128] He had been rather cryptically congratulated 'on discovering a new kind of bird' in the December 1936 issue.[129]

SIXTH FORM

Douglas became a History Grecian in January 1937.[130] History was taught by David Roberts who lived off-site and sometimes held his classes at his home. Roberts had a broad idea of his role and taught his subject with a strong view to its cultural side. He told Douglas's mother that her son's poetry 'lacked depth of feeling' and thought that Douglas would become a novelist. Douglas responded with acerbity. Such a view, he thought, proved its holder 'astonishingly insensitive',[131] but he became a regular visitor to Roberts's house. He also had a new housemaster, H. R. Hornsby, whom Douglas learned to trust. Hornsby and Douglas talked at night when the rest of the house was asleep. Increasingly Douglas opened up about his mother's poverty and his father's silence, about real or perceived injustices, and, of course, about H. L. O. Flecker. Hornsby encouraged his young protégé as, without their conversations, he felt that Douglas would 'blow up'. As Graham says, 'Hornsby listened, sometimes gave an opinion, and Douglas returned to bed. Hornsby's clearly defined character had few pretensions and it was typical of him to write thirty years later that, apart from the friendship between them, he did not think he had taught Douglas "anything worth tuppence. He taught me far more."'[132]

Certainly in 1937 Douglas performed well academically. He won the Grinling Prize for History and Roberts remarked on his end of year report that Douglas had 'a most refreshing and original mind' and that his work was 'clear-cut and critical'. Roberts predicted that he would get a good university scholarship and Hornsby reported that Douglas's work was 'consistently good and interesting'. Douglas's only surviving Christ's Hospital school report from these years was written in summer 1937. In it Hornsby wrote that he was 'very satisfied' but added a warning note: 'he has a great deal that he can contribute to the house and I hope that next year he will make that contribution. At present he is a bit too critical of any existing school institution and needs to be a little more tolerant.'[133]

Douglas certainly didn't behave well towards authority figures, but those figures didn't behave particularly well towards the young rebel, a fact that was acknowledged by the assistant master of Lamb A, C. A. Humphrey. Humphrey wrote to Jo that Douglas's various conflicts had been the responsibility of those in charge as much as they had been Douglas's and that he was settling in well to his new house: 'He is certainly very happy, and both his housemasters are quite satisfied with the way he settled down at the beginning of term and with the way he has behaved since then.'[134] Hornsby also wrote to her to reassure her that her son was settling down 'uncommonly well'. Douglas wanted to make amends but his desire to impress the authorities with his prowess at rugby,[135] swimming and his OTC activities didn't affect his artistic and literary ambitions. He was runner-up in summer 1936 in the school's Lamb Essay prize and his involvement with *The Outlook* deepened with each issue. Jo's recollections weren't completely reliable – she wrote that Douglas had edited the magazine[136] although there's little evidence of that[137] – but she described her son's life at Christ's Hospital in a way that just stops short of hagiography: 'He designed decorations for his House Day Room & for programmes of School Plays. He was keen on acting & interested in producing. He took a great interest too in the School Band & though not a performer (officially) he attended practises & played various drums – Tap dancing was another of his interests & he would like to have learnt ballet dancing. He loved to design Decors & always intended to obtain some good training in this branch of art.'

Certainly Douglas's (as Raps) linocuts of a jazz band and of a figure and shadow adorned the cover of *The Outlook* for the next four issues until he left Christ's Hospital. Apart from the cover design Douglas contributed three other items to the March 1937 edition, a linocut, a short story and a poem. The linocut depicts a traditional oast house, of which the oldest surviving example is near Tunbridge Wells. The short story, 'Fragment – Death of the Squire', is an account of the final moments, the final dreams more accurately, of an ageing huntsman. The story can be seen as an extension of Wilfred Scawen Blunt's poem, 'The old squire', which Douglas knew.[138] Blunt's squire, as Douglas's, loves the noises of the countryside. The poem, 'Triton', reflects a recently acquired literary maturity. Douglas begins with a quotation from the Russian writer and religious thinker, Dmitri Merejkowski:

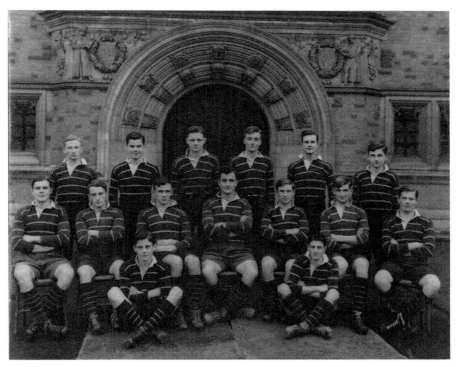

Christ's Hospital first fifteen, 1937. Keith Douglas is in the middle row, second from the right; his friend Norman Ilett is on the same row, second left.

'Not so long ago, on the island of Chios, some washer-women from the convent did find on the sea-shore a veritable ancient god, a triton with a fish tail, with fins, all in scales. His head was grey, his eyes glazed, like those of suckling babes. When they saw he was old, feeble, in all probability ill, they gathered round him, the low-down scum, surrounding him with their Christian prayers, and beat him to death with their rollers; this ancient god, mayhap the son of Poseidon.'[139]

The first stanza of Douglas's poem follows the story as told by Merejkowski:

> The old god, lying on the white sand,
> and his face whitening with extreme age,
> lying in the sun which is not his element,
> where the women, carefully coming, beat him;
> Poseidon's prodigal, returned to no fatted calf.
> This old god, this I can see so clearly,
> with his squameous and kindly whisker.

('Squamous', misspelt in 'Triton', appears to have been a favourite word. He used it in 'Song of the Fisherman'.) The following stanza brings the narrative right into the poet's life in the present, perhaps the first time we have heard Douglas address his own reality so directly:

> More clearly than I can see,
> on this June evening, when the tennis-court
> is divided like bathing-tents with black and red shadows,
> you and you who stand there who really love me.
> Why tell you of the old god? You would not
> understand, dear.[140]

Douglas was discovering the attractions of the opposite sex. In 1937 he wrote 'An Unfinished Autobiographical Fragment' which described the young poet at the age of fourteen:

He was now, at the age of fourteen, tall (some five feet nine inches), and fair, with very white skin and large brown eyes, long-lashed. He sat now sprawled on a stone seat, whose white stone shone back the sun at him disconcertingly. Sunlight, the blue glare of the sky and far off cricketing sounds mingled, coming gently to his notice through eyes half shut and dreamy ears, moving him to an indescribable feeling of melancholy and longing, which both compelled and defied analysis. He began stumbling in his mind after this ignis fatuus discontent. This definite and indescribable disquiet, and suddenly caught up with it: suddenly he knew that it was a desire to share beauty, the pleasantness of this summer afternoon, with someone else, someone to understand not this only, but every tossed thought and ambition. This would be a girl evidently: he pictured her for many days after that.

Walking along Eastbourne front in the holidays, he looked carefully at the faces of the girls who passed him. Some, freckled and pleasant, attracted him instantly: any one of these might have been his sympathiser, and he turned heavily into the swimming baths, wishing that one of these faces belonged to an acquaintance.[141]

The June 1937 edition of *The Outlook* (with a cover design by 'Raps') shows this new preoccupation perhaps for the first time. There is a linocut of a deer[142] but the two poems (by 'Flip') concentrate on different aspects of love. The first, 'For E. B.', is a simple, heartfelt lyric. Perhaps it is not the most gallant of love poems but Douglas was nothing if not honest:

> You are the sun. He smiles
> With your face out of his blue fields:
> Leaves shared your lips with me. Green miles
> Of earth your country yields.
>
> I have grown so to hate
> The typical, print dress and hair in reels;
> Unlearn'd, you satisfy. You sate
> My yellow ambition. Your honest ideals
>
> Only include what they all knew. Inventions,
> Theories, don't interest you. To kiss
> After a gallop, and the best intentions
> Thrown in the hedge, that is our bliss.
>
> So like new land, I will take seizin, tithe,
> A handful, armful of you, all I can carry away.
> Your other lovers, sun and wind, I will share you with,
> Since these must give you up at the end of the day.[143]

'E. B.' was Liz Brodie. She was the fifteen-year-old daughter of Captain and Mrs. Brodie who had a farm at Southwater, close to the school, and who welcomed Christ's Hospital boys. As Ilett recalled: 'They had a few horses and took us to Pony Club dances, hunter trials etc. A laugh really. Not our scene at all.' Desmond Graham says that 'For E. B.' is a 'farewell to love'[144] but I don't find anything especially valedictory about it. If anything the poet is welcoming love but accepting that love's subject, in this case, has feet of clay.

Where 'For E.B.' is a celebration, however earthy, of an actual person, the other poem in the July 1937 issue, also by 'Flip', is a Hopkins-like celebration of the state of being in love:

> Now the new airs and winds, fulfilled
> With poems call
> The trees stretching from sleep; new leaves
> Sing, crack out youth's trumpet. Eaves
> Swallowful, Earth swelled
> Elemental. All
>
> New in this: fish in his sea,
> Salamander lies
> Flat in his fire; lark is lifting,
> Climbs his air. Earth, drifting
>   Ball in blue sky, be
>   Crass conies' place.
>
> Desire leans over in waterfalls
>   (No shadow flatter
> To hide in the lichen), lies
> In the hay, and humming flies
>   Abroad with gnats, calls
>   In cuckoo's clatter.[145]

Douglas made only one contribution (apart from the cover design) to the December 1937 issue of *The Outlook*. For the poem, 'Villanelle of Gorizia', he returned to his Italian holiday with a eulogy of sunlight and wine. William Scammell points to a few failures in the poem but celebrates its overall technical success: 'The bringing together of sunlight, flutes and wine achieves a verbal and emotional synaesthesia expressive of delight in the relaxed pleasures of the Italian town. Assonance, alliteration, internal rhyme … all work to heighten the musical sense of repetition.'[146] The poem as first published in *The Outlook* is better than the version in *Complete Poems*, if only because the final stanza is better:

Over and over the street is repeated with sunlight,
the oxen tire even of the leaves,
the flutes sound in the wineshop out of sight.

The sky is apathetic like a kite
that cares not how the string below it weaves
over and over; the street is repeated with sunlight

Till only doors are dark among the white
walls that outstare the sun. And noon achieves
the flutes' sound in the wineshop, out of sight.

The town cannot remember when was night,
the trees droop for the subtle-coloured eves,
over and over the street is repeated with sunlight.

The short shades of the avenues invite
the monk with his umbrella, who perceives
The flutes sound in the wineshop, out of sight.
All this the bottle says, that I have quite
poured out. The wine slides in my threat [sic] and grieves.
Over and over the street is repeated with sunlight.[147]

As Vernon Scannell said, in 'Villanelle of Gorizia', he shows how 'rapidly he is mastering the control of prescribed forms and how cunningly he can play rhythmic changes on a regular iambic line.'[148]

Douglas was starting to think of the future beyond Christ's Hospital. He had already considered entering Sandhurst and, finding that it was financially practical, wrote to his mother about it in December 1936.[149] It looks as though he was talked out of the army (by Roberts in particular) and in January 1938 he wrote to Edmund Blunden at Merton College, Oxford. He would have been aware of Blunden as a distinguished poet (Blunden was published in *New Verse*) and as an alumnus of his own school, but he was encouraged to write to Blunden in the first place by his history teacher, David Roberts. He showed Blunden's reply to Roberts and to W. R. Macklin, his English teacher. He told Blunden that Macklin had suggested that Douglas study one of the Christ's Hospital old boys who was less popular in the English curriculum, Leigh Hunt. Macklin had already started Douglas on a course of Elizabethan drama and some pre-Elizabethan mimes and miracle plays. Blunden had suggested something slightly different (work on all the Christ's Hospital alumni authors, including Coleridge and Lamb) but Douglas hoped that a compromise between Blunden's plan and Macklin's would suffice. 'I have already begun the drama, which is keeping me very busy,' he wrote. 'I hope this does not seem to you an impatient and impertinent rejection of your advice: if you still think it would be better for me to take all the O.B. [Old Blue] authors I can start work on them as soon as your letter arrives to say so.'[150] For all his bluntness with authority figures he knew how to be polite when he needed to. He wrote to Blunden again in May 1938 to give him a progress report:

> I began by reading some miracle plays and various early comedies, Ralph Roister Doyster [sic] and Gammer Gurton among them. Simultaneously with these I studied Leigh Hunt's life and works and wrote an essay on him and another on his poetry. I also read Allardyce Nicholl on Masks, Mimes and Miracles, and on The Development of the theatre ... I read two plays each of Lyly, Peele, and Greene, and wrote on all three of them together. Then I read Nashe's Lenten Stuff and reread Tamburlaine taking notes on the verse. After that I wrote a very hasty essay on the Verse of Tamburlaine ... In the holidays I read a long essay on Lyly by Bond, and all his plays, and wrote notes on them, from which I am now writing an essay. I managed to read Heywood's Woman Killed with Kindness – and Sense and Sensibility and Amaryllis at the Fair as a change.[151]

There was some activity behind the scenes. On 3 May 1938 Blunden's friend at Christ's Hospital Hector Buck wrote to Blunden to invite him to the school to talk to Roberts's History Grecians: 'He [Roberts] has a secondary string to his bow, inasmuch as he'd welcome a chance to talk to you about Douglas, that highly promising but difficult young man you're taking at Merton in October. The things to say about him are not easy to put on paper and would proceed more comfortably by questions and answer. Chances of an action for libel would be reduced, and so forth.' Blunden replied on 16 May: 'I wonder what scathing records he [Roberts] is going to pour on me concerning the Douglas.'[152]

Douglas was preparing diligently for entry to Oxford, as Blunden acknowledged in a letter of 16 May 1938: 'It looks as though you have been digging in with excellent energy. I shall not know how to employ you when you come up!'[153] Meanwhile his contributions to the school magazine continued. The April 1938 issue, with cover design by Raps, contained a linocut of a horse by K. R. D., two essays by 'Keith', 'New Year' and 'Going away', and two poems by 'Keith'. If there is little throat-clearing in Douglas's poetry there is a good deal of it in his essays. 'New Year' struggles through several paragraphs of non-event before finally reaching a sort of point, which is that New Year may have had a certain importance in Celtic Britain, 'when Druids performed strange ceremonies by torchlight among their squat stones, and the old year ended for many unfortunates with a ritual knife-stroke.'[154] But after a brief reminiscence of the 'interminable' chant of 'Ave Maria' in Gorizia the essay concludes that New Year is inherently pointless. We know from the references to Yeats and to Hopkins that he had been reading those poets. 'Going Away' is scarcely more pithy: it still uses a lot of words to say very little about the art and purpose of leaving.[155] In the poems, however, Douglas shows great confidence. 'Point of View' uses the countryside as a point of reference but is no longer haunted by Pan.[156] The sonnet, 'Here where the years stand ...', barely pauses for punctuation:

Christ's Hospital Grecians, May 1938. Keith Douglas is second from the left on the back row. Flecker, the headmaster, is in the centre of the middle row.

Here where the years stand under us in the valley
We can look down upon the shops and vineyards
And honestly say, we would rather be like leopards
Let loose in one direction, who cannot be silly.

This simple evening moment, when the shallow
Echoes stagger against Big School, it is awkward
Realising happiness seems just to have started
And now we must leave it, live like trees or charlock.

One of us will be the kettle, past care of tinkers,
Rejected, one the tip-top apple, the winking
Sun's friend. It will be that way, and Time on our ground

Will sweep like a maid, and where we were be clean.
Shall we find room to laugh, if turning round
We see where we have walked, how wrong we have been.[157]

    This poem was later collected as 'On leaving school' and it forms a natural valedictory companion to 'Going away'. Douglas was preparing to leave Christ's Hospital but he had two more poems published in the next issue of *The Outlook*. 'For E. B.' begins with a quotation from Ronsard's famous poem, 'Quand vous serez bien vieille', which sets the tone:

For E. B.

Direz, chantant mes vers, en vous esmerveillant:
Ronsard me celebroit du temps que j'estois belle.

Thank you for a present you have given;
Sweet eyes and mouth, deigned me on certain days
Which out of dull years and the dull seven
I will recollect, my treasure a hundred ways.

This be my duty or pity; I give you my blessing,
Paid thanks, such prayers as I make, or what you would.
The charm outworn, there is no shame confessing,
Or standing glad for minutes that were good.

No drug or prayer will get this gift again,
This hour filled with gold others as we
Have found a torch, too hot with lovely pain;
Only to taste is this defended tree.

No use repainting, the dainty days are gone;
Only dreams gilt them with that simple light.
In this less happiness let us muddle on,
Not to forget until the black night.[158]

This is an altogether more gallant love poem than the earlier one to Liz Brodie. The other poem (by Raps) is entitled 'Kristin' in *Complete Poems* but is merely 'Poem' in *The Outlook*. It celebrates young love against the backdrop of events in Europe and elsewhere:

Yes, futile to prolong this natural instant –
Black days lean over, hours curtailed with fear.
But look, while these flowers imbibe the rain
A little forlorn magic has homed again.
Take this, these limpid days will not be constant;
They will forsake you, will not reappear.[159]

Kristin was what Douglas called Christine Woodcock, whom he met at a New Year's Eve dance in 1937. He wrote to her in January 1938, proudly announcing that a poem of his had been accepted by Grigson's *New Verse*,[160] and it is clear that they had connected immediately at the party. 'I shall love writing to you because we never had to make friends,' he wrote, 'we just were more or less immediately, and I know there's nothing I need leave out of letters to you. There are millions of things I can't tell mother & long to tell someone, so I shall never lack any material for letters.'[161] This long letter to Christine provides a useful description of his environment:

I am writing during prep: in my study – a dirty little room which I will describe. It is wooden mostly – partitioned off from the dayroom in which most of the house work. It has a half glass door, & windows looking into the dayroom as well as outside. All these are curtained with white stuff which has a green repeating pattern woven into it. The wooden and plaster walls are green (dark) up to about waist high & then yellow plaster, or window. These walls are covered with initials and burnt lettering of various kinds (particularly the lower part of the door, which is brown). Indelible finger-marks of past owners are profusely distributed. I have a little table, a lot of books, an armchair, a deckchair and a settle. The wall is decorated with a large curtain (same stuff as the others) hiding where I wrenched away a hideous fixture school bookcase, & elsewhere with various small coloured reproductions of Van Gogh, and 1 by Pollitzer, and a large tempera picture by me of soldiers at bayonet practice. This picture dominates the study and catches anyone coming in full in the eye … Also in the study are a card table, covered with a rug of the Douglas tartan, (mainly green), and a dirty fireplace, with a fairly cheerful fire in it.

The reproduction of a Sigmund Pollitzer piece on his wall may have had some influence on the linocuts he made for *The Outlook*, particularly the oast house and spearman. In this letter, having described his study, Douglas goes on to describe his school uniform. He is dressed in 'a long coat of blue kersey, white linen bands at my throat, fourteen silver buttons down the front of me, black knee-breeches and yellow stockings. I have black velvet cuffs turned back with more silver buttons.' After some more ruminations he turns to Christine's dress: 'You could look (to use your favourite word), marvellous, if you would only wear the right clothes for your figure and colouring. I would hesitate to tell you in a way because you would be surrounded with boys in no time and forget all about me.'

He should have hesitated longer, but he didn't:

First, never wear dresses when you needn't. Your figure is either willowy or skinny. If you wear a roughish, but well-cut tweed coat and skirt, brown or dark green, plain or check (small check), you are willowy and lovely open-air lady immediately – lipstick and nail-polish to match would help. In your thin dress you are skinny & unhappy-looking. Go in for checks and autumn sort of woven scarves & you would be the best of yourself, & attractive. You may despise sporty people, but they dress well … You wear a pale blue polo sweater, but you would look yards better in dark brown or green. Your colours are the colours of woods and fields in summer & autumn – open air colours – the best colours in the world.[162]

We don't have Christine's reply to this clumsy fashion statement, and we have only one more letter to her from Douglas although there are (typically artless) references to Kristin in later letters to female friends. Perhaps he realized that he was not making the best of cases: 'Chris don't be offended by all this', he continued, but he couldn't keep it up: 'I would love you to look as nice as I know you could. The reds & yellows you wear now are the good clean eternal colours that the medieval people & the Greeks – the best dressed the world has ever seen – wore. They weren't thought of until mass-production and state-run brothels were invented. Will you do this thing <u>for</u> me and dress like this, (if your mother will let you).'[163]

Not many relationships survive the insinuation that the woman wears mass-produced clothes favoured by prostitutes. There's not much indication that this one did, although they seem to have been seeing each other until late in 1939 at least.

During the Christ's Hospital years Douglas wrote poems that did not appear in *The Outlook*. A number of them are published in *Complete Poems*[164] but it seems that Douglas didn't think particularly highly of them. He wrote on the manuscript of one 'I don't like this much myself KCD', and on 'Famous Men' he wrote, 'Cut this out too if you like'. But 'Famous Men' is worth lingering over if only because it is perhaps the first of his poems that displays the effect of the modernist revolution, that ability to strip as much out of a poem as the poet dares, sometimes too much. 'Famous Men' is almost Poundian:

> And now no longer sung,
> not mourning, not remembered
> more under the sun,
>
> not enough their deserved
> praise. The quick movement of dactyls
> does not compensate them.
>
> The air is advertised of seas
> they smote, from green to copper.
> These were merciful men.
>
> And think, like plates lie deep
> licked clean their skulls,
> rest beautifully, staring.[165]

As Scammell says, 'this poem is so pared-down and compacted as to make interpretation difficult, yet its intriguing and powerful ending invites attention … the poem points forward in some ways to "Simplify Me When I'm Dead" and the skulls that litter the desert writings.'[166] That's true, but one wonders what the poem is 'pared-down' from. The first line implies that there was, if only in the poet's head, some introductory material that gives some context. Who are the famous men whose skulls are staring? Who (or what) licked their skulls clean?

Douglas found time to review *Christ's Hospital* by G. A. T. Allan in the November 1937 issue of *The Blue*, and revealed his affection for the place that had been his real home for the previous six years:

> This book must never lie on the same shelf as those old tomes in the school library, familiar only to moth and rust, which men of other centuries have written about Christ's Hospital. Mr. Allan's style is so far and beautifully removed from them; he has handled a mass of material in a conversational way … Tripping gaily down the centuries, with Mr. Allan always ahead opening strange and stranger factual doors, we who live with the present school can almost feel that we have shared this journey through time to the Sussex woods. Going about our business we look upon the statues, long familiar to us, with new understanding. For we have seen them in their habit as they lived a century ago before the 'glaring red-brick settlement' rose by Sharpenhurst.

Douglas concluded his glowing review by thanking Allan 'because it will no longer be necessary to draw from a copious imagination when showing visitors rounds the school; though, indeed, all sensible visitors will have read the book themselves.'[167]

Douglas had a poem published in the last edition of *The Blue* to appear while he was at Christ's Hospital. It is called 'Dejection':

> Yesterday travellers in summer's country,
> Tonight the sprinkled moon and ravenous sky
> Say, we have reached the boundary. The autumn clothes
> Are on, death is the season, and we the living
> Are hailed by the solitary to join their regiment;
> To leave the sea and the horses and march away
> Endlessly. The spheres speak with persuasive voices.
>
> Only to-morrow like a seagull hovers and cries,
> Shrieks through the mist and scatters the pools of stars:
> *The windows will be open, and hearts behind them.*[168]

This poem was published in *New Verse* in March 1938.[169] Graham thinks this an 'identikit' thirties poem[170] and if you see it only as a response to the bet with Ilett that seems a fair comment. But the poem is more than that. For a start behind it lies the growing tension in Europe. Everyone expected a war to start imminently, Douglas included, and 'Dejection' showcases the poet's gloom about his own chances of surviving it. As Ted Hughes says, 'In a sense, war was his ideal subject: the burning away of all human pretensions in the ray cast by death. This was the vision, the unifying generalization that shed the meaning and urgency into all his observations and particulars: not truth is beauty only, but truth kills everybody. The truth of a man is the doomed man in him or his dead body. Poem after poem circles this idea, as if his mind were tethered.'[171] Nature itself, in the form of moon and sky, tells us that we have reached a limit. Death beckons. As Scammell says, it is in the nature of youth to be haunted by death[172] but in Douglas's case this is not a poetic pose for the sake of publication in *New Verse*. It is part of his firm belief that he was not going to survive the war.[173]

Towards the end of his time at secondary school Douglas wrote about his plans for the summer of 1938. He was spending quite a lot of time with horses. Brenda Jones, who met Douglas in 1937 when he came to ride the horses at her father's farm, recalls that he was 'very exciting to be with but a very kind person really … he was very bold. He'd try jumps, all sorts of things that perhaps he shouldn't have done, but that was Keith. He always had to go on to something else to prove himself.'[174] He had 'arranged to jump Nabob' one evening (in July). 'We had to remove a hind shoe first,' he told his mother, 'and after much wrenching got it off.'[175]

Chris had come down to the school with friends on the previous Saturday and George Cunningham, an American boy whom Douglas was looking after to earn some money,[176] had returned to the school from Henley and told him that he was going to Norfolk for a week in August. 'I said I thought I could go, but would possibly have to go for only 4 days and come back early. The people are allowing me £1 for fares, 5/- [shillings] a day for entertainment and 16/- a day for food. I doubt if I'll eat all that so I ought to make a bit on it. They don't seem to expect any change. So I can come back after camp and take the boy for the 4th and 5th and go up on the 6th stay the week and come back. He will get as much of me as he would have before.' He wrote to Chris the same evening and was less full of advice than he had been earlier in the year:

> I have had a telegram from Mrs Rochfort to say that she can't have me until the 29th, that is, Thursday. So I am staying on here [Stakers Farm, Southwater] until then but it doesn't matter, we'll have a week. In that case I will come on Thursday evening – would you have the time & inclination to meet me and come out to a film and/or supper? If you would like that reply,

by returnish, and say what film. It is poss: I shan't have the money, in which case you'll have to take me & I'll pay you back … I am rather hard up at the moment, because Mother promised to send some money & forgot to enclose it. So I have only about my fare … In spite of the busy farm life etc, I don't seem to have nearly as little time for letters as you do. I think little of you.[177]

The charm offensive over, he told Christine about his recent activities. He'd spent an evening with his ex-history teacher eating mushrooms and telling ghost stories. The Munich crisis, for once, was not a topic of conversation. He'd ticked Lizzy Brodie off for behaving in a 'queenly' way, greatly appealing to the Dutch girls who were staying at the farm. The car had broken down on a trip to the Brodies and they had to push it 'about ¾ mile in very wet darkness to a garage'. A visit from some people from the school to the farm had gone well and he'd been to the gym with a master who had 'just come back from learning the real dirt in Denmark'. At the last minute Douglas seems to have remembered who he was writing to: 'Darling I am sorry I can't come today. I'm longing to see you again you sweet person. Rite me a nice luving letter, you're on my mind & in my heart.'

Douglas's mother and his friend John Adams recalled a late, and typical, controversy. Before he left Christ's Hospital Douglas complained directly to the War Minister about the failure to equip the school's OTC with gas masks, so contravening the rules of both Corps and school.[178] But his main preoccupation appears to have been horses. He wrote a story in about 1937 which gives an indication of his lifestyle at the Brodies:

> Pierrot turned his lovable enquiring face to peer round one bright black shoulder as Jerry rattled the door. Six foot Jerry with a red face of real healthiness was glad too to see Pierrot. He set down the saddle and stroked Pierrot's enquiring nose. Pierrot reared his rubbery upper lip outward, waggling it, searching for bread & salt. He was a horse who had never learnt about sugar. This was the way of it many mornings, but never was there a morning so clear, as clear and exciting as a sword; they were both freshly feeling the gift of strength and the prospect of speed.
>
> Pierrot made trouble with his bridle as a matter of course. He was as anxious as Jerry to be about in the field and over the jumps with a shout, but this formality must be gone through. He stuck his head up & nosed the roof. Jerry pinched his nose with a practised hand, brought down his silly black face under the bridle, opening Pierrot's mouth with two fingers & slipping the

snaffle bit inside. Next he took Pierrot outside & could vault into the saddle. He took him into the field in a sidestepping way. The two of them were one piece and that one like a dancer. Pierrot was pleased with his field. He was allowed to trot, going up and down like a Rolls Royce on his long pasterns. Jerry touched him lightly into a canter, but Pierrot was impetuous and said he would straightway gallop. They argued. Jerry sat just as easily through the high bucks, the cow tricks, & the twisty ones. He brought Pierrot to a stand still. Pierrot laid back his ears & made faces.

The inclination to gallop was in the wind and Jerry put him fast at five feet ten of sticks. Pierrot cleared it hilariously, all but one crazy hinder hoof, which brought a couple of poles down. He took his chance & set out at a rebellious gallop, in a circle so small that his hind leg flew from under him, & he pulled himself up by the sheer strength of his forelegs. Pierrot looked anxiously round them, & Jerry eased up. He decided to take an excited horse to cool down along the edge of the road.

The sun was just getting hot then, hotter than yesterday's intense heat, and the rain of last week was drying fast. Not long before it should be too hard to jump even the poles & Sussex gates in Marlpost woods. Pierrot walked with the air of putting his best foot forward, inspecting all the morning had to offer, with a lively interest. He wanted to stop and converse with the children who were in awe of him & who expressed in their wide eyes utter agreement with the voice of the smallest of them, saying coo, orse, in a mazed way, repeating it. Clara the ancient black-avised Shetland wasted her furious glances across the hedge on Pierrot, for he ignored her, & was engaged in stretching his muscular neck down to watch his feet passing at close range. Then he continued to look about him with every sign of happiness, to step daintily, & to ignore the rudeness of little dogs. His excitement was exchanged for interest, and Jerry thought fit to canter. He laid his leg on lightly and started Pierrot very collected along the springy black path. Jerry began almost to be overcome with the unconfinable joy of movement, of his movement being a part of the graceful and muscled shining movement of Pierrot. The tradesman in his van passed two beings where happiness made them like deities in the young world.

Now Pierrot would not be passed by such a poor vehicle as Potter's van, he lengthened his pace & put his foot in a hole & rolled in tumult, his legs were flying and his frightened face was underneath all of him. Jerry rolled frantically to escape the mass of horse that filled the sky & rolled down upon him like the heavens themselves. Pierrot got up & shook himself. The cantle of the saddle was broken, the maringale snapped and hanging. Pierrot was grey with dust, and his nose bled slowly through it. Jerry sat without thinking & watched his arm turn red.[179]

The closeness of rider and horse in Douglas's story is reminiscent of the relationship of the dreamer and his horse in Stephens's story, 'Etched in Moonlight'.

Douglas's differences with Flecker didn't prevent the headmaster from writing a positive testimonial before Douglas left Christ's Hospital:

I have great pleasure in writing a testimonial for K. C. DOUGLAS, who has been a member of this School since 1931 and has borne a good character.

He has done very well indeed intellectually as was proved by his success in winning an Open Exhibition [minor scholarship] in Modern History at Merton College, Oxford. He really has a gift for writing and I believe that, with the broader scope of the university to help him, he may well do brilliantly in that way. His career has been marked by a number of School prizes for English and History and he has a genuine gift as an artist.

DOUGLAS is also a good athlete. He has been a member of the School First Rugby Football XV for the past two seasons, a member of the School Swimming VIII and he is a keen rider. He has also reached the position of Senior Sergeant in the O.T.C. He has a real gift for this type of work.

DOUGLAS has distinguished himself in other ways. He has been a Monitor for some time and has done his work well.

This unusual combination of qualities has created great possibilities for his future.

I believe that his father had a distinguished record of service in the War. I know that Mrs. Douglas needs all the help she can get to see the boy though his University career and I therefore have no hesitation in recommending him to the Trustees of the Lord Kitchener National Memorial Fund.[180]

Flecker understood Douglas. He wrote to Douglas's mother on 11 May 1945: 'These youngsters with a streak of genius are, I think, always difficult in the early stages. If they are treated differently from other people, that may have the worst possible reaction upon them: if, on the other hand, one treats them just like anybody else, one is likely to do them grave injustice.'[181] And he fully appreciated Douglas's genius. He wrote to her again on 23 April 1947: 'It [*From Alamein to Zem Zem*] strikes me as a work of quite remarkable maturity and balance, with a note of sincerity and a power of mental analysis that are very unusual in any but long established literary craftsmen.'[182]

Perhaps the last word on the end of Douglas's school career should go to *The Blue*. In July 1937 an anonymous colleague wrote: 'Entomology is all the rage this term ... Nor has Douglas held himself aloof from these proceedings, and if you are very lucky you may see him capturing a Caeruleocephala or a Chrysorrhoea with a deft sweep of his mighty arm. Most of the time, however, he is elsewhere; for long periods he is absent, and then, when we think he is gone for ever, he returns, smelling strongly of horses.'[183] And in December 1938, when Douglas was long gone, another colleague (who turned out to be Ilett[184]) wrote: 'Douglas has gone where he can work on the floor without either splinter or rebuke; no longer does the welkin ring with the strains of some almost recognisable ditty, and no longer does the homely smell of horse pervade our changing-rooms and dormitories. Only an odd spur or riding crop here and there remains to recall the glories of the past. We miss him.'[185]

3

THIS CITY EXPERIENCES A DIFFICULT TIME[1]

Douglas arrived at Merton College Oxford on 7 October 1938. He lived in room 2:2 in Fellows' Quad. In September he wrote to Edmund Blunden with the usual set of undergraduate anxieties – accommodation, protocol and money:

> 1. I have received a notice requiring me to come into residence on October 7th. Is this an earlier date than the day on which the whole college comes up? I have heard that freshmen are required to come up earlier, and was not certain whether October 7th was the earlier date or not.

> 2. Would it be unusual for me to have luggage, etc., sent to Merton 2 or 3 days before I am required to come into residence?

> 3. I have not been able to get a list of College rules – to whom should I apply for these?

> 4. Some months ago I had sent me from Merton College a statement that the amount of my Exhibition was £30 p.a., and that a further grant was to be made, of £50, subject to adjustment if 'further emolument' was obtained. Well, further emolument has been made, but I still need the £50 p.a. Would it be possible for you to find out what adjustment, if any, has taken place; and can you tell me how this money would be paid, or allowed me?

> I am sorry to buzz at you with so many queries, some of which must seem to you pointless – but I shall be bewildered enough even when all these are answered. When I see you I shall still be loaded with a charge of more particular enquiries.

My address will be the one at the top of this letter [The Rectory, Withyham] until the 19th, from which date until the 27th September I shall be at Stakers, Southwater, Horsham. After the 27th until I go up to Merton I shall be at St Hugh's Cottage, Oakleigh Rd., Little Common, Bexhill. Not the least of my difficulties is this continual migration while I am making arrangements.[2]

The 'continual migration' merely mirrors his mother's.

One of Douglas's first jobs at Oxford, at Blunden's suggestion, was to make contact with the senior undergraduate poet, Margaret Stanley-Wrench. Her *The Man in the Moon* had won the Newdigate Prize, awarded to Oxford undergraduates for the best poem (not exceeding 300 lines), in 1937. Douglas wrote to her in the October with typical passive-aggressiveness: 'I said [to Blunden] that you would be too busy & know too many people already; & if you are & do, I shan't be particularly put out if you don't answer this.'[3] He added: 'PS. You won't have to read my poems.'

She did reply, inviting Douglas to her rooms at Somerville College at 4 o'clock the following Sunday. That meeting must have been acceptable to both parties because they became friends for the rest of Douglas's short life. She wrote to her mother that he was a: 'very opinionated young man, but not unpleasantly so, because he has a lot of sense. He is remarkably mature and confident. He must be only nineteen, if that, but looks quite twenty or twenty-one, fair, with hair falling over his forehead in half curling locks, rather like a mane, a fresh complexion, in glasses, thickish brows, pleasant features, tall and long-legged.'[4]

Margaret Stanley-Wrench's *The Man in the Moon* is not a good poem, and it is about as far from the late 1930s zeitgeist as you could get. It is doubtful that Douglas, if he had read it at all, would have been impressed. He might have read her first collection, *News Reel and Other Poems*, published by Macmillan in 1938 while she was still an undergraduate.[5] Although not an accomplished book, there are many horses in it so the poems might have endeared themselves to Douglas. Graham says that he read her poetry on his first visit to Somerville and that he didn't like them.[6] John Waller damned her with faint praise in his two-part essay, 'Oxford poetry and disillusionment', in *Poetry Review* in 1940. Stanley-Wrench was, he said, 'pleasing in character and appearance, more productive than most poets, and … wrote with a high level of competence. But she had the misfortune to win the Newdigate Prize, which … is in Oxford almost a taboo, a spiritual death.'[7] In May 1940 Douglas wrote in *Augury: An Oxford Miscellany of Verse & Prose*, a selection of work by Oxford students which he co-edited with Alec Hardie, a passage which might have described Margaret Stanley-Wrench's poetry, though he was writing of the poetry of undergraduates generally: 'most of these poets survey the world still as placidly as one should who looks out from such an ancient standpoint as this university. The emotions expressed are as a rule about more ordinary and permanent things than the situation this year, and, though not introspective, most of the poetry is pleasantly personal. If it leaves no great thoughts or thunderous lines in your mind, at least it may in mass reflect a kind of solidity and some comfort.'[8]

The poetry of Margaret Stanley-Wrench is represented in *Augury*[9] but it is doubtful if she ever had a saner review. Douglas wrote to Toni Beckett on 25 March 1940 that the proofs of *Augury* looked 'very nice but VERY thin. There are some nice misprints such as Joan [for John] Waller and no one having a more insensitive appreciation of Oxford poetry than Basil Blackwell.'[10] Douglas became good friends with Hardie, a Merton student who went on to become an academic and taught, like Blunden, in Hong Kong. He spent the New Year of 1940 with Hardie's Scottish family, much to his amusement.

Douglas's philosophy of poetry was developing:

Poetry is like a man, whom thinking you know all his movements and appearance you will presently come upon in such a posture that for a moment you can hardly believe that it is a position of the limbs you know. So thinking you have set bounds to the nature of poetry, you shall as soon discover something outside your bounds which they should evidently contain.

The expression 'bad poetry' is meaningless: critics still use it, forgetting that bad poetry is not poetry at all.

Nor can prose and poetry be compared any more than pictures and pencils: the one is instrument and the other art. Poetry may be written in prose or verse, or spoken extempore.

For it is anything expressed in words, which appeals to the emotions either in presenting an image or picture to move them; or by the music of words affecting them through the senses; or in stating some truth whose eternal quality exacts the same reverence as eternity itself.

In its nature poetry is sincere and simple.

Writing which is poetry must say what the writer has himself to say, not what he has observed others to say with effect, nor what he thinks will impress his hearers because it impressed him hearing it. Nor must he waste any more words over it than a mathematician: every word must work for its keep, in prose, blank verse, or rhyme.

And poetry is to be judged not by what the poet has tried to say; only by what he has said.[11]

One wonders if any of the poems selected for *Augury*, even those by Edmund Blunden, F. T. Prince and C. S. Lewis, passes this rather severe test. *Augury* was announced in *Oxford Magazine* of 26 October 1939: 'There is a danger that war, though it increases the demand for serious literature, may tend to stem the supply. In a hope to counter this tendency, and also to record the reactions of Oxford at the present time, it has been proposed that some publication should be made of literary work written since the war began, dealing with any subject … Contributions should be sent to Mr. Alec M. Hardie, 16 Longwall Street.' The 25 April 1940 issue of *Oxford Magazine* trailed *Augury*: 'The miscellany of Oxford prose and verse, of which mention has more than once been made in these columns, is to be published next week by Messrs. Basil Blackwell under the title *Augury*. Keith Douglas, several of whose poems have appeared in THE MAGAZINE, is joint editor with Alec Hardie, and the contributors include C. S. Lewis, Nevill Coghill, E. R. Appleton, Ian Robertson, Joan Yeaxlee, Penelope Knox and Basil Blackwell himself …'[12] *Oxford Magazine* carried a positive review of *Augury* in the 23 May 1940 issue.

Graham writes that 'much of this first term was given over to meetings, generally over tea at Fuller's, discussing the miscellany's contents with his co-editor Hardie, Blunden, the other members of the editorial committee, [the biographer and children's writer] Roger Lancelyn Green and Daphne Aye Moung [who contributed one poem each], and the eventual publisher, Basil Blackwell.'[13] Douglas contributed two translations as 'K', 'Horace, Odes I:V' and 'Head of a Faun' from Rimbaud, four original poems, 'Villanelle of Spring Bells', 'Pas de Trois' (first published in the 9 November 1939 issue of *Oxford Magazine*), 'Stars, for Antoinette' and 'Haydn – Military Symphony' as well as the notes on poetry. The medieval scholar Nevill Coghill wrote an essay on Oxford amateur dramatics, E. R. Appleton, the father of Betty and Joan, wrote a reactionary essay on women's issues and Blackwell wrote about a Sanskrit scholar's sudden death. *Augury* is, as Graham says, 'anti-miltaristic, even anti-serious, offering an indication that the simple and civilized pleasures of life still mattered.'[14] The ongoing war does not feature in *Augury*. It is deliberately ignored.

Douglas spent the holiday after his first term at Bexhill with his mother. He wrote to Margaret Stanley-Wrench after Christmas to thank her for her card, to complain about their accommodation and to give her his vacation news: 'Excuse pencil because I have no writing materials, being stranded at a Tea-Room with nowhere to go, until we can find a house or flat. I exercise horses every morning: there is a skewbald pony (mare), a 17-hands hunter mare with 8 inch ears, a chestnut thoroughbred mare, a black pony, a grey gelding and a gloomy little bay mare. They are respectively Peggy, Jill, Gail, Gipsy, Abbott and Molly. All but Molly are very fresh and provide some excitement. I have bought a red navvy's dinner handkerchief & a check cap, also a lovat weskit with brass buttons and so look very horsey indeed.'[15]

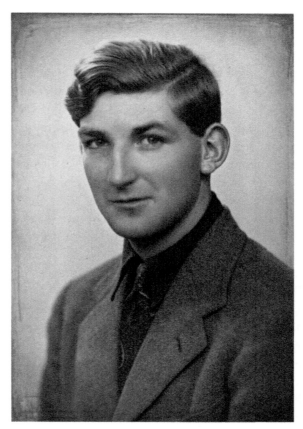

'*I ... look very horsey indeed.' Studio shot, late teens*

DOUGLAS AT OXFORD

Douglas did little to distinguish himself academically at Oxford. He wrote to Blunden during the Easter holidays of 1939 that 'the week of no exams during P. Mods was more taken up than I expected, because I had to do some of Hamo's share of preparing for Anglo Saxon, since he was busy about his other subjects.'[16] Hamo Sassoon was Siegfried Sassoon's nephew and an early friend of Douglas's at Oxford. He was a near contemporary of Douglas (born on 22 February 1920) and educated at Sherborne School. He joined Merton College in October 1938 and was in the Army from 1940 to 1946.[17] Douglas and Sassoon were planning a cycling holiday together in France, where Douglas was going to finish his own essay. Presumably Douglas had already come under Blunden's scrutiny. Hector Buck wrote to Blunden on 16 March 1939: 'Sorry about Douglas. HM [Headmaster] says, if *kindly* talk is required Hornsby (his late housemaster) is the man: but if a "round turn", then he himself will act.'[18]

Douglas wrote a postcard to his mother from the quay at Dieppe in April 1939. He and Sassoon had landed there at 2 o'clock that morning and slept on the boat until 8. The crossing had been warm and calm and the next stop was Amiens.[19] He wrote another postcard to his mother from Amiens Cathedral announcing that he and Sassoon had arrived there separately as they had been parted in a crowd listening to Edouard Daladier, the French prime minister, who was telling them that Hitler had broken the Munich Agreement. Sassoon recalled that Douglas was less concerned about the money that he had left with Sassoon than he was with whether or not Sassoon had followed the direction he had left on stones on the route to Amiens.[20]

Blunden advised Douglas to think harder about his course during the vacation: 'Think well over your whole course ahead while you are seated on some Normandy hill in the sun. You have now had 2 terms and time runs away. Consider exactly what the Statutory scheme of the English school is, and apply your powers to it as to any other problem. Map out a way of progressive reading, such as will cover the great authors and particular works which the examiners require, and allow too for any special tastes of your own. But the chief thing to aim at is a continuous view of English literary achievement, with its "beautiful variety", in which there is still method and unity. You can only just cram the necessary reading in, before the Schools will be upon you.'[21] He had taken home Chaucer, Gower and Saintsbury but there is little evidence of Douglas taking Blunden's advice. The surviving letters, even those to Blunden, show virtually no inclination to work, although he did tell Blunden in September 1939 that he had read 'a lot of Saintsbury Literary History, some Dekker, Utopia, T. Tusser, Defense of Poesie, John Heywood, and other early drama filling in where I got to at Housey. Malory has also taken up my time. Just lately I have been too occupied for anything in the way of reading, but now I know what's being done with me I have nothing to occupy me until I'm called up'.[22] He doesn't appear to have been particularly motivated by his subject. He wrote a card to Toni Beckett (undated but November 1939) saying that he had been trying to read *Othello* but that another student had come in and found him asleep over it.[23] He wrote to her later in the term to announce that he had written a 'short and brilliant' essay on *Othello*, with no quotations at all in it and no facts at all.'[24] Margaret Stanley-Wrench told her mother that she occasionally saw Douglas in lectures but that he was bored and unattentive.[25]

After Douglas's death, Blunden wrote to Buck on 5 October 1944:

> ... he [Douglas] lived largely for the arts, and literary endeavours of the place [Oxford] and was always on some new venture. He was capricious we know, but in one thing was remarkably constant, viz. love of C. H. (he even wrote a tribute to Leigh Hunt which I guessed was because L. H. was a Blue.) You know how outspoken he was – & his letters to friends of his own age were rather astonishing in that, he expected a lot of human nature, and by heaven he sometimes got it. He had ideas of returning to college and becoming a good Scholar – there's no doubt he *could* be diligent. Though in some essays he was so grown up, & could cut through stuffy and troublesome business with a hard judgement, he was largely the boy, who saw the world as a rich orchard where surely many rosy apples would be flung to him by fairy hands.[26]

If Blunden had doubts about Douglas's academic diligence he had none about his poetry. He wrote a tribute to Douglas which was intended for *The Blue* and enclosed it with the October letter to Buck:

> ... one special characteristic is clear – [Douglas's poems] were the work of a painter–poet, and highly pictorial. His thought and fancies were curious, his emotions were not everybody's, and he strove to present these in sharp designs of image and allusion. His observation of the arts, no matter what the period or the place, was extremely keen, and provided him when he wrote verse

with these figures and their strong colours. As yet, his topics were principally personal, yet his mind's eye saw in them the recurrence of experience of wider range and longer date than his own … Some of his latest pieces are (I think) his best; the complexity which overlaid much that he meant has gone, and he is 'governed by the great argument of the time', – that becomes the rhythm and the feeling of his lyrics. But still the singular touch of his pictorial sense signs the poems.

He hated decoration without anything behind it, but his verse is decorative, and thinking of it I think of figureheads and lamias, or of the masks which he devised so eagerly; yet it was his real aim in pleasing the imagination thus to impress truths of human affairs which he came at in his independent way. He did not wish to startle us with novelty, but to fashion his work well as best suited his way of thinking, whether that were unanticipated or after all an ancient way. The very look of his manuscripts is interesting as a help to understanding his poetic mood; they are written freely and gracefully, as if he saw his abstractions as definitely as physical objects. And this he maintained throughout his varied circumstances on active service.[27]

The respect was reciprocated. Douglas's Christ's Hospital history teacher, David Roberts, wrote in his obituary that Douglas was 'instantly drawn' to Blunden: 'In his letters and in his talk there was never any doubt about the debt he owed to Blunden. There were very few men or women of whom Keith spoke with unqualified admiration. From the start Blunden was among the few.'[28]

In part Blunden was repeating in his letter to Buck what he had already told Douglas in a letter of 21 May 1940 in which he returned the typescript of the poems Douglas had selected for a possible collection: 'I restore your MSS., no, TSS. with the assurance that you have here produced a most attractive series of poems, interesting alike in the way you think about things, the painter's quality in the treatment, and the originality with which you vary normal metres … there is scarcely any item which it would be best to exclude, the vitality of eager feeling and shaping seems to me to be present in nearly all.'[29]

Douglas's lifestyle doesn't seem particularly conducive to academic achievement. He wrote to Toni Beckett towards the end of 1939:

Well, I've been out getting drunk again … I consumed some port in the J. C. R., went to the East Gate, met Ilett, Abu, Pennock. There I put away a quart of beer and some port and lemon, and went back to Pennock's room. Here we went mad. The table and chairs were put back, Abu strummed negroid rhythms on the piano, and we all danced and tap-danced. Pennock took over the piano sometimes, and at other times we had the radiogram. We've broke a lot of Pennock's crockery, and I painted pictures of lewd dancers on the lampshade, with the wrong end of a pen and Pennock's ink. After that we all reeled out again, said goodnight to Ilett, and went off down the High and along the Corn singing and crashing into policemen and soldiers. We ended in the milk bar, where we sobered up, and where a pathetic old man sold us obsolete communist propaganda, and I gave a shilling to him.[30]

Not much room for Blunden's interests there. On 8 January 1940 he confessed in a letter to ex-girlfriend Yingcheng (see p. 129) that he had lost self-control during the previous term, 'did no work of any kind, ate and drank far too much, and hardly took any exercise'. After a party he had 'climbed to the top of the Logic Lane railings and after swaying backwards and forwards some 7ft above the cobbles, was violently sick and fell back into University College, somewhat gored by barbed wire.'[31]

He told Toni Beckett in May 1940 that he hadn't got the distinction he expected in the paper on Milton but that he wasn't going to resit the examination because he had done his best and doubted that another term's work would improve his answer.[32]

THE CHERWELL

In the Trinity (summer) term of 1940 Douglas became the editor of *The Cherwell*, the weekly non-political newspaper for Oxford undergraduates that had been founded some twenty years earlier. The outbreak of war had not caused the newspaper to cease publication, despite the vastly reduced number of undergraduates at Oxford, but by this point *The Cherwell* was severely diminished, with some rumours that the Conservative Association would take it over.[33] Becoming editor of *The Cherwell* was not without its problems. The editor of the *Oxford Magazine*, Robert Levens, seemed to think he had Douglas under contract.[34]

Douglas had already done some theatre reviews for *The Cherwell*. A terrible review (by 'K') of Bernard Shaw's *Geneva* at the New Theatre appeared in the issue of 17 February 1940. It has all the hallmarks of Douglas's criticism: Shaw 'now exhibits intellect in decay as conceitedly as he did in its prime, with a doddering wit. Indeed his wit and the action are well nigh stationary until the last act, when they become vigorous, but saving some sparse quips, obvious and cheap ... As constructive criticism of the world, Geneva has nothing new: as a criticism of people, chiefly of English people, it has a little value but no more originality.'[35]

Perhaps this was the tone *The Cherwell* wanted because Douglas was immediately promoted. He became sub-editor from the next issue. The editor was his Merton colleague David Beaty. 'K' contributed another theatre review to the issue of February 24, this time of the comedy drama *The Late Christopher Bean* at the Playhouse. He lauds the acting of Betty Hardy but deplores the rest of the cast as well as the producer: 'In fact Miss Hardy has again carried on her shoulders a play which would otherwise have failed. If this company are to survive, they must learn to act more like people and less like actors, and must take in hand only what they can achieve. They must find someone capable of producing a play as a whole, not as a gallimaufry; and who can restrain himself from using the plot as a background to his own wit.'[36]

The 2 March issue carried Douglas's poem 'The Creator' and, as 'K', he contributed an essay, 'The undergraduate fallen from his high estate', in which he berated his student contemporaries for gutlessness, lack of intelligence and taste, for their sheer lack of imagination, and finds explanation for it:

> There are reasons for the lack of confidence and drive behind undergraduates in such a world as this. Youth cannot so easily indulge in its fine dreams in a town full of newspaper sellers who cry out the world's doom as clearly as Solomon's Eagle. The university is impoverished and her soul changed by government action. There are no longer so many rich fathers to pay for your enjoyment with a knowing smile, and you yourselves are no longer sure of your position. The undergraduate even ten years ago lived in a city where every member of the university and the trade in Oxford knew his place ... The type of undergraduate has changed too. There are so many who are here only to get through work which they could have done as well by correspondence, to whom the university as an institution is nothing but a means to a dull but lucrative position. When they stop work, their recreations shew that they have no intelligence outside their own subject and no imagination at all ... These are some of the abuses of the university as it struggles to exist at present, and they and their causes resolve almost into one defect: apathy.[37]

If the university was struggling, the issue of the decline or otherwise of *The Cherwell* wouldn't go away. The editors printed a piece in the same issue on the subject. With 'debit' and 'credit' quotes they add: 'The editors apologise for this apparently quack advertisement. We want you to make up your minds if THE CHERWELL is worth saving. If it is, please help us by writing, reading and buying it. If it isn't, then we shall stop issue.'[38]

As Beaty's deputy Douglas quickly made his mark. It's impossible to believe that he did not have some influence on the decision to make the next issue a poetry issue. His poetry certainly dominated it with 'Caravan' (written under the pseudonym of Peter Hatred), 'Sonnet' ('Curtaining this country the whispering rain'), 'Japanese' ('Ono-no-komache the poetess'), 'Horace Odes 1:5', again as Peter Hatred, and 'Stranger, for Y.C.S.'.[39]

By April Douglas was the editor. He struggled to find suitable contributors and wrote much of the paper himself, under a series of pseudonyms. His poems had been published by *The Cherwell* since the previous term, but now, as Graham says, he 'took on the role of spokesman'.[40] Douglas wrote in satirical vein in his article 'Jeunesse Oblige' in the 27 April 1940 issue that 'the words pacifist and coward will soon be as synonymous as they were a quarter of a century ago. In no time at all it will be once more *de rigeur* to put nearly everyone against a wall: and the Englishman with his traditional modesty will consider himself the salt of the earth and the saviour of it. Not the Englishman who fights, but he who stays at home and doesn't know what we at Oxford are coming to. And as long as he and his kind condemn us and rant at the enemy and the pacifist in terms of the last generation but one, we may be satisfied that to be young is still as always the most useful and heroic occupation. It is still the part of youth, as far as possible to stem the foolishness of a dying generation and in time to redress it. Why youth is so soon forgotten is more than we can say. Perhaps we shall know when we ourselves have forgotten it.'[41] But it is the desperation of the plea that follows this bravado that strikes the reader now: 'This term we hope to produce a consistently improving CHERWELL, in the intransitive sense. But there must be more material from which to construct it. You are still urged to give evidence that more undergraduates can produce something worth the notice of the rest of the university. Linocuts, woodcuts, wood engravings, and any other form of illustration which can be printed from the illustrator's own block, will be welcomed; and we are anxious to print them, though a fairly high standard will be set … We have tried to assemble a staff this term which drinks less sherry and does more work, and hope their efforts may content you.'[42]

Keith Douglas, studied Oxford undergraduate

The same issue of *The Cherwell* carried Douglas's poem, 'Famous Men', and his translation of Rimbaud's 'Le Dormeur du Val' as well as several of his short stories. 'Drunk' is a black comedy that is reminiscent of Edgar Allan Poe. A drunk soldier tells a story about a drunk poet and it is hard not to see Douglas himself in it. The poet's 'largest ambition was to have a poem accepted by one of those exclusive little magazines which live chiefly on the subscriptions of their contributors. When he was twenty-two he wrote something he knew was really good: the long words and similes fell over one another delightfully, and when he had written it he thought of a meaning for it too.' The soldier quotes four lines from one of Douglas's poems, 'Villanelle of Gorizia', the final stanza excluded from the version in *Complete Poems*. The drunk poet wins a competition run by one of the little magazines (we inevitably see Grigson's *New Verse* here) with the wrong poem, but by the time his victory is announced he has broken his neck in his drunken stupor. 'Drunk' has some memorable lines. The soldier's voice is 'as harsh as the claret' he is drinking; his head is 'covered with a black and yellow handkerchief, making a wasp's face at me.'[43] 'The Angel' also has a Gorizian theme. A small boy sees a massive angel straddling the valley of the Isonzo, which had seen some of the most devastating battles of the First World War, and is apparently rescued from his vision by an 'exceedingly potent pill' administered by one of the monks at the local monastery. 'Coutts' is set in an Oxford college and is a dark tale of insanity, death and mysterious letters, and 'A Present for Mimi' is set in Paris. Vincent van Gogh is befriended by a beautiful but morally suspect waitress. She returns with one of her lovers to the café where she lives: 'In the little room upstairs Mimi lit the gas and surveyed herself in the peculiar mirror. Behind her Gaston grunted, not too pleased. "What is the matter, darling?" asked Mimi. "Another of your admirers has seen fit to send you a present," said Gaston. "I shall go out again and find you a better one." "Don't be silly. You can't possibly get anything now. But you may buy me the ring with a little face on it, in the window opposite, to-morrow morning, my sweet." She was busy undoing the wrappings. Inside the first of them was a note in clumsy script – "A present for Mimi." Inside the second wrapping was Vincent's right ear, so fine and large, like an elephant's.'[44] The short story, 'Profile', is unattributed, like 'The Angel', 'Drunk' and 'Coutts', but it has Douglas's macabre hallmarks. He praised the production of 'Romeo and Juliet' at the Playhouse in his theatre review as 'the best the Playhouse has offered since it was rebuilt',[45] although, as we shall see, that largely positive review came back to haunt him. And the issue of 27 April concludes with 'Farewell Poem', by 'K', which, as Scammell says, can be read alongside 'Canoe' as a sort of Song of Innocence against the Song of Experience of 'Canoe'.[46] Douglas's contributions make up about half of his first issue as editor. It wasn't vanity; he just couldn't get the contributors. Perhaps he was getting a reputation for necessarily using pseudonyms. That issue published two poems by Shotaro Oshima and he quickly had to defend himself against readers who suggested that Shotaro Oshima was 'a figment of the editorial imagination designed to attract readers from those who love the exotic.'[47]

The following week he tried a more informal start: 'Hey, Persephone, have you forgotten? The first of May and what happens? You forget your cue, and instead of reporting your entry we have to put in a fable instead.' He tells a fable about an artist and an omnivorous cow and announces the moral, which is that 'there is more than one way of beginning an editorial'.[48] True, but the editor was still desperate for contributions which were 'urgently requested': 'From to-day you are asked to regard all older persons with hostile and critical suspicion for at least two hours a week, and to submit the results of your scrutiny in writing to this paper.' These contributions were solicited for a 'Contempt For Our Elders' number which never materialized. Douglas concluded his editorial more in hope than expectation: 'The Editor would be glad to hear of anyone who is prepared to contribute a weekly article, report, or story, to **THE CHERWELL** … Meanwhile being still without such contributions the editor must leave his editorial and contrive to fill some more blank pages further on.'[49]

The issue had started with a poem by Shotaro Oshima and Douglas's translation from Rimbaud's sonnet, 'Au Cabaret-Vert':

> For eight days I had worn my boots out
> on the cobbles of streets. I entered Charleroi
> and at the Cabaret-Vert bespoke a cut
> of bread and butter, some warm ham, no more.
>
> Content, I stretched my legs under the green table
> and contemplated the ingenuous designs
> of the carpet. Also it was delectable
> when the girl with the enormous breasts and sparkling eyes –
>
> – she wouldn't be frightened of a kiss, that girl –
> brought me my bread and butter all with a smile,
> some warm ham in a decorated plate,
>
> some pink and white ham, touched with a perfume
> of garlic: and filled me a great glass, its foam
> gilt with a glimmer of belated sunlight.[50]

I think the short story, 'Sin', attributed to 'J', is by Douglas. Later in the term there is an essay on Leigh Hunt by 'John Oligarch' that is close enough to Douglas's definition of poetry to ascribe confidently to Douglas.[51] And Douglas had a habit of using the initials of his pseudonyms. Most tellingly, 'Sin' sounds like Douglas:

> The morning was as yet barely begun, and a low, diaphanous mist still shrouded the grass, which was wet and shining with the heavy dew. The sky was pure blue and cloudless, sure promise of a fine, sunny day. Arthur was crossing the lawn when a mischievous zephyr teased him; but for that, all

might have been well. In that moment he forgot everything, including the careful washing and meticulous toilet he had undergone yesterday afternoon; and with a yelp of satisfaction, he threw himself over and rolled on the grass, luxuriating in its damp softness.

While he did so, the mist gathered up her ethereal skirts and waltzed away, swaying gracefully in the grasp of her partner the zephyr, like a stately lady of old. The tulips, the object of all the gardener's care, his pride, the talk of the country round, kept time to the graceful dance, bowing and pirouetting to the music of the nearby hazel copse. The wallflowers smiled, demure yet stately, from the shelter of the old stone wall, watching with half-approving, half-disdainful eye the gaiety of their companions. A solitary daffodil, alone, fading, on the bank where she had once blushed among a thousand companions, hung her heavy head, and sulkily repulsed the wind's blandishments.

Arthur stopped rolling, and erect once more, sniffed the tang of the morning air. And then, with the most delicate of touches, a thistledown brushed by. He was young, and the white voyager was new to him. He chased it, right across the lawn, the dew flying from his feet in a shower, across the drive in a scutter of gravel, headlong into the tulips to land asprawl among them. The wind had dropped, and the thistledown hung lazily, anchored to the gorgeous blue bloom. He made a sudden grab, but his eager rush disturbed it, and it skipped away. He followed after, regardless of the bleeding stalk of the great tulip, unconscious of the ruin in his wake. Backwards and forwards in the bed he charged, until the rising wind carried the fluffy ball away. He watched it go, panting.

The starling called derision at him from the elm, but he never heard it. The sunlight filtered through a cranny in the wall and tinged his coat with gold, but he never saw it. A spider waited patiently in his lacework web, waiting for the fly that buzzed about Arthur's head. He cared for neither, for a consciousness of his guilt began to dawn, deepened as he heard a horrified voice calling him by name. Then, tail between his legs, he uncoiled himself and trotted shamefacedly back to the house.[52]

Douglas didn't normally write about dogs, but the style (and the irony of the title) is his. The fact that it is attributed to 'J' may be to break up the 'K's in the contents or it may be a sign that he was not particularly proud of it.

The next piece, 'Rejoice in the Lamb', is an altogether more accomplished essay on the eighteenth-century poet, Christopher Smart. Douglas published this 'to bring to notice this poem ["Rejoice in the Lamb"], which though it has now been published, has not received much attention from ordinary readers.'[53]

The story that follows the essay on Smart is 'The Gnome' by Peter Hatred, so Douglas occupied the first seven pages, almost exclusively, of the 4 May issue. 'The Gnome', like 'Sin', is not particularly distinguished but it has some characteristic Douglas stereotypes, including an irascible old landowner, an idiotic local policeman, a permanently inebriated ex-gamekeeper and villagers that are straight from a novel by Thomas Hardy. The celebrated gnome, belief in whom is much derided by the landowner, proves to exist however and is duly shot by the landowner. 'Get off my land', he shouts, and continues, apparently unaware of the irony, 'I don't believe in fairies and I'll have no damn fairies on my estate.'[54]

The rest of the 4 May issue has two further poems ('Dejection' and 'Head of a Faun', another translation from Rimbaud) by Douglas, and a film review (of *Ninotchka* at the Ritz).

The issue of 15 June was Douglas's last as editor. He published four of his own poems in it ('Soissons', 'Shadows', 'A Mime' and 'The Deceased'), a largely positive review of Shaw's *Man and Superman* at the Playhouse and an encouraging review of the film *Balalaika* at the Ritz, which delighted him with 'brilliant moments' although the accompanying spy film was 'banal'.[55] He finished with a characteristic Douglas flourish: 'Do not forget to carry your identity card with you. Officious people on buses will ask for it, and if you have it not, you must crawl to the police station, and there confess your delinquency to the formidable constable outside before you can even enter and make your excuses.' One feels the heat of Douglas's own experience here.

From October the translator Michael Meyer was editor. It seems that Douglas was not the wartime entrepreneur that *The Cherwell* needed. Meyer was a contemporary of Douglas's at Oxford. His tutorials with Edmund Blunden were held in a pub, The Bear, from six o'clock in the evening to ten o'clock, closing time in that era. 'Mostly at these drinking sessions,' he recalled, 'we talked about living poets, his friends such as Sassoon, Eliot and Graves, and the younger ones, Auden, Spender, MacNeice, Day Lewis and Dylan Thomas, all of whom he admired ... He mentioned another pupil of his who had been to his old school, Christ's Hospital, and who he said was an interesting poet who edited the university's literary magazine ... I should, he said, meet this young man, Keith Douglas.'[56]

Meyer submitted a poem to *The Cherwell*, and Douglas accepted it, no doubt gratefully.[57] Meyer went to meet Douglas at *The Cherwell*'s office near Folly Bridge, and so began a short quasi-professional relationship. Meyer's recollections of the new editor of *The Cherwell* strike a familiar note. Douglas was:

> … lean and tough, a year older than me but infinitely more mature. For one thing, he seemed to know about girls, and as often as not had one on his knee as he sat at his desk. He was not an easy person, cynical, abrasive and pugnacious. Once I found him with a large piece of plaster on his face; when I asked if he had had an accident, he said: 'No, a fight.' He returned contributions which did not please him with sarcastic comments, and frequently insulted individuals and institutions in his editorials and reviews. One notice which he wrote of a revue at the Playhouse was so abusive that the theatre withdrew not only Cherwell's weekly pair of complimentary tickets … but also its weekly advertisement, for which I seem to remember they paid 5s. 10d., almost the equivalent of the sale of twelve copies … This abrasiveness of Keith's, not surprisingly, concealed a raw sensitivity and great tenderness.[58]

Douglas didn't know the new poets who arrived in Oxford during 1939 and 1940, Drummond Allison, John Heath-Stubbs, David Wright and Sidney Keyes in particular, and although he published new poetry in *The Cherwell* (helped out by a supply of new poems by Edmund Blunden) he was notoriously hard to please.

The hostile review must be of *Romeo and Juliet*. What is most startling about the 4 May 1940 issue is the letter from John Eyre of the Oxford Playhouse, protesting at some remarks in Douglas's review of *Romeo and Juliet* the previous week, and Douglas's defence of it. Quoting some remarks of Douglas's about production being allotted to the 'best boy of the week' Eyre wrote:

> I find that this cynical statement when examined is extremely inaccurate. The producers at this theatre during the last two terms have been, first Willard Stoker, a professional producer who is now producing plays with another company; then Geoffrey Tyrell, who could not possibly be termed the best boy of the week and whose productions of Mr. Emlyn Williams' two plays were well appreciated in most circles; thirdly, Ian Dawson, who at the time was not a member of the company and who came down specially to produce a play; and finally Leslie French, to whom your reviewer attributes 'the hand of a good producer.' This passage which I have analysed is dangerous because

it catches the eye and suggests that the Playhouse is not fulfilling its purpose, whilst in reality the particular suggestion implied has no sound basis in fact.[59]

Eyre's letter is fair enough. Douglas was 20 and knew virtually nothing about theatre, professional or amateur. Willard Stoker went on to become a well-known director who gave young working-class actors the opportunity to star; Geoffrey Tyrell became an actor in 'Saloon Bar' in ITV's *Television Playhouse* and as Mr Jorkins in *David Copperfield*, as well as roles in *Dixon of Dock Green* and *Z Cars*; Ian Dawson was a well-known television actor; and Leslie French was a famous Shakespearian actor who made a name for himself in British films. But Douglas was unrepentant, unapologetic and arrogant. His off-hand reply fails to accept that his review may have done some damage:

> In answer to your claim our reviewer [Douglas himself, of course] draws your attention to the word 'seems.' Being ignorant of the considerable qualifications of Mr. Stoker and others whom you mention, it did indeed 'seem' to him that the task of producing was allotted without an eye to capability. You see, he noticed that, in plays he had reviewed, the producer was often to blame for not taking proper advantage of the play: or, in the case of *Midsummer Night's Dream*, for taking so much advantage of it as almost to rewrite several scenes, and to turn the whole into a travesty of a Christmas pantomime. Such spectacles as that have admittedly soured our reviewer, and after the performance of *Midsummer Night's Dream* he might even have suggested, as you say he does, that the Playhouse was not fulfilling its purpose. Another play in which producing and acting vied in their amazing inefficiency was *The Late Christopher Bean*, which only Betty Hardy's acting saved. It is not too much to say that very often the Playhouse is not fulfilling its purpose, and that more than once during the past year performances have been given which would shame amateurs. The balance has been more than redressed at other times, particularly in the last production. Our reviewer apologises if his remark has created rumours of raffles behind the scenes at the Playhouse. No one even among our clientèle of admirers does not realise that there is often (but not always) excellent acting and production evident there. With your permission the hand of a good producer is still attributed to Leslie French: what a pity that Geoffrey Tyrell cannot possibly be termed the best boy of the week.[60]

It's difficult not to agree with Max Beerbohm's caustic view of Oxford undergraduates in *Zuleika Dobson*: 'Youth all around prancing, vociferating, mocking; callow and alien youth, having to be looked after and studied and taught, as though nothing but it mattered, term after term.'[61]

Keith Douglas at Oxford

Douglas's editorial the following week returns to the behaviour of those undergraduates, who he had argued on 2 March had become so supine. It appears that they had been woken up, but by the wrong movement. He gives a faint cheer to the May Day celebrations: 'The riots seem to have been an exhibition of bad taste which is to be deplored, but they also represent energy which seemed to have left the University.' But the university's Labour Club was behind the students' resurgence, and that was not a good thing:

> The Labour Club, and in particular the working class, have as false an idea of many of those outside their ranks as many outsiders have of them. No one but a fool will mistake the intense bitterness of these people against those who have been unfairly favoured. They are forced to live in an economic and political world, and their economics and politics are sounder than most. But there are some to whom all economics and politics are still unnatural, just as there were those who deplored the passing of a more leisurely age, whatever its appalling reproaches. You have only to watch one of many Russian propaganda films to

see what is wrong with the rule of the working class. Where the capitalist and the aristocrat still flourish the world is bad and inefficient, but human: where the workers of the world unite, the last barrier of humanity will fall: even art and poetry, as we have already seen it, will be enslaved to utility. It is a world in which some of us could no more live than in the middle of the sun: and though we understand the injustice which inflames the daily worker to action, and condemn the mass of hypocrisy in which we live, we must fight to avoid a world run by labour as we would fight the devil, in whom even atheists still believe.[62]

Douglas makes the mistake of confusing the Labour movement with Russia but has no qualms about tying his colours to *The Cherwell*'s mast. The same issue carried an account of the May Day Communist march and the attendant violence, by D. E. Morris:

The flaming red banners demanded universities for the people, called for higher doles, and, inevitably, urged the workers of the world to unite. With the banners came grim unemployed, earnest undergraduettes, ardent undergraduates, sad-eyed middle-aged women, bearded men, a few children, and two smiling policemen … when the head of the column passed Long Wall Street hell broke loose. Oranges, tomatoes, apples, eggs, flour, smoke bombs, water and lemonade cascaded forth from every window in the High. A bellowing mob attacked from the pavement. Traffic was reduced to chaos. Shouts, boos, cheers and hisses made a shattering noise. Vicious fights ended in the gutters, and a brief excursion into politics was repaid with a bloody nose … And so we came to St. Giles, where, according to *The Times*, *Daily Telegraph*, *Daily Mail*, *Mirror*, and *News-Chronicle*, the Communists abandoned their meeting. That, quite simply, is a lie, doubtless perpetrated for reasons best known to the reporters concerned. For half an hour, it is true, no speaker could be heard, banners were torn down, brawling shook the street, and policemen removed the unfortunate … The meeting was finally rendered innocuous by the continued arrival of more and more police, whose numbers, perhaps wisely, increased in inverse ratio to the size of the crowd.[63]

This report was accompanied by a sane letter from John Biggs-Davison, then a Lieutenant in the Royal Marines:

It was alarming to read in this morning's press of the anti-democratic hooliganism exhibited in Oxford on the First of May.

The change from the undergraduate liberalism general in recent years is indeed frightening. Red-baiting has been in every country now plagued by dictatorship, the first stage on the road to totalitarian intolerance.

If it is evil things that we undergraduates in uniform are enrolled to fight, let those blurred with happier surroundings remember that they are not necessarily confined to Germany.[64]

Biggs-Davison had been a member of the Communist party while at Oxford. He became a right-wing Conservative politician after the war.

Having delivered his anti-Labour rant Douglas returned to the more familiar territory of contributions to his newspaper, the quality of which he acknowledges to be improving while the variety and quantity is not: 'You may have noticed that THE CHERWELL has for a long time now been written by so few people as could not possibly represent the whole amount capable of making contributions of a high enough standard. This is your magazine, and … one of its most important functions should be to reflect your opinions. But the number of people who have anything to say does not at present reach an average of one a week.' He doesn't seem to recognize the irony of this. If *The Cherwell* was truly to represent the opinions of its readers he shouldn't have concluded the previous paragraph's rant with the confession that 'there are very few of us who think like this.'

Douglas ends his editorial with a defiant justification of his own administrative incompetence: 'Among the letters to the editor lying unanswered in THE CHERWELL office are some notes from would-be members of THE CHERWELL staff. None of these people has ever tried sending the magazine to press, with all the attendant collecting, correcting, typing, and proofreading; or none of them would imagine that the editor (who is responsible for all this as well as the careless witticisms which litter these pages), has time to reply to the communications of people who cannot be bothered to come to the office and work themselves onto the staff.'

The following issue led with Douglas's essay on *The Yellow Book*, a piece that got him in the national press, and not in a good way. He had written the essay at school[65] and, to be fair, it is no celebration of *fin-de-siècle* decadence. Like butterflies the contributors to the 1890s quarterly were attractive but meaningless: 'The decadents who produced the *Yellow Book* became entangled in their own complications, as the eye is entangled by the involved patterns and lines of their drawings, or the ear bemused by the innumerable turns of their literary style. Their quest was splendid, but their methods were necessarily corrupt; and their book is the record of a vain search, doomed from the start, carried out with the consciousness of impending fate.'[66]

This not very controversial piece provoked an attack on Oxford undergraduates generally, and *The Cherwell* specifically, in the *Sunday Chronicle* of 2 June by Beverley Nichols, of *Down the Garden Path* fame. Nichols was in Oxford for the Eights Week debate at the Oxford Union. He saw in a shop window a copy of *The Cherwell* which, he says, 'does not pretend to be a magazine of weight or authority'. Nichols was amazed and disgusted by Douglas's 'leader' on *The Yellow Book*: 'It can't be possible! That precious, over-thumbed symbol of the decadents of the 'nineties? Perhaps there's some mistake? Perhaps it's a punning title on Germany's latest white book of lies? But no. This leading article … which I read with glowing [sic] astonishment, as the armoured cars trundle past in an incessant stream … really *is* about "The Yellow Book" … that the principal undergraduate journal … should choose this moment of all moments to flutter the dusty pages of "The Yellow Book" … it's incredible.' After a pointless anecdote about his old college (Balliol), his incredulity at a sign notifying visitors that the chapel was not gas-proof and the notes on the notice boards Nichol turns to the students:

'I am more and more amazed by the weirdly dressed youths who are thronging past … When I saw, emerging from a high-powered car, a youth wearing pale yellow corduroy trousers, Riviera sandals over bare feet, a pale pink silk blouse and hair that needed not only cutting but bobbing, I felt that the proportion was a little distorted … There were a great many like him. They drifted down the streets in droves.'[67]

Nichols's point was that Oxford's undergraduates were completely out of touch with the war, and were making fun of the privations of their fellow citizens. The *Sunday Chronicle* gave Oxford the right to reply and the university pointed out that of the 3,000 potential recruits 2,362 students had immediately volunteered at the outbreak of war. But Oxford's reply was too little for Douglas. This time he sprang to the defence of his fellow students in 'No Cuddling' in *The Cherwell* of 8 June 1940. 'We might ignore Beverley Nichols' maiden-avuncular criticisms; it can cause us no anxiety that he should condemn us, though his praise would indeed mark us down,' he began, disdainfully. 'But there is evidently a considerable force of opinion independent of, though now perhaps fanned by, Nichols, which holds that Oxford is the home exclusively of totally exempt conscientious objectors, that we callously ignore the sufferings even of those who a few months ago stood here with us, and almost that we are responsible for the disaster in France and Belgium.'[68] Nichols's ridiculous charges needed no rebuttal but Douglas clearly believed that his brand of sarcasm was precisely the rejoinder needed.

This is to imply then … [that] any patriotic student will leave his work and join one of those semi-civilian organisations for wasting taxpayers' money of which there are now so many. Let us look carefully and see what good this could do. In the first place almost every undergraduate is registered already for one or more forms of national service: several wait up at night to greet hypothetical I. R. A. men with fifteen rounds of ball and a bayonet: farming and forestry schemes will occupy numbers of those who are not absorbed into the services during the long vacation. Any further activity would probably be discouraged. And in any case most of us might be allowed some amusement during the last few weeks we are able to get it. Moreover, a great part of the conscientious objectors will be doing work with ambulances a good deal more dangerous than that of several patriotic heroes who joined up at the outbreak of war to do office work in uniform … Our critics outside will probably not concede that there is any use in preserving a university magazine which treats of such shocking subjects as the decadence of the eighteen nineties at this stern season: or in encouraging wittiness at the Union, or in performing plays and good music … There is further the accusation that if we had been less apathetic in the past we should have been more ready for invasion now. It is hard to see the very smallest evidence of reasoning or justification behind this amazing statement. If the government were largely composed of undergraduates or even of Dons; if it were even aware of the fact, that some undergraduates are sensible, and if it were eager to take their advice on major point of policy, then we might bear the accusation of apathy with justice. But in this curiously arranged country, everyone is legally a zany until he is twenty-one. A man may be taken away and blown up at an age when he is not allowed to lead an independent life in his spare time. All we are permitted to do is further to show our youthful foolishness by writing our names under offers of service to the government of our elders – not even in sarcasm can we bring ourselves to add – 'and betters.'[69]

Douglas returned to the fray in the same issue with an article (signed 'K. W. R.', but presumably by Douglas) entitled 'Pansies or Petunias *or a University Quisling*', which ridiculed Nichols for hypocrisy and peddling fake news.

I talked to Beverley Nichols about the hoax [about forming a local *Down the Garden Path* club] which had taken place in Balliol gardens that same afternoon [that Nichols had addressed the Union]. Beverley Nichols knew nothing about it, and until I showed him my invitation card he had never seen one. I can still hear the silvery tinkle of his girlish laughter, as he expressed his delight, and said how certain he was that I was the perpetrator. But he must have a card as a memento; he would so love one, and so a girl friend of mine ran back to her college at eleven o'clock that night, to get him a spare one. If she had not he would never have possessed the card which, in his article, he threw down in disgust on his dressing table, as he was changing for the debate. In the article in last Sunday's paper my girl friend has become a pained and disappointed mother, and Beverley Nichol's [sic] girlish delight has changed to pseudo-manly disgust.[70]

Douglas hadn't finished, even in this issue. An endnote says as much: 'the law of libel, which allows him to cover the pages of Sunday newspapers with unfounded and malicious lies, will not permit us to say what we will of him. But next week Quentin Dobson and Peter Hatred and anyone else who submits worthy work, will do their best. If Mr. Nichols considers returning to Oxford any time soon, he had better wear an old pair of trousers.'[71] The 'Quentin Dobson' piece is an unpleasant attack, that is not averse to insinuation. Dobson wrote that Nichols 'must have been lucky to see so many long-haired extravagantly-dressed would-be aesthetes wandering about in your very short visit – we suspect that your admirers had all turned out to see you.'[72] The Peter Hatred piece does not appear but this may not have been deliberate. The editor of *The Cherwell*'s office was chaotic. On 8 June Douglas apologised to readers: 'The Editor apologises for a confusion in THE CHERWELL of June 1st, which attributed the poem 'This Known Land' to Geoffrey Matthews, and in the table of contents, the linocut on p.88 to Peter Hatred. The linocut was by Jocelyn Jacoby, the poem by Gordon Swain.'[73]

Meanwhile, *The Cherwell* needed filling. The 18 May issue carried a scoop about the German invasion of the fictional country of Ruritania. The 'Special Correspondent' who wired the news from 'Bittach on the Ruritanian border' was doubtless Douglas himself, and the editorial that accompanies it, 'Scoop', was almost certainly written by Douglas: 'This week THE CHERWELL is first with the news of the invasion of Ruritania: in actual fact our reporter was not on the spot, but he has evolved a formula for reporting invasions which is as infallibly correct as anything out of a geometry book.'[74] Although Nichols's piece was gratuitously unpleasant you can see what he was getting at. There was enough going on in the summer of 1940 without inventing and satirizing fictional German invasions of nonexistent countries. The same issue carried two of Douglas's poems, 'Images' and 'Canoe'.

It is impossible to know how much of *The Cherwell* was written by Douglas in the summer term of 1940. It is clear, however, that by the 25 May issue he was getting pretty fed up:

> Every week the editor is more and more struck with the futility of writing anything at all in this paper. Every week he must sit opposite a typewriter which is too heavy to carry about out of doors, and compose so much poppycock, which is read by very few: and deserves to be read by fewer, very often. Even on those rare occasions when the editorial wit contrives to scintillate for as much as a page, and perhaps prefixes some excellent work by surer pens, hardly anybody notices … At least until after the war, extensive distribution and advertisement will be impossible: but it is in the interest of that small group who do still enjoy one or two of THE CHERWELL's contents, to see that more people hear of THE CHERWELL, buy it and read it. For this reason: that a man who knows that he is speaking to no one at all, unless he is mad, will not go on speaking. And an editor who knows only too well that he and his contributors are addressing a dwindling minority, will presently lose heart, and no longer be bothered to do his best.[75]

That issue carried his reviews of *Patience* at the New Theatre, the Playhouse Revue at the Playhouse and the film *Babes in Arms* at the Ritz,[76] as well as his poem, 'A Round Number':

> The monotonous evil clock
> Is creeper climbing on my heart
> and with rank ivy will pull down
> my hope of happiness and renown.
>
> My sacred lady who needs no art
> gives an idiot place to mock.
>
> I know the fragrant girl is dead,
> and perished with my innocence
> and died two hundred years ago:
> or twice that time if Time is slow.
>
> And so reflect for recompense
> she only lived inside my head.

Then she is gone. I still remember
my early promise, looking for
obliging fame to make amends
and here my last existence ends.

For I can't feed hope any more
And Time has reached a round number.[77]

As Scammell says: "'hope of happiness and renown" go together: his unluckiness in love is part and parcel of his unworthiness as a poet. The "rank ivy" of the opening stanza, which contrasts with the "fragrant girl" of the second, is literally time, but also a type of lust for sexual and literary favours. Unlike those who have time to sue for grace and win the bays by years of devotion, Douglas is up against the fast-forward motions of a poet in wartime, for whom last week or month is already "two hundred years ago".'[78] In other words, Douglas felt by 1940 that he didn't have much time.

The evacuation of Allied troops from the Dunkirk area happened from 26 May to 4 June 1940. *The Cherwell's* response to it was Douglas's editorial, 'The Happy Fatalist', in the issue of 1 June:

The happiest person at such times is presumably the fatalist: what he loses in the enjoyment of high hopes he gains in immunity from despair. The advantages of his philosophy are still more those of freedom from panic and the ability to be unprejudiced by what has happened, what is happening, and what will happen. There may be those (apparently there are) who can still believe in God as a benevolent divine uncle: and by all means let each find comfort where his reason allows him. But even for the fatalist the facts of good and evil remain, and he should be able to appreciate them better than anyone else.

For he is not that hopeless castaway he sometimes appears, he does not trust in nothing, nor is he faithless. He rather believes in the most evident and omnipotent deity of all, whose ways are not inscrutable, who moves in a wonderful but not a mysterious way, and who is as fundamentally just as any other deity has ever been. To some the fatalist may still seem to be cold and inhuman, and as far as reason and impartiality are not the true characteristics of humanity, he is inhuman and superhuman.

Happy fatalists can listen to the news and the rumours and enjoy in spite of them the occasions which even war cannot make less pleasant. Here at least there is still pleasure and activity for a good many people, and it would be foolish to let any forboding [sic] spoil either.[79]

One can't imagine that Beverley Nichols would have enjoyed this editorial much, nor would he have approved of the article on the poetry of Leigh Hunt by 'John Oligarch' in the same issue. Douglas had written on Leigh Hunt at Christ's Hospital and his essay in *The Cherwell* draws much the same conclusion, that Leigh Hunt was a poet who never drew conclusions but merely described his experiences.[80]

Apart from the anti-Nichols diatribes, Douglas contributed (as 'K') a review of Shaw's *The Devil's Disciple* at the New Theatre to the 8 June 1940 issue. On 15 June Douglas returned to Nichols: 'Undergraduates – you have hissed Beverley Nichols [Nichols had complained of being hissed during the Union debate]. You have been seen in sandals and bare feet at this critical time, when every youth should help the nation to his utmost by wearing shoes and socks: you have allowed this immoral paper to lie on the very same bookstall as the SUNDAY CHRONICLE, and to contain articles on literature, without publicly burning every copy of it.'[81]

Douglas continues to lampoon Nichols mercilessly in his leader, and *The Cherwell* goes further in the following article, 'The Tragedy of Mr. Nichols', by J. M. Rampton: 'To think of the career of such a superficial person as Mr. Nichols in terms of a tragedy will probably bring a sardonic smile to the lips of most people, but whoever it is, it remains profoundly tragic when early success booms boomerang-like on a writer and blights the rest of his career.' According to Rampton, Nichols had been an honoured guest of artists, politicians and society hostesses alike but his image became tarnished as the bright young things of the 1920s hit the 1930s:

> He first turned rustic and cultivated the primitive delights of our countryside, and wrote *Down the Garden Path*. But the escape to the cottage in the country, away from the coarse utilitarian life of the city, soon grew wearisome and he became an hysterical convert to emotional pacifism, and wrote *Cry Havoc!* But how soon the novelty of that wore off, and he tried once more to forget himself by burying his permed locks in the bosom of the Church, and wrote *The fool hath said*. But even religion, that supposed panacea for the aging neurotic, never provided satisfaction and there began his inclination towards Fascism – the weak man's desire to lose himself in the corporate state and flight from the introspection of middle-age, and after a series of articles in *Action*, *News of England* was written.

But 'none of these novelties' provided Nichols with lasting satisfaction, according to Rampton, so he turned on Oxford, where 'the gangrene of success first set in':

It is not hard to imagine Mr. Nichols jealously resenting the lives that the undergraduates still lead. It would bring back very bitter memories of the success and hope for further success that once was his. But however intelligible that article is in terms of personal psychology, it is in no way excusable. Mr. Nichols did not harangue the Union in khaki but in the suave get up of the society lounger. He was not writing a bitter indictment of the civilian population from the front line in Flanders but a ten guinea article from the safety of Fleet Street. For a middle-aged gentleman, not himself militarily occupied, to accuse young men of lack of seriousness towards the war, is merely asking for a return of the accusation.[82]

Douglas knew Rampton at University College, to which Merton undergraduates were moved when Merton was requisitioned for war work. Rampton was born on 19 March 1921 and matriculated in Modern Languages (English in his last term, taught by C. S. Lewis) in October 1939. In 'Chez des Artistes' Rampton ridiculed Oxford artists, particularly those from the Ruskin and the Slade School of Art which had been evacuated from London to Oxford: 'I ought to explain that the Art School has divided itself into self-contained cliques. The clique that I knew had and has still as far as I know as its centre Ajax. It was to Ajax's room that I used to pay my visits. I used to go to his room and see the artists filling his arm-chairs and littering the floor.'[83] Ajax is derided by Rampton, along with his friends, Cyril, Monica, Felicity, Leslie, Hugh and Hector. 'If any of them reads this and has keen enough noses to recognise its source, they will not, of course, agree with my estimation of themselves, but they will with what I say about their fellow-members of the clique. They will not, of course, understand a lot of it, but they will agree with the tone I've adopted. And those I've not mentioned will be particularly nice to me at our next meeting. Not because they are frightened of what I might write concerning them in the future, but because they are so pleased that I've dealt sufficiently viciously with the rest of the clique.' Douglas added a rider as the editor: 'To put it very mildly indeed, this is a one-sided view. We would like someone to write the other side of it, to appear next week.'

Douglas himself replied in 'Another Art Gallery', as Peter Hatred, in the issue of 25 May: 'Of course, Ajax is very much on the edge of my circle, but

I doubt if what you say is so, and it doesn't coincide with anything I've heard … I know Ajax by sight, because he is a friend of Inez, whom you could not have included in your Philippic, because not even your promiscuous mudslinging could stick any on her. Her recommendation is enough to clear Ajax too, for most of us.'[84] Douglas goes on to defend the artistic talents of his friends 'James', 'Bill', 'Sidney' and 'Nan' and concludes magisterially: 'These images, then, I set up against yours, not as a direct answer to you (although you shall have that) but simply to make the whole discussion appear more accurately. I do regard these people with a certain amount of affection, but I have tried to be impartial in portraying them. That, you must appreciate, is a harder task that you set yourself, for to destroy is always easier than reproduction. And I imagine that you are immune both from the sentiment of affection and from the affection of others.'

Another riposte to Rampton, by G. B. C. Webb, appeared in the same issue. This could have been Douglas again, especially given his freely expressed disdain for both Rampton and Beverley Nichols. The main reason for suspecting that G. B. C. Webb is Douglas is the article by Rampton, 'Rampton comes again', in the 1 June issue. (The *Oxford University Gazette* reports no matriculation of G. B. C. Webb in the period so it is safe to assume that the name was used as a pseudonym.) Webb is attacked with such hostility that one must assume that 'Webb' is Keith Douglas. Webb's:

> … prose is overloaded and such a stew of dreary clichés that to disentangle his arguments is wearisome and difficult. A few examples from the first paragraph alone – self-important nonentity, beastly little ego, bored unconstructive young men, a few neurotic young men, crude excesses – show Mr. Webb as worthy as any one to write leaders in the tabloid press, which he seems so vigorously to deplore. But that is incidental. Mr. Webb tells me I am reactionary, thinly-veiled. From his language one would conclude that Mr. Webb is a baby Blimp, cutting his first venomous fang, who in the true tradition of his forefathers will eventually descend – as he suggested of myself – to pacifist-baiting.[85]

It is difficult to believe even Keith Douglas to be this direct with one of his contributors. In 'Rampton comes again' Douglas also attacks another critic, Walter Douglas, who had written 'Rampton raised' in the 25 May issue. Walter Douglas was close to Keith Douglas: 'I drink my tea in my studio and write this … mostly because but for me Mr. Rampton would never have written "Chez les artistes" … That my friend the Editor of THE CHERWELL should print such writings [attacks on his Van Gogh article published in *The Cherwell* on 11 May] is regrettable but not strange. He is endeavouring to keep afloat, in a time of crisis, that most easily debased of all forms of literature, an undergraduate literary magazine.'[86] Walter Douglas goes on to attack Rampton's lack of loyalty ('He, who has allowed himself to be disloyal to those about him, has ended by being disloyal to himself') and his sex-obsession.

In 'Rampton comes again', Rampton mocks 'Webb', 'Walter Douglas' and 'Peter Hatred' and claims the high ground:

> After this war most of the useless superstructure of the university will be lopped off. Oxford will be reorganised on a drastically more democratic basis. Intelligent people as a whole will welcome it, firstly because of the intrinsic merit of such an action, secondly as a simple necessity, but no one will welcome the prospect of Oxford becoming a mere governmental department, run by pin-heads of the Civil Service. If the public become convinced that these people are typical of Oxford, then there is the probability that Oxford will become a bureaucratic department whose members, as a writer in THE CHERWELL said last term, could as well do their work by a correspondence course.[87]

When Meyer became editor the following October he was forced to assure the Playhouse that *The Cherwell* would take a less aggressive stance. Copy and advertisement sales had so declined under Douglas's editorship that the owners had decided to cease publication, but the new editor's father guaranteed any losses the magazine made. It was not an offer that Keith Douglas's father would have made.

In his memoir, Meyer quotes Douglas's poem, 'Canoe', which, as he says, 'perfectly captures the atmosphere of Oxford around the time France fell.' 'Canoe' was published in *The Cherwell* of 18 May 1940:

> Well, I am thinking this may be my last
> summer, but cannot lose even a part
> of pleasure in the old-fashioned art of
> idleness. I cannot stand aghast
>
> at whatever doom hovers in the background;
> while grass and buildings and the somnolent river,
> who know they are allowed to last for ever,
> exchange between them the whole subdued sound

of this hot time. What sudden fearful fate
can deter my shade wandering next year
from a return? Whistle and I will hear
and come another evening, when this boat

travels with you alone towards Iffley:
as you lie looking up for thunder again,
this cool touch does not betoken rain;
it is my spirit that kisses your mouth lightly.[88]

TRAGEDY AT UNIVERSITY COLLEGE

The Government requisitioned Merton College in 1939 and by the new academic year, in October 1939, Douglas was staying at University College. Parts of Merton had been ceded to the military authorities at the outbreak of the Second World War. In September 1939 the Ministry of Works formally requisitioned Grove and St Alban's Buildings, staircase V of the Front Quadrangle and staircases I, II and III of the Fellow's Quadrangle (where Douglas's room was). Most of the requisitioned rooms were unoccupied until November 1940 when the Ministry of Aircraft Production took them over. By the summer of 1940 only 30 men lived in Merton and 50 had been sent to University College. Blunden was Principal of Postmasters and College Fire Officer from June 1940 to June 1943 when he resigned from the college; not very glamorous positions for someone who had seen active trench service in the First World War.[89]

Douglas wrote to Margaret Stanley-Wrench that he was 'at present parked at Univ. and sharing a room with someone who does nothing but play bridge with a lot of noisy friends and I don't like him much … Just now I am sneezing violently and very miserable. Shortly I shall go out and buy some rum, in the hope that it will do me good.'[90] The alliance between Merton and University Colleges was close and friendly. The two colleges operated joint sports teams and according to Robin Darwall-Smith, 'University–Merton collaboration was of a more novel kind. Peter Bayley (m. 1940) had created a play-reading society on coming up; that summer Merton Floats, Merton's drama society, wished to perform *The Comedy of Errors*, but lacked enough men. To make good the deficiency, Bayley created the Univ. Players … Preparations for war, however, did not cease. The Chapel windows were taken down, and blackout regulations enforced. The most time-consuming war work for undergraduates was fire-watching. Every night, they took turns sitting on its roofs looking out for passing aeroplanes, some sitting in boredom, others enjoying plane-spotting.'[91] But increased rationing gradually affected College life '... members received two-course dinners, rather than three. One undergraduate remembered lunch becoming "something of a disgrace – frequently no more than a bowl of soup or (not 'and') a black pudding, supplemented by bread (unrationed) and one's own butter, cheese, etc. as required."'[92]

Tragedy visited University College on 17 May 1940. Some undergraduates walking out from Hall into the Main Quadrangle after lunch were shot at by the undergraduate occupant of a top-floor room directly opposite. Charles Moffatt was killed and two of his friends were wounded. Historian Joshua Levine takes up the story: 'Charles Moffat was shot in the abdomen. As he fell, groaning, another shot struck him in the neck, killing him. The second shot also hit Dennis Melrose in the chest. A third shot missed, but a fourth struck Pierre de Kock in the calf. John Fulljames was not firing indiscriminately; his targets were all part of a particular college "set". After the shooting Fulljames walked up to the dean of the college. The dean asked whether he knew from which room the shots had come. "I'm afraid they came from mine," said Fulljames. "Do you know who had the gun?" "I'm afraid I did. What do you want me to do, sir?"'[93]

According to Levine, Fulljames was a quiet man who had performed well at school but had recently become 'moody and apathetic'. He was a pacifist but had tried to enlist in the Territorial Army. He told a friend that he 'might get a kick out of killing' but had had to leave the Bette Davis film, *Dark Victory*, because of his dislike of bloodshed. According to the historian of University College, Robin Darwall-Smith, one of the victims, Melrose, who became a leading heart surgeon, thought Moffat 'was "playing dead", but when Melrose tried to lift him, he was hit himself in the chest, saved from death only by the bullet ricocheting off the fountain pen in his jacket pocket. The killer ... apparently believed that one of his victims played loud music and entertained girls in his rooms nearby especially to annoy him, but Norman Dix also remembered breaking up at breakfast that day an argument about conscientious objectors, with the killer defending them against Melrose and his friends.'[94]

Fulljames had written letters to friends in other colleges before the shooting so the murder was premeditated and when asked by the dean (the economist William Beveridge, who later inspired the British welfare state) if he was ill replied negatively. In spite of this he was remanded to Brixton Prison where he was diagnosed with early paranoid schizophrenia, although he was well enough to stand trial, which was in early July.

> Counsel for Fulljames ... submitted that when his client fired the four shots, he did not know that what he was doing was wrong. He presented the concept of schizophrenia to the jury by referring them to 'the famous horror story' involving Dr Jekyll and Mr Hyde. 'The mind,' he said, 'disintegrated and the whole personality was withdrawn from reality into a world of fantasy.' He called an eminent psychologist, Dr Henry Yellowlees, to give evidence that Fulljames was insane in law. In rebuttal, the prosecution called the senior medical officer from Brixton Prison, who restated his opinion that the schizophrenia was not advanced, and that Fulljames *had* known, when he fired, that what he was doing was wrong. The jury was presented with a straight choice. The young man's life rested on its decision.'[95]

The jury retired for only 25 minutes, after which time it returned a verdict of guilty, but insane, meaning that Fulljames escaped hanging but was committed to Broadmoor. Apparently he smiled as he left the dock. The medical authorities at Broadmoor did not believe that Fulljames had ever been insane and recommended his release after just five years of imprisonment.

Whatever the rights and wrongs of the case itself, Douglas was clearly affected by it. Alec Hardie recalled coming across Douglas in the quadrangle at University College just after the incident and being surprised by how badly shaken he seemed,[96] but no account of the murder appears in any of Douglas's surviving letters. His rooms were then on Staircase VII, room 2 on the ground floor so if he was in his room at the time he would have had a perfect view of the shooting. Why anyone should be surprised at such a reaction to a fatal shooting isn't explored.

BETTY SZE

Through Margaret Stanley-Wrench, Douglas met Jean Turner and Joan Appleton, who became his friends. He invited Jean Turner for tea at Merton and to an exhibition and she invited him for an English Club tea at St Hilda's College.[97] Joan Appleton's family lived in John Masefield's former house, Hill Crest, in Boars Hill, just outside Oxford, and he became a frequent visitor there. Indeed he gave it a plug in the 27 April 1940 issue of *The Cherwell*:

Comparatively few people in the University know of the existence of a private theatre at John Masefield's ex-house on Boars Hill. Performances of ballet by the pupils of Lydia Sokolova, and of music by members of the university, were given there last summer term; in which the majority of undergraduates showed a characteristic lack of interest. This term it might be used again, if there is any support for the idea. Two nebulous schemes are under consideration, both of which (or one of them) may be put into action. They are (a), that a professional ballet company under the direction of Madam Sokolova and including Harold Turner and other well known dancers, probably from the ballet Rambert, should be asked to dance at least one miniature ballet, and various divertissements. (b) That a programme of English masques, including Dryden's Secular Masque, *Comus*, and a new masque by Edmund Blunden, should be given by members of the university and others. Anyone who is interested in dancing, reciting, or singing in the masques, or in watching professional ballet, should write to THE CHERWELL, or to Miss Joan Appleton, Hill Crest, Boars Hill, as soon as may be.[98]

The masques had already been performed in Oxford. The 30 November 1939 issue of the *Oxford Magazine* announced that: 'The Merton Floats, who two years ago won high praise for their production of *The Ascent of F6*, have this term joined forces with their reception college, University, to produce Fielding's burlesque of restoration tragedy, *Tom Thumb the Great*. The play, being of less than full length, will be preceded by Dryden's *Secular Masque*, which has been set to music by Mr. Kenneth Brooks. A prologue has been written by Mr. Edmund Blunden, who will also, in the Masque, demonstrate vocal powers hitherto unsuspected except by his neighbours in the Bach Choir.' Douglas helped paint the scenery for the masque and made masks for it.[99] There were three performances, one on Tuesday 5 December, at 8.15, and two on Thursday 7 December, at 2.15 and 8.15. As Graham says, 'the choice [of drama] could hardly have been more pointedly pacific and backward-looking.'[100] It was as though the war had done nothing to disturb Oxford's preoccupations. Blunden recalled the Dryden production in his introduction to the Faber & Faber edition of *Keith Douglas, Collected Poems* in 1966:

Another engrossing scheme was a performance of Dryden's *Secular Mask* – on the ending of an old age and the beginning of a new. Now we realized, if we had not already done so, that Keith was deeply devoted to the stage; he assisted us in all the preparations for this operatic piece (a shame that there was no part for him to act), spending many hours unseen to us in attempting to supply papier-mâché masks. These were revealed and had merit, but unfortunately collapsed before they could be displayed to the audience. After the show Keith used all his art (and he was a painter always looking about for some opportunity, some untried nicety) on a decorated poem in honour of the cast and, if I may say it here, of the senior member who played Chronos with a beach-ball as the globe he was compelled to carry.'[101]

In February 1939 Douglas started a relationship with Betty Sze, who was an undergraduate at Lady Margaret Hall. Her father, the prominent Chinese politician and diplomat Dr. Alfred Sao-ke Sze, had been the first Chinese ambassador to the US and was thoroughly Westernized. He himself was educated at Cornell University, and Betty's schooling had been at Cheltenham Ladies' College. Douglas fell in love with her but Betty (or Yingcheng) refused to marry him and remained the unrequited love of his life, and arguably the focus of his best romantic poetry. On 15 May 1939 he wrote to her a poem, 'To a Lady on the Death of Her First Love' as it was titled in *The Cherwell* when it was first published there on 27 April 1940:

> So death, the adept subtle amorist,
> Has taken from you what I might have kept
> Fast in the queer casket of my heart.
> You were beguiled to grant him that part
> That was the whole of you. Then death crept
> Like a secret jeweller, and the amethyst
>
> That I diligently sought, he took and stored.
> O rich man, death, you sent your creature
> From your demesne, disguised with life, to steal
> A gem you never wanted. You cannot feel
> Its worth. And she, making the first gesture
> Of waking, gave it you, the wicked lord.
>
> It was death's emissary who took your love
> To hoard it in the quiet land, nowhere.
> He followed death's instructions from the start,
> And when he had it of you, went apart
> And tendered to his master death the fair
> And gentle plunder. Death will keep it close enough.

> Still I, the loving fool and last courtier
> Attend you, and my service is still yours
> For all the profit you enjoy of it,
> Use my emotion and occasional wit
> To colour each opaque hour, the course,
> Despoiled princess, you must complete here.'[102]

One infers, from the elegiac tone of this poem, that Douglas already suspected that her love for him was no match for his for her. Indeed he wrote to her, again with a poem, with a third-party self-characterization that says as much:

> These lines ['What in the pattern of your face …'], written by a famous poet in his youth, just before he went to the dogs over a woman, are more sincere than they sound. The trouble with him was that he always fell in love with the wrong girls, and wrote no novels about it. After his affair with a Chinese girl, who treated him shockingly, the poor poet cracked up completely, and was sent down from Oxford, where (of course) he had just commenced a promising career … Do you remember which piece of wall we sat on, where for 10 seconds you became one of the world's great heroines? I shan't bother to go and sit there but my shadow will be on duty for me. When you have given me up and spoilt the [here there is the sketch of a heart with blots on it] few good bits there are left in my heart, you will see that shadow every time you come past late at night.[103]

On 15 July 1939 Douglas wrote to Yingcheng that he was still 'seeing about a car, which I shall buy for use in vacs, if poss. The chauffeur here has a Riley, same date as ours, bought for £25 with a new hood; and he has tuned it up to do 33 to the gallon and 75 m.p.h. It just shews. He is only licensing it for 2 quarters and says it comes to about 3/6 per quarter more than licensing the whole lot at once. So I think Mother might manage tax and insurance if I do the actual buying.'[104] Yingcheng recalled to Desmond Graham a visit with Douglas to Christ's Hospital in 'a sporty little Riley roadster that he and I chose secondhand', an ambition that he had long wanted to fulfil.[105] 'To complete the effect', Yingcheng recalled, 'he made me wear a Chinese dress – determined to emphasise the exotic!'

Douglas was in love with Yingcheng, although he confessed later to Toni Beckett that 'it was because Betty was as strung up as I was that we were continually biting each other's heads off.'[106] By June 1939 Douglas had wanted to formalize his relationship with Yingcheng and had bought her a silver engagement ring, 'St. George and the Dragon carved in a shield shape' according to her.[107] The holiday in Paris was not a success. Yingcheng came to feel that his dependency on her was emasculating.[108] She went to Bermuda and he returned to his mother at Hadlow Down in Sussex, where Jo was a companion to an elderly lady. He wrote to Margaret Stanley-Wrench in October 1939 to apologize to her for neglecting her during the previous term: 'As a matter of fact I neglected everyone except, of course, the Chinese girl Betty Sze, with whom I fell very violently in love. We became unofficially engaged and went to Paris on a still more unofficial honeymoon, after which Betty went on to Bermuda and became properly engaged to a rather rich American inhabitant of the island.'[109] He wrote to Jean Turner at around the same time: 'Betty Sze has given me the air.'[110] After the 'unofficial honeymoon' in Paris he returned 'to England for some months of brokenness and boredom. For eight weeks or so I scarcely spoke to anyone under forty. Betty hardly wrote, and when she did, it was only to say what a good time she was having and how many handsome young men there are in Bermuda. Her last letter complained of me insulting her, said she had only been kind to me because she thought I needed encouragement as an artist, and now I could go to hell.' Later, he wrote somewhat tactlessly to Toni Beckett, his fiancée at the time, that the period spent in Paris had been 'a wonderful adventure, and I enjoyed it. But what I enjoyed was being in Montparnasse, the haunt of Romance, among artists and Bohemians to be as Bohemian as any of them, and Betty was a piece (a big piece, but only a piece) of the Bohemian atmosphere: it was the same, on a larger scale, as when I took her to Christ's Hospital.'[111]

Yingcheng had introduced Douglas to Toni Beckett in October 1939. A friend from Cheltenham Ladies' College, Toni had just come up to Lady Margaret Hall. 'Have you seen *Carnet du bal* yet?' she wrote to Beckett. 'If not and you would like to go, I wonder if you would allow a very charming friend of mine to take you? His name is Keith Douglas, he's second year, reading English, a poet and artist and quite respectable (should I have said that?) anyway he's longing to meet you and I said I'd introduce you to him.'[112] Douglas threw himself into the new relationship. He wrote to Toni Beckett straightaway: 'Apparently it's Betty Sze's idea that you should come and see *Carnet du bal* with me, because she's decided she doesn't want to see it again. An entirely undated latter from Betty which arrived sometime yesterday says, "Toni Beckett can come tomorrow but that's the only day she can manage;" and I'm to say when I can meet you at L.M.H. Well, if today's the day you can come I'll meet you outside L.M.H. at 4.0 and take you out to tea first … I hope you'll like the film, even if you find me unpleasant.'[113]

By 25 October he was declaring his love to Toni: 'I need someone like you so badly that is you *are* kind to me, I shall study to repay you the only way I can, with complete devotion; so that once I've let it happen, only you can stop me loving you for the rest of my life …'[114] He went on to describe his previous love life: 'I've only been in love with two people so far: the first I forced myself to be in love with because she seemed to be in love with me and I hadn't anyone else. Afterwards it turned out that we were both dutifully behaving, each as we thought the other one wanted. The next was Betty, and she held me because she was strange and really summed up in herself the satisfaction of my desire to go and see places like Bali and Hawaii and bathe in tropical moonlight etc. etc. à la Rupert Brooke. I knew she never sympathised with me or really understood me.' Within a few days Toni was 'Darling Antoinette'.[115] By the end of October he wrote to her that he'd 'thought about nothing else than you ever since I saw you yesterday, and I'm still just as sure I'll go on wanting you.'[116] He soon began to lecture Toni about not writing to him as frequently as he would have liked: 'Any relationship between a man and a woman is most due to each realising what the other wants, and when. The more hints we can give each other the better time we can have. And I can't help thinking that I haven't got an awful long time before I leave this lazy life, possibly for good.'[117] The frequency of the recurrence of his death wish, or mortal foreboding, shows that it was no mere seduction technique. As Declan Ryan wrote in the *Times Literary Supplement,* many of his university poems are 'written in what reads like the near-certainty of approaching death.'[118] Keith Douglas genuinely didn't expect to survive the war and told both Betty Sze and Joan Appleton he would be killed in the war.[119]

Toni Beckett recalled Douglas as presenting himself as 'one who could expose the stupidities of the social world to which she belonged and mix equally on every level of society. His talk was constantly about his school, its routine and character rather than his troubles there, and about the blindness of people with money.'[120]

Douglas's feeling for Toni was reciprocated. He wrote to her hoping that she would continue to feel as she did about him then: 'There are some things which thrill, surprise or excite you now, which will stop thrilling you when you get used to them. But for compensation, you'll find some other things about me that you never knew, every day if you know me for years.

And other things you'll go on loving and become so used to loving that you will find that I am indeed a part of you and when I go, part of you goes too, and part of me stays behind.'[121] This newly-discovered confidence in his relationship is refreshing but was soon overtaken by financial realities: 'we shall have to start making money or spending yours ... or just not spending.' He suggested cutting out morning coffee and not meeting until the afternoon and in addition, sought employment: 'Please do your best to get me a job, through your guardian or someone. My qualifications are – I can coach in French, German, History, Latin, English, Art, Greek (if necessary but not very advanced) teach riding, swimming, P.T., drive a car and teach anyone else to drive. I can also do housework, and might make a good 2nd footman.'[122] He was sometimes painfully honest about his love life. He wrote to Toni from University College:

> Darling I don't think you are quite sure I'm not just taking the first I get, are you? Straight away though, you can be quite certain of this – even if I only keep you until I no longer need your sympathy, it'll be for the rest of my life, if you want it to be, because it's not over the Betty Sze question I need help, it's over everything. And I'll make you sure I love you for good soon. You'll see I've only implied a proposal. I'm not going to ask you to marry me till I've seen you again a few times, because I want you to be sure, and you must hear a bit more about me too. But in case you think I only want a university affair, I really do want to marry you ... I knew my only chance of getting over this affair [with Yingcheng] properly was to get someone quickly. Also I was determined not to fall flat for any one person. So I arranged all sorts of meetings, some through Betty and some on my own. But unfortunately they rather fell through when I had that evening with you on Wednesday; and ever since I first heard of this bust up with Betty I've been trying to make myself fall for several girls – four in fact. I tried very hard because I was terrified of having no one, but it didn't work. As soon as I got away from each of them I knew it was no use. But I never tried to fall in love with you. I only came to have a pleasant outing, thinking that after Betty I wasn't running after any more ex debs.[123]

He had known Toni Beckett for only about four weeks. He wrote to his mother on 14 November 1939 to explain his new relationship:

> I think Toni & I have thought of everything you put down [in Jo's letter to him] – & since we look like having to be engaged for at least three years, we ought to be quite sure of our minds at the end of that time. Either of us can

terminate the engagement at any time during the three years, so I haven't tied her down particularly. What with the things Dadda did that were mistakes, & the mistakes of other people which Toni has heard about, & the mistakes I made with Betty, we have had plenty of things to think of that we will not do. Toni, I'm afraid still thinks I am going to get tired of her. So do most of my friends, so does her guardian, & so (I think) do you. All this is bound to make me very nervous of getting tired of her, because she is such a very nice girl, and she is so much in love with me she can't help it any more. But it also makes me quite determined to do my best not to. It is possible I could meet someone who is both very intelligent & very original & very beautiful, & in love with me, & that such a person would suit me better. But it is very unlikely indeed that I should meet a person like that, and not certain they'd suit me better if I did. Toni is not by any means unintelligent or bad looking … The chief difficulties of marriage for us seem to be three – one of which you mentioned. The one you mentioned is the difficulty of getting a job – particularly as Toni wants to have children as soon as possible. The second is her finding it a strain to keep up with me intellectually, and the third, I am quite sure after seeing some photographs of the lady, is her Mother, who luckily is in India at the moment with her Father, a judge in the Punjab.[124]

He thought he could get round the perceived intellectual disparity and told his mother that Blunden thought he could get him a job at the *Times Literary Supplement* when he had finished at Oxford, but it seems as though he was making the best of a *fait accompli*. In the same month he wrote of his engagement in a far lighter tone to Jean Turner:

> She is probably going to chuck me quite soon, but at the moment parental and guardian opposition are stimulating her to stay engaged. Once again I have ensnared a member of the upper ten, a last year's deb. With the imposing Christian names of Antoinette Gabrielle. She is very determined at the moment that my brokenness shall make no difference, but let her once meet again the vastly rich young gentleman whom I have cut out, and off I go again in quest of further beauty. That is as it should be, for I feel much less left out in the cold being engaged, and at the same time there is no prospect of getting married for at least 3 years, by which time the thing will obviously have gone up in smoke, so I am not really so very tied down, or up.[125]

But to Toni at least he claimed that their engagement had brought him a kind of ecstasy. He wrote to his 'darling fiancée' that 'from today and this enchanted evening we are promised to each other, and we will be able to walk at will in our own fantastic paradise. On either side of us our friends will go, even touching us and talking to us, and we shall not be with them. On Sunday we'll celebrate – at supper we'll just drink wine, but afterwards we'll drink to our love, outside, from our own glasses; and when the toast is drunk we'll smash the glasses, over our shoulder against the wall. And some prosaic passing people who hear the tinkle, will wonder what it was.'[126] His professions to Toni of an all-consuming love don't match the cynicism with which he wrote of it to Jean Turner but they do have the ring of authenticity: 'I almost wish I had some control over my emotion towards you. But not quite. I know I am content to be lost in love, and passionately anxious to continue so lost for ever. It's like being picked up by a huge hand or a wind out of heaven and moved helplessly. It's an enchantment, and yet I know everything in this fairyland is quite, quite real. I don't think you can ever make me feel conceited over having you: for when I consider your love for me, this person I know so well, I am utterly abased. We are two very emotional, sentimental people – and because of that we're like gods. Goodnight my darling Toni, there are no words or combinations of words to tell you how very very entirely I am filled with love for you. Bless you and thank God, or whatever made you exist, for your existence and your love.'[127] If he was acting he played his part very convincingly. He compared his relationships with Toni and Yingcheng in a letter to Toni:

Your photograph is on the table looking at me in a quizzical kind of way, and beside it I've put Betty's. How utterly different they are. You certainly put some love in your eyes when you looked at the camera and Betty I think in a way has shewn her state of mind for she is looking rather pensively sideways as much as to say, now look what I've landed myself with. And when I think of that ham she's engaged to, I must say I think she'll be sufficiently punished before she's finished with her happy married state. It seems impossible to credit, that I should have loved Betty so much, and now care nothing at all for her, and love you. But it is actually fairly easy to explain. I seem to be made up of two very different parts: I'm almost two people. One wants exoticism, travel, adventure. That's why I loved Betty, and why I still love the person I pictured her to be in my imagination, when she was away. It's why I want you to do something very well, to be original and outstanding, and to be looked at, and why I have a terror of perishing into an ordinary existence without having tasted a hundred strange pleasures and experiences; that's why I'm afraid of us getting fat: because fat is not romantic, or adventurous, it's either a nuisance, or ludicrous, or disgusting, according to how much there is of it.

There is always in my mind an ideal companion in these adventures, and I love my ideal with one part of my love, very intensely. Betty is too cheap to fit that ideal, but you aren't; for you're sincere, and you don't want to be ordinary any more than I do. The other part of me is tired of fighting, wants to be settled, to have a real aim for the rest of my life, above all wants a companion, someone to sympathise with me and to love me, and to whom I can give all my love without fear of being hurt and to make you happy. And you don't know how I love to do things for you, and to do things with you. That is real love and companionship which I only had with Betty for one day during the whole time I knew her. And I wonder if it was really true then. It's there all the time between you and me. You feel it too, don't you?[128]

It's possible that Douglas foresaw the reason for Toni's dissatisfaction with the relationship. He advised her: 'as long as we're sure of each other we'll be safe against anything. We must share everything too, all our friends and our thoughts and occupations. There mustn't be any secret corners in either of us, not even a little bit that the other doesn't know and understand, because secrets are what make the trouble. That's why I've introduced you to my friends and why I shewed you mother's letter and my poems. We must become so that we can change minds and think just as easily from each other's point of view. Loving each other as we do, there'll always be some easily found reason if things go wrong. And we must have enough perception of each other's thoughts to feel it.'[129] This idealized view of a relationship was not very practical and things did indeed eventually 'go wrong'.[130]

Before they did, Douglas wrote Toni a poem, which was first published in *Oxford Magazine* on 30 November 1939 with the title 'Addison and I':

The stars still marching in extended order
move out of nowhere into nowhere. Look, they are halted
on a vast field tonight, true no man's land.
Far down the sky with sword and belt must stand
Orion. For commissariat of this exalted
war-company, the Wain. No fabulous border

could swallow all this bravery, no band
will ever face them: nothing but discipline
has mobilised and still maintains them. So
Time and his ancestors have seen them, So
always to fight disorder is their business,
and victory continues in their hand.

From under the old hills to overhead,
and down there marching on the hills again
their camp extends. There go the messengers'
Comets, with greetings of ethereal officers
from tent to tent. Yes, we look up with pain
at distant comrades and plains we cannot tread.[131]

We don't know how Toni reacted to this poem but it has a distinctly martial rather than romantic tone.

Douglas spent the new year of 1940 with Alec Hardie's family at Hadlow House near Winchester. He wrote to Toni that 'I am driving the Hardie car, a massive wagon capable of 90 m.p.h. up to town on Wednesday, for the day, so I hope to get my Greek lunch.'[132] He was amused by their, to his mind, cartoon Scottishness, which he found 'almost unintelligible':

Alec's name is in fact Ollick as they say it, and although no-one has yet said 'Hoots mon' they habitually employ 'canna and didna' and say things like 'ye're no' fou the noo onyhoo'. Last night cousin Davie appeared and said such things as

The fouk wis ta'en, the bisem wis ga'en
The barry widna row its lin
An' siccan a sos ye niver had seen
As the muckin o' Geordie's byre

And Pop sang, quite truthfully 'I'm fou the noo, I'm absolutely fou'.[133]

He wrote again on 5 January: 'I haven't got any riding here because of ice on the roads – but ice or no ice I took the Hardie car out to the New Forest to look for riding schools and in spite of skids touched 76 m.p.h. Going to London tomorrow I want to reach 85 if I can, which is about its maximum – but it'll need a very long straight with no ice … I must say I think it's most trusting of Mrs Hardie to let me drive the car on icy roads without Mr Hardie knowing. He was down for Hogmanay, a very large, heavy Scot – and got drunk and kept trying to kick me – much to the shame of Alec and Mrs, who tried in vain to prevent him.'[134] He wrote to Yingcheng with some more entertaining details about his drive to London: 'we were held up at 5 miles an hour for some time behind what appeared to be an entire battleship on a 32-wheel lorry. When we eventually scraped past I prepared to make up for lost time but we ran into a lot of antiskid sand, at about 76 m.p.h., and it contrived to make a sort of paste with the wetness of the road, so we braked rather erratically. Coming back ... culminated in my being directed up a wrong road. As I was a good way up it before anyone realised, I tried to turn, only to find that this vast car was as wide as the road, and that we were dead opposite a lamp-post. My efforts to batter this down having failed and reduced Mrs Hardie to hysterics, we were pushed gradually round by various bystanders, and set off once more.'[135] It's probably just as well that Mr Hardie didn't know about Douglas's cavalier approach to driving. Douglas also wrote to Kristin effectively to end their relationship by explaining about his engagement to Toni. She didn't reply.[136]

Douglas's letters to Toni present him as deeply in love with her, but his letter to Yingcheng of 8 January 1940 reveals his uncertainty: 'I think I have a fair chance of as much happiness as I can get now with Toni. But you, however cheaply you behave, and whatever other people think of you, will always be the only person I love completely – you'll become almost a goddess or a mania if you go away ... So if it's a matter of months or years, you can get me any time, *unless* I've taken so much from someone else that I owe it to her not to leave her. I shall try not to get married for sometime. I pray constantly, as far as such a completely faithless person can pray, that you will come back, though I can't believe you will.'[137] He urged Yingcheng to burn this letter, and said he would never forgive her if she let anyone else know of its contents. If Toni had got hold of the letter I doubt she would have been particularly impressed. In any event she was beginning to have doubts about her relationship with Douglas. She regarded him as self-centred and annoying, and she suspected him of a serious inferiority complex.[138] The split was on the cards. He wrote to her in late February or early March 1940:

> I came to take all my stuff back – reckoning that you'd be out so it needn't worry you again. I feel all this, though it was the third time, was for no reason but just flared up. It was all so unnecessary, when you had come to see me feeling so happy, and brought me a plum. Then I was horrid and didn't take the plum and went on at you, and now I feel like death. I've just wandered round Oxford ever since – I can't believe it, or couldn't at first, but now it's coming into my mind and I'm done. I've tried and tried harder than I've ever done anything, to make a go of this, and I'd go on trying for ever. I love you so much I feel knocked out. You asked me to write you a real love letter and you seem to be getting it. I must see you again darling – I can't bear it – this very usual stuff is enough to make anyone sick of me but I can't.[139]

He was clearly very needy.

In March he went to Cheltenham races with Yingcheng and visited Cheltenham Ladies' College. He appears to have patched things up with Toni temporarily and wrote to her on 21 March giving details of his visit to her (and Yingcheng's) old school: 'I met a peculiar tough egg called Miss Wilson at C.L.C., also the matron of the San and a female skeleton, (unidentified). On one occasion I got ushered into a roomful of multi-sized girls, causing instant confusion. I visited the Prefects room, which smelt like a Prefects room, St. Margaret's, St. Austin's, and various corridors: and I was privileged to catch a glimpse of Miss Barham or Barret or Something, forging along on a bicycle … judging from Miss Wilson's conversation, you and Betty are the only 2 old girls not married.'[140] The relationship was still alive in early May 1940, when he wrote to her ingratiatingly: 'You make an awful lot of efforts for me now, and although I'm sometimes sorry that they have to be efforts, I'm very appreciative, though I mayn't appear so. I was also very impressed with you for not losing your temper with me in the Indian restaurant, and altogether you're very sweet.'[141] But later that month Toni told him that she was unable to put up with his jealousy any longer and they split for good, apparently after a scene outside Lady Margaret Hall in which Douglas threatened to shoot himself.[142]

By summer the war had caught up with him and Douglas's time in Oxford was over. He left Oxford in June 1940. He could, according to Meyer, 'hardly wait to join the Army and start fighting professionally. I never saw him after he went down that June, except once, in uniform across the floor of the Café Royal, entwined with a girl, not many weeks before he was killed.'[143]

He wrote to Blunden in June 1940 from Hadlow House in Sussex: 'I'm not to report for a week or 2. I shall have time to clear things up a bit. My poems are packed up and in transit here by goods, with the rest of my stuff – but when they come I think I shall send them to you for safe keeping … I am going down to Housey to get as much riding as possible before I actually get to the cavalry, and to learn up Cavalry training and Horsemastership.'[144] He wrote again to Yingcheng before he joined up and told her that he would never fall in love as deeply as he did with her: 'So I suppose I shall love you hopelessly till I die … I still fall tremendously in love with people while the circumstances are right and romantic, but you're the only one who survived the cold light of reason.'[145] So much for Toni Beckett, to whom he had been sending passionate love letters until just a few weeks previously. He was going to Edinburgh on 18 July to join the Scots Greys, and he didn't think he'd meet Yingcheng again. He wrote a little bitterly to Jean Turner in December 1940 that 'Betty Sze broke my heart for no reason at all, blast her, because she isn't going to marry her smooth Bermudan after all. So she'll be an old maid, in all but the technical details, I expect: or else a society wife. Poor silly girl.'[146]

4

THE FILTHIEST SCRUFFY HOLE I'VE EVER FALLEN IN

Keith Douglas joined the British Army in July 1940 as a Cavalry Trooper (an equivalent rank to private) at Redford Barracks in Edinburgh. He described his journey to, and arrival in, Edinburgh to his mother in a letter of 19 July: 'I slept about 4½ hours, & arrived on time in pouring rain. I hung about the station after having a bath & a shave & breakfast & eventually met another Oxford man who came in on a later train & borrowed a mac from his cousins who live here. I had lunch with him & tea with the cousins & we reported about 5.30. We are issued with uniform tomorrow, & I believe begin to ride at once.'[1] He went on to describe his new environment: 'Work will obviously be very hard & I shouldn't like to have it indefinitely but I ought to stick 4 months. These are huge barracks & take some finding your way. There are several jockeys here and we have a dummy horse in our bedroom like a full size rocking horse, to do exercises on … I have a very shifty-looking jockey next bed to me, who looks as though he'd pinch anything he could, so thank goodness I've got a padlock. We have a beer room, restaurant, smoking room, & bedroom with 24 beds, about the size of a housey [i.e. Christ's Hospital] dormitory with a wireless going all day all over the barracks, and a locker over each bed.' In other words he returned to the communal life he had long been used to, since he joined Edgeborough School at the age of six.

During the Easter vacation he had collected his poems and sent them to Blunden. Blunden returned the typescripts on 25 May 1940 with a letter that expressed thanks 'as a reader' for 'the pleasure and quickening your verse gives me, and this is naturally all the better to reflect upon in view of our old C. H. We have had some pretty good poets, Peele, Coleridge, Lamb, Hunt, but the line must be extended! and I think you can do it.'[2] But Blunden had no idea what to do with them, particularly in time of war: 'But now, what is to be done? Will you send the MS. up to a publisher? It is a ghoulish moment for such matters … I would suggest (1) J. Cape or (2) Faber. With Mr. Hart-Davis of Cape I have an ancient friendship, & can speak to him of you and your work, – but I have no real contact with Faber, and indeed my name *there* might only cause Mr Eliot (who perhaps 'reads' for the firm) to suspect you were in some sort of my poetical platoon, and do nothing.' Douglas thanked Blunden in a letter of June 1940 and urged him to send the poems to Cape. He wrote again to Blunden a few weeks later to thank him for accepting 'the protection of my poems … I doubt if I shall write any more for some time – I am now trying to learn Cavalry Training and the Manual of Hosemastership [sic] by heart.'[3]

In September and October he was training at the Army School of Equitation,[4] near Weedon Bec in Northamptonshire. He spent two weeks at Boars Hill while recovering from an injury sustained at Weedon when a horse wounded his leg,[5] and in November he moved to Sandhurst until January 1941, where he was an Officer Cadet, and from where he wrote to his mother on 4 November 1940: 'This week we have been doing the theoretical part of a petrol engine. Next week we spend taking engines to bits and the week after, driving. After that we have an exam. Not passing it is our first opportunity of getting sent back to the ranks. Then we go to Lulworth & are finally judged on our Gunnery marks there. When we come back (we go about the end of Dec.) our course is virtually over, for better or worse … Don't be surprised if you only get very short letters for the next 3 weeks because this is the main part of the course, & after that, Lulworth is almost as important. I may get some Christmas leave in between but I don't know where I can go. Oxford term ends tomorrow. I've heard no more of my poems.'[6] He had swapped horses for tanks. In December he complained to Jean Turner that army life wasn't suiting him:

> I have been in the mill for 4 or 5 months – it might have been as many years, it seems so long since my previous existence ceased. I have all the disadvantages of army life, but at present, no advantages. At least if I had as much money as most officer cadets I could hire or seduce an obliging young lady to spend my leaves with me. But I haven't even got anywhere to go if and when I get leave. I had a touching but painfully moral romance with a girl in a hat-shop, when I was a trooper in the Scots Greys in Edinburgh. She still writes to me devotedly and rather illiterately. Hence I just work, though in very luxurious

surroundings, and hitchhike to Oxford on Sundays. There I walk desolately about trying to find people in, until it's time to come back ... I shall pass out of here into a tank in a month or two, and that I think will eventually be a final exit.[7]

Douglas would have sympathised with Gavin Ewart, who wrote in 'Oxford Leave':

> The 'Lamb and Flag' was closed, so I went to the Budolph Hotel
> And saw there several faces that I remember too well,
> Wartime and peacetime faces, R.A.F. operational types,
> Girls who were arty and tarty – and several blokes with pipes.[8]

A change had come over Douglas. He was no longer enjoying the training and his wireless instructor recommended that he pay more attention to his appearance, which he had been complimented on at Redford.[9] The life could be very boring. The 'Home Front' section of *The Terrible Rain*, Brian Gardner's selection of Second World War poetry, bristles with the tedium of being a soldier away from the war. As Robert L. Chaloner wrote in 'Home Front: 1942':

> These carry now the future in the heads
> Fouled with the daily drug of great events;
> Discuss is in their buttockbiting beds
> Or argue in the damp despair of tents
> While hired wireless sets dictate aloud
> The paths which must be followed by the crowd.[10]

Life seems to have been particularly unexciting in the countryside, where Douglas found himself frequently before he sailed for the Middle East in June 1941. Here is Michael Barsley in 'Rural Sunday':

> With vacant stare in the market square,
> Tricked out in a lilac suit,
> The villager stands with great hands
> And chaffs with a raw recruit.
> The heat comes down on a sleepy town
> Like a blanket over the head,
> And a church clock beats in the silent streets
> Saying 'Dead, dead, dead'.[11]

Douglas and Jean Turner had trouble meeting. He wrote to her again on 10 December 1940:

I'm very glad you've appeared again, only I'm sorry I didn't know in time for last Sunday. I *was* over and I only just managed to find someone in. I may be booked next Sunday but anyway I think you'll have gone by then … I'm leaving about next Sunday week either for a gunnery course at Lulworth (Nr. Bournemouth) or else on a week's leave. Anyway I shall be at Lulworth till after you return from Oxford. But if you can get here from wherever you are, before the Sunday after next, let me know. I can escape next Saturday afternoon, and I shall probably be free on Sunday but don't know yet. After that I'm free on Wednesday next week. If I get a week's leave, would you come and spend some of it with me, if I could find anywhere? This is not an improper proposal, particularly – but I may well have to spend my leave alone otherwise.[12]

There's no disguising his loneliness. He wrote to Blunden in December 1940 to thank him for sending his collection of poems to Eliot and to explain his recent training: 'I have just finished learning to ride a motorbike in 2 lessons. The first was more or less in private, the second began on a main road, and took us through a town, across a blasted heath, up and down very steep wet sand tracks and through a pinewood, going in and out among the treetrunks. I have driven a tank about 4 miles, but there's more of that to come.'[13]

By the time he wrote again to Jean Turner, from Lulworth Cove, his disillusionment with his women friends and with army life had both reached new nadirs:

Well, you horrid girl. Why didn't you write back – you're no better than the rest. I may be pretty grim but I did think there was someone who would write and cheer me up, at least if they were asked. However I seem to be wrong. I really must raise some more (girls). The present list is a bit depleted – so –

~~Betty Sze~~	cancelled
~~Kristin~~	cancelled
~~Toni~~	cancelled
~~Jean~~ (you)	too lazy to write
Netty (Scots shop girl)	occasional illiterate scrawl
~~Natasha~~	too lazy to write
~~Joan Appleton~~	too lazy to write
~~Deirdre~~	cancelled[14]

'I have the face of a parrot.' Douglas in army uniform

The tank gunnery course at Lulworth was no better:

This is the filthiest scruffy hole I've ever fallen in. It's a concentrated army
nightmare. We're put on charge for having a bath. We have to scrub out
lavatories. We have to sweep rooms, clean washbasins, make beds. We have to
walk everywhere through at least a foot of mud. Everyone either swears at us
or is very grim or morose. We have to walk 300 yards though a blizzard and
queue up for 20 minutes to get a plate of dirty grease and a few lumps of offal
or gristle, as the case may be. We are kindly allowed to spend our miserable
pay on doughnuts made without sugar and unrecognisable tea. Occasionally
a cold ex-fried egg may be bought for an exorbitant price and anything up
to ¾ hour waiting. We are pulled out of bed (if it can be called a bed, being
3 planks raised 6 inches off the floor) at 6.30 by a lance corporal. And so it
goes on. This is because we are officer cadets. When we were troopers we had
spring beds, got up on our own, had 4 good meals a day and got off every
evening.[15]

Clearly there were elements of communal life that were beginning to pall.

He had a joint twenty-first birthday party with David Lockie, a fellow Sandhurst trainee, roping Jean in to help. He asked her to invite a long list of people to their party on Saturday 1 February at The Noted Snack Bar on the High Street, Oxford. He wasn't confident of success, confiding in Jean: 'Personally I think it'll be an awful flop – David and I aren't the sort to give parties.'[16] He invited Blunden, giving a different date from that in the invitation: 'The party is to be on January 21st (Saturday) from 5.0 onwards. Birthday presents *in the form of bottles* will be gratefully received. We are having some difficulty in finding anywhere to hold this gathering, but when we do I'll let you know.'[17]

Meanwhile he was getting closer to the war. He wrote to Jean Turner that he was to be commissioned to the Second Derbyshire Yeomanry (Armoured Cars) stationed in Ripon, on 8 February, after a week's leave.[18] In Ripon the race course had been adapted as Regimental Headquarters and totalizator buildings had been turned into dormitories.[19] Douglas wrote plaintively to Jean from Ripon:

> I am so sorry that this letter is not enclosing a present for you – but I shan't buy just anything. Partly because it would be waste of an opportunity for spending an enjoyable time choosing, and partly because if I bought just anything it wouldn't [be] worth having or be likely to give you much pleasure. In the end it will probably be a ring of some kind, because I am more likely to manage in sending it safely to you … I wish there was someone whom I could ask to meet me somewhere suddenly, and know they would. I had vaguely thought of a day in London with you ever since before Christmas: perhaps because you described in a letter how you enjoyed (with John Hyde wasn't it?) almost the same things as I wanted to do. Well I did them; with Mother. It was nice and anyway she certainly enjoyed it. But you know the difference. Perhaps you really were sorry because you couldn't come. I was.[20]

He painted a picture of life in Ripon in another letter to Jean: 'As for Ripon – I've hardly seen it: we're quite busy and though I've passed through it I've never been there longer than ¾ hour and that in the dark. We are under some feet of snow here and there's quite a lot to do with the cars, and guns. We have just finished firing – rather a farce: after a whole afternoon and morning working on the guns and driving 6 miles through a blinding snowstorm, we fired for perhaps 10 minutes and returned, to spend another evening and morning cleaning.'[21] He went on to describe part of the dynamic at Ripon:

I had my first row with my troop sergeant. He was troop leader before I came, as there was no officer available, and has got too used to being on his own. Today I ordered a parade in one place and at the last moment he found one of the guns needed cleaning again, as the barrel had sweated. So he and the troop never turned up. This was, I realised, the crucial point, etc. etc. If I had let him get away with it, I should never have caught up again. So I had a good snap at him, which required some courage, as he knows much more about a lot of things than I do so I'm dependent on him over car maintenance etc. However I snapped my snap, and smoothed things over as soon as I saw he'd got it straight, so I hope to God I won't need to do any more snapping. I followed it up with an incredibly authoritative tactical lecture, just to show I know more about some things than he does, and I hope all is now well. Because he's an excellent chap and the troop are all very cheerful and amiable, though 2 of them think by numbers, and with a good pause between each thought.

His loneliness shone through his letters to Jean. In another written from Ripon he wrote: 'I am feeling most fed up, as usual. Why is it that I always want other people's women? I hope it isn't just because they're other people's. But I begin to wonder … I went to a dance last night at a hotel in Harrogate and met someone with whom I danced every dance but 3 for the rest of the evening and those 3 we sat out. She looked marvellous, she talked sense and she's the best dancer I've ever danced with. And so, of course, she's married, and probably has been for years … Why do I always pick on those sort of people?'[22] He wrote to his mother about the same dance but put a more positive spin on his dance partner: 'She danced better than anyone I've ever danced with and we hardly missed a dance for the rest of the evening. She was also much better looking than anyone else in the room & since I don't suppose many people realised she was married, and not to me, I must have been most envied … Today I am going to Harrogate again to meet Pennock's girlfriend Lorna. I really must get one of my own. The last 5 I've taken out have been other people's. It's an outlay of money for nothing.'[23] He wasn't looking forward to his next move. He wrote to his mother that he was expecting 'a terrible journey down. We are the last squadron of the Regiment and the whole Division is moving in a column nearly 18 miles long, even if they keep closed up. Since everyone here seems to know where we're going and how, we shall no doubt be dive-bombed.'[24] In the same letter he wrote that

> I'm getting very fat again due to eating & drinking such a lot to keep warm, and getting no exercise. We had been snowed up until today, & though I've done a lot of standing about in it, I haven't done much walking. We did a scheme (the Squadron) for the Commander in Chief Home Forces, Gen'l Brooke. The great man did not actually speak to anyone himself, but the Divisional General, McCreary [sic] asked me a lot of questions, in fact I was the only person in the squadron who was spoken to at all. I answered them all satisfactorily & the Colonel (our Colonel) [Barnes] was tremendously pleased with me, as he had expected me to be frightened of all the Red hats. As I was able to bob down into my turret again the moment they asked me anything I didn't know, & as I was disguised in thousands of scarves, overalls, glasses and earphones, I felt quite safe.[25]

On 15 February 1941 T. S. Eliot wrote to him encouragingly:

> I have been somewhat delayed by illness in considering your poems which Mr. Blunden sent me some time ago, but I have now read them several times and with continued interest. The seem to me extremely promising, and I should like to keep in touch with you ... My impression so far is that you have completed one phase which begins with the very accomplished juvenilia and that you have started on another which you have not yet mastered ... I think that you have definitely an ear. What I should like to see is the second phase which you have begun developed to the point of formal mastery, and meanwhile I think that it would be useful to get poems in periodicals outside of Oxford ... I shall be very glad to draw the attention of the editors of *Horizon* [Cyril Connolly and Stephen Spender] to your work. If you are still writing I should like to see something.[26]

Such an endorsement by the high priest of modernism was invaluable for a young poet. Douglas's rather cynical response to Jean Turner was 'How much can I sell his autograph for?', although behind the cynicism he does seem to have been genuinely excited by Eliot's apparent enthusiasm.[27] That excitement seems, however, to have been tempered by unusual self-doubt. Douglas wrote to Blunden in March to thank him for returning his poems, which he was going to read through to assure himself that 'I really used to write poetry once'. He asked Blunden if he took Eliot's letter 'as an excessively polite refusal to have anything to do with my efforts? I really think I give up – I may try and write a novel but I doubt it. As a poet I seem to lack the correctly exotic style and don't really get on very well with the present rulers of poetic society. I am inclined not to *destroy* my poems as yet, but another reason for returning them to you is that on impulse I am quite likely to burn them.'[28] Douglas's concern is ridiculous: Eliot's letter is a model of encouragement, and there's little evidence of any attempt to even make contact with 'the present rulers of poetic society'.

It was a brief stay in Ripon and the regiment was moved to Gloucestershire from March to June 1941, with squadrons quartered in the villages around Wootton-under-Edge. Douglas was quartered in Wickwar, about four miles from the regimental headquarters. As he wrote to Jean: 'We are now cut off from the world, in a remote hamlet of Gloucestershire where everyone knows everyone else.'[29] He was stationed with a local family, the Thayers, and he quickly made contact with their next-door-neighbours, the local squire and his wife: 'I cadged acquaintance with Squire', he wrote to Jean, 'or rather Squire's wife, Lady Gunston.' Thayer was the local bank manager and he lived at Hope House, at the other end of the High Street from the White Horse Inn, which served as the officers' mess. Douglas shared a room with another officer but was rarely in the house. He was kept busy 'driving armoured cars', he told Jean, 'at top speed all over Glos. with one wheel in each ditch. Whatever happens, it won't be suicide because nothing I hit can make the least impression on a Guy (touch wood).'[30] From the officers' mess in the White Horse he wrote a progress report to Jean on 21 March 1941: 'I'll tell you what I've been doing – what is known in the army and elsewhere as sweet F. A. for most of the time, and some dangerous driving thrown in. The other day we walked over to the remains of a German plane and the rather less amusing remains of its crew, which stank. One of them was hung in a tree some yards away from his own head.'[31] As usual he was contemptuous of authority: 'Next week we go to Bristol for a week. Although we are only 16 miles away, and Bristol is blitzed about every other night with heavy casualties, and although all we have to do there ends at 4.30, we are ordered to stay there to save petrol. Possibly when half this squadron is blown to hell they'll let the next squadron off going there. I can't say I mind very much, or am very surprised. One expects that sort of imbecility from any authorities, army or otherwise. Anyway it'll do me good to come in contact with a bit of the war and all this British heroism.' In any event he needn't have worried about staying in Bristol. As he wrote to Jean Turner after the event: 'We have just returned from a week in Bristol during which not a bomb fell. But last night the whole sky was lit up with A. A. fire, planes, bomb explosions, and a fire which seemed to stretch all over Bristol.'[32]

The regiment used the tank range at Linney Head in May for a gunnery course and learned to use the armament of the train load of 54 Guy Armoured Cars that it had taken delivery of the previous November.

In the early summer of 1941 Douglas's regiment continued its travels, first to Charlwood in Surrey and Rusper in Sussex, where the soldiers 'did a lot of work, travelled immense distances and learned a great many lessons',[33] and then to Maresfield Camp in Sussex, where, according to Jones, 'it was soon apparent that something was in the offing … Cross-country runs, fitness tests, motor cycle trials and troops leaders competitions took off our surplus flesh and it was a very fit and much rejuvenated Regiment that came into being. The first stand-to for overseas service came in the early spring of 1942 but proved a false alarm. The second was destined to be more real. Then followed hectic days of embarkation leave, packing of vehicles and the thousand and one things so necessary until, in May 1942, we were off at last.'[34] Douglas didn't, however, sail with them. He was sent to a course, presumably on army lorries, at Karrier Motors in Birmingham from 17 May to 24 May 1941, where he met and fell in love with a sixteen-year-old girl called Diana. He and Diana became engaged but Douglas wrote to Jean Turner: 'Diana and I are engaged, but I hold out no hope for the engagement, from either end. It is simply for these reasons, that we really would like to get married, and are in love, and that being engaged gives a very slender extra chance to both of us, to exercise a certain amount of self control and wait. But it's a long time, and she's very anxious to get married and start having babies straight away.'[35] By the end of 1941 he confided in Jean Turner that Diana had written to him twice 'and I am inclined to cross her off (which to tell the truth I am glad to do with such a clear conscience) … She is a very kindly placid sort of girl but I never meant to get engaged to her.'[36]

Engagement notwithstanding Douglas sailed from Southampton for the Middle East, according to his army form, on 25 June 1941. He wrote with a Port-induced hangover to his mother early in the voyage that 'I & all my goods are still together and I have a fairly comfortable berth with a window onto the boat deck & an electric fan. I share it with one chap (Michael Hutton) who is underneath you'll be glad to hear.'[37] He was unenthusiastic about his engagement in a letter to Blunden: 'The wonders of the ocean are a little diffident but present themselves now and then; and the sun and moon have been doing strange things. I have at last begun a novel but it bores me, however I'm plugging away. Unfortunately I can't manage verse as well so that is stagnant. There is very little in the line of duty and not much excitement. People are pretty boring and identical. I share this cabin with a love sick young man who uses me for a sort of confessor of which I get heartily sick. I pull his leg without compunction but it will stretch to any length apparently without his noticing. Myself, I narrowly missed being married before I left, and am very relieved still to be independent. Though I should like to think I was stinging the Pay Office for a marriage allowance.'[38] He went on to tell Blunden about the voyage: 'I'm over sunburnt and very sore ... I force myself to do some P. T. every afternoon and so counteract to a certain extent the four huge and excellently-cooked meals a day. We get most of our entertainment (a few of us) from watching the rest. Many of my former mentors at the Equitation School provide more than most ... There are occasional concerts, of the sing-song-music-hall variety, but none touch great heights, although we have on board a professional accordionist, a very good performer on the banjo, and the composer of the once celebrated Penny Serenade ... I'm bored, healthy, and only kept from pining away by a rumour that there are women on one of the other boats. If they're there I wonder if the Samuel Goldwyn moonlight has the same effect on them.'

He wrote to Jean Turner, in a letter that is postmarked 6 September 1941 but was written presumably while the boat docked at Freetown in Sierra Leone, that:

> We are beginning to look like heroes already – considerably thinner and pleasantly tanned. The voyage is by no means over, and already has been interesting and at times mildly exciting. The first spectacle was provided by porpoises, and very soon after that flying fish, at first singly and then in shoals, began to leap out practically from under the ship. They are quite small, about 7 inches long and 14 across the wings, or less, and reflect the sun brilliantly when they fly. So far no sharks, no whales. At the moment we are at a sort of halfway house port, confined to the ship, with very little to do except buy unripe fruit and vegetables at exorbitant prices from natives who wear very scanty and ragged but colourful clothing and sing snatches of the Lambeth Walk as a sort of reckless chant.[39]

There was some social life. He told Turner in the same letter that the previous evening he had consumed 16 whiskies and soda in the Chief Officer's cabin but the prevailing theme seems to have been boredom and inactivity,[40] punctuated by prodigious meals: 'we are still being given meals calculated to keep out the December snows, and we sit and steam as we eat them. However it's probably very slimming – in fact it certainly is. Even some of the officers who looked as though they had to wear brassieres when they came on board, are now comparatively tolerable to look upon. It's amazing how much less revolting tanned fatness is than dead white neverbeenundressed English skin. Myself, I am quite bony.'[41] They had bought a monkey, Chica, in Sierra Leone: 'she had all the usual attractive – & unattractive – simian traits,' he wrote to his mother. 'She was affectionate & had an amusing little face; most of the affection of course cupboard love. When a mango was brought into the cabin she would stand up & hold out her hands, making a sort of impatient clicking noise. She liked apples too. But as a monkey, so to speak, she was rather a failure. She would not swing on the trapeze we put up for her but fell off it most ungracefully whenever she was put there. And when she made a mess in someone's seaboots we were glad she hadn't stayed in the cabin. She was fondest of a cockney member of the crew who always addressed her as 'well yer ugly barstard' with more success than any of the other sailors' endearments had.'[42]

The crew had a 'riotous'[43] ten-day holiday in South Africa. It was, he wrote to his mother,

one long & very expensive holiday. There is plenty of hospitality for the troops & for anyone who is content to return for that 10 days ashore to a homely comfortable family life. For the rest, girls are booked up like taxis for several days ahead, & having set out to go to a dance the first night, we came back at 10.30 without having had a single dance. The social & entertainment life of Durban is something like one has seen in American society films. We connected on the second day with a retired Colonel in a seaside village called Isipengo Beach. There we used to repair whenever possible; we hired a 27 h. p. Studebaker for 21/- p. d. between 3 of us & flashed backwards & forwards in it to the bright spots of Durban, the Hotel Edward, the Stardust, The Athlone, the Roadhouse, the Doll House, the Blue Lagoon. At these places we danced or sat in the car in the moonlight while Indian waiters brought relays of toasted egg & bacon sandwiches. In the day time we bathed at Isipengo beach or in the seawater baths on the front at Durban, or at Tiger Rocks, where the surf pulls you out into deep water unless you keep about 6 ft. from the beach, & sharks swim hopefully up and down in the calm water outside.[44]

He went to the Durban Gold Cup meeting which was a big disappointment after Cheltenham. He found South African taste in dress 'appalling', and the atmosphere lacking: 'There were no tic-tac men no bookies shouting –

everyone placed their bets in stolid Dutch silence. Even towards the finish of the race scarcely everyone cheered.' Most of all he was disgusted by the South African accent:

All you heard was Afrikaans & South African English with continually the peculiar exclamation 'Ach, sis man' – Africander women call each other man or rather 'men' as they pronounce it. The S. A. accent is a little like Southern American with a touch of English nouveau riche. It sounds more like someone imitating an accent than a natural way of speech. 'Our David, ah think yuh bett' pork you' caw they.' They never pronounce the plural of woman any different from the singular 'Look at therse woman owr' they'.' They can't say there or hair or where. It is always they' & hay' & w'ay'. One gets used to it in time … In South Africa there is more fruit than they can get rid of. One night we went up to Durban University to look down on the whole town, lit up. It was a lovely moonlight night (almost every night was the same) & there are hundreds of crickets which cheep regularly as you hear in American films. Sometimes we used to drive up the south coast in the late evening and just swing the car down on to the sands. There is no shingle. Beauty spots are Hill Crest & the Valley of 1000 Hills, where the floor of the Valley is a set of little humps & hollows said to have been made by an angry giant, stamping to kill pygmies. The town is full of a hotch potch of races. In the non-European quarter are several sorts of negro, including of course a few Zulus, though most dislike the town & stay away, & between the common nigs & the white population is a sort of half-way population of Indians & Chinese.[45]

The censor who read this letter presumably didn't have access to Douglas's army record. If she or he had it might have called into doubt the implied cosmopolitanism in the poet's assertion that he spoke French and German, had written Greek and Italian and had travelled in Italy, France and Switzerland.[46] In this letter Douglas went on to describe the second part of the voyage, up the east coast of Africa: 'We are now on rather a luxury boat, with the additional complication of 200 women passengers who are causing a certain amount of trouble & strife … The last lap is as unlike being at war as any of the others. Action must still come as a hell of a jolt.'[47]

The South African activist, Mary Benson, was one of these women. She, like Douglas, was just 21. She boarded the ship at Durban and found it to be full of English soldiers bound for the Middle East. It is difficult to imagine a more romantic situation. 'Sailing northwards through tropical seas, we could have been in a movie. In a shady corner of the deck, a young lieutenant sat cross-legged at my feet, reciting ['Remember me when I am dead']'. The young lieutenant was Douglas, 'thick hair tumbling over his blue eyes', but as so often he didn't make a positive first impression: 'Though flattered when he went on to read one of John Donne's love poems to me, I thought him too solemn and shy and had no sense of the complex nature of the youth who would become the war's finest poet.'[48]

As soon as Douglas reached Cairo he was hospitalized. He explained the circumstances to Blunden in a letter postmarked 10 October 1941. His injury was nothing to do with the war:

> I'm writing in bed in the 23rd Scottish (very Scottish) General Hospital somewhere (and having been brought here in the dark and a stupor I don't know myself where) in Palestine. In Cairo (than which I never expect to find a more unsavoury habit of more unsavoury people) I picked up some bug out of a swimming bath, which with the casual aid of the RAMC deafened me, gave me a temperature and provided more agony than I have ever had in my life. I was posted to a Regiment shortly afterwards and not wishing to be left behind I set out with the others eating Vegenin [sic] tablets in much the same way as people used to think Americans chewed gum. By the time when, in the early hours of the morning, we arrived at the particular stationless spot in the wilderness where the Regiment lives, I had run out of dope, and was therefore staggering like a drunken man and at my wits end. I spent the rest of the day with millions of flies and tons of sand, on a camp bed and in the evening set out in an ambulance for what the M.O. said would be a 2 hr drive to this hospital. How anyone unconscious stays in an army ambulance God knows. I hung on and after 3 hours by my watch, when we had stopped about 10 times I asked the driver if he had any idea where he was. After making him repeat his answers several times I found he didn't know, and it was only by sheer luck it turned out that we were already in the hospital grounds. Here I still am after, I think, about 3 weeks.[49]

Reasonably enough he felt something of a fraud in hospital. As he wrote to Jean Turner: 'I'm only here with bugs in my ears out of a swimming bath in Cairo, and everyone else is bandaged and riddled with bullets from Greece and Abyssinia and Syria, all with a hundred gruesome tales to tell.'[50] He was recovering slowly. 'I've been here a month', he told Jean, 'with terrific agonies and stone deaf most of the time. They don't know how it happened or what it is. I don't either really. Thank God it's nearly over … I've been up for a day or two but haven't got used to walking again as yet. And today I tried to run 20 yards and nearly passed out. In about a week I'll join my new regiment.' They, and he, did know what it was. He told Brenda Jones that he had otitis

'Deaf, dopey and dead to the world.' Douglas in the army.

which kept him 'deaf, dopey and dead to the world for a month'.[51] He was looking forward to joining his new regiment. 'I shall then be a Sherwood Ranger', he told Brenda, who lived on a farm where he used to ride horses at school. 'This is a more recently unhorsed regiment and retains 8 officer's chargers for the officers to ride in their spare time. So I shall be quite happy.' He wrote to Blunden on 26 October 1941 to send him two new poems. He took the opportunity to update Blunden on his convalescence 'which has consisted of doing nothing but sunbathe and bathe in the Mediterranean … I return to duty and the Notts. Yeo. m.e.f. the day after tomorrow. I gather from rumours that duty even then is not over heavy and I may still get an occasional bathe … I have been for some very long walks along the shore and on although it's Palestinian winter it's hot enough in the day time … in a day or two I shall once more live among sand, lizards, flies and mosquitoes, not forgetting the feverbringing diminutive sandfly. I have not had sandfly fever yet so I must have one or two "goes" of it before I become immune I suppose.'[52] He wrote to his mother the same day to tell her the (presumably) good news that he was to 'escape from the final (convalescent) clutches of the RAMC the day after tomorrow', that he would be 'quite near where Uncle Gordon died', and to give her more detail about his progress: 'The last few days I have been basking by and bathing in the Mediterranean, and am once again, in spite of three or four weeks indoors, noticeably sunburnt, and covered with salt and sand most of the time. I usually walk several miles along the sands (with intervals of rock, they stretch indefinitely, and finally bathe (sans costume) with some four miles of shore to myself.'[53] He told a similar story to Jean Turner at about this time (the envelope is postmarked 'Oxford 20 November 1941').[54]

So far he had had a pretty easy time of the war, what with the training in the UK, the 'pleasant and interesting' sea voyage to the Middle East and the extended convalescence that began almost as soon as he got there. All that was about to change.

* * *

He had written little poetry while training but at Sandhurst he wrote one of his most famous poems:

Simplify me when I'm dead

Remember me when I am dead
and simplify me when I'm dead.

As the processes of earth
strip off the colour and the skin
take the brown hair and blue eye

and leave me simpler than at birth
when hairless I came howling in
as the moon entered the cold sky.

Of my skeleton perhaps
so stripped, a learned man will say
'He was of such a type and intelligence,' no more.

Thus when in a year collapse
particular memories, you may
deduce, from the long pain I bore

the opinions I held, who was my foe
and what I left, even my appearance
but incidents will be no guide.

Time's wrong-way telescope will show
a minute man ten years hence
and by distance simplified.

Through that lens see if I seem
substance or nothing: of the world
deserving mention or charitable oblivion

not by momentary spleen
or love into decision hurled
leisurely arrive at an opinion.

Remember me when I am dead
and simplify me when I'm dead.[55]

'Simplify me when I'm dead' is more than merely a young man yearning for recognition by later generations. It is not meant to be uplifting. It presumes that its author will not return from the war, and it is an objective meditation on the consequences. It doesn't assume that its author will die a heroic death, or that he will be much remembered afterwards. In a sense it is Douglas's own elegy on his death. This poem locates the individual as a microscopic being, prey to natural forces, but still an individual. It is disturbing because it is so unemotional, so uninvolved in the poet's own demise, and because it makes deliberately limited demands on those who knew him. William Scammell points to some possible sources such as Shakespeare's sonnet 81 ('No longer mourn for me when I am dead') and C. H. Sorley's sonnet 'When you see millions of the mouthless dead', but believes that Douglas had in mind in particular Christina Rossetti's sonnet 'Remember' and Rupert Brooke's iconic First World War elegy, 'The Soldier'.[56] Scannell writes: 'Poor old Rupert Brooke has had enough mud thrown at his 'The Soldier', but, quite apart from the dignity, intelligence and economy of Douglas's poem compared with Brooke's sentimental advertising copy for good English fertilizer, it is instructive to note that the First World War poet's sonnet begins with the conditional clause, 'If I should die …', whereas Douglas writes '… when I am dead', and the removal of any question of survival places him squarely before the bone-hard reality of his subject.'[57] This poem, according to John Carey, is 'a plea that suggests Douglas's unease about the yearnings and resentments that rankled beneath his well-polished buttons. But it also amounts to a request to have his complications put on record … Much of his best poetry grows out of this conflict between the urge, on the one hand, to reduce himself and other people to objects … and the claims, on the other hand, of emotional involvement that he could not withstand.'[58] 'Simplify me when I'm dead', underneath its brutal account of bodily decomposition, is a moving and sensitive questioning of the poet's 'substance or nothing' that leaves the reader with the strong impression that its author genuinely didn't know the answer.

THE DESERT

It will become a staid historic name,
That crazy sea of sand!
Like Troy or Agincourt its single fame
Will be the garland for our brow, our claim,
On us a fleck of glory to the end:
And there our dead will keep their holy ground.

But this is not the place that we recall,
The crowded desert crossed with foaming tracks,
The one blotched building, lacking half a wall,
The grey-faced men, sand powdered over all;
The tanks, the guns, the trucks,
The black, dark-smoking wrecks.[1]

This is from John Jarmain's poem 'El Alamein'. Inferior poetic talents described army life in the desert better than Douglas did. Here is Terence Tiller on lecturing soldiers:

They sit like shrubs among the cans and desert thistles
in the tree's broken shade and the sea-glare:
strange violent men, with dirty unfamiliar muscles,
sweating down the brown breast, wanting girls and beer.
The branches shake down sand along a crawling air,
    and drinks are miles towards the sun
    and Molly and Polly and Pam are gone.[2]

In 'Lecturing to Troops', we feel the strangeness of the situation, the gulf between the 'clean cleverness' of the poet and the sullen patience of the soldiers. But what Douglas caught better than anyone else was the *moment*, whether stumbling across the body of an enemy soldier in 'Vergissmeinnicht' or the soldier he shoots in 'How to kill'.

In September 1941 the Sherwood Rangers were at Karkur camp in Palestine, training to be part of the 8th Armoured Brigade. As T. M. Lindsay put it: 'Flash Kellett was still Colonel and, as one of his officers wrote at the time "most efficient – so much so that I am afraid we shall lose him." Major Donny Player was second-in-command. The squadron commanders were: "A", Major Stanley Christopherson; "B", Major Michael Laycock; "C", Major Stephen Mitchell; "H. Q.", Major Lawrence Biddle. Hard training and continual tactical exercises were the order of the day.'[3] Douglas joined the regiment on 14 September 1941, according to his army record. He wasn't so sure of Kellett's acumen as Lindsay's anonymous officer. He wrote to Jean Turner, now in the Women's Royal Naval Service, in a letter with an envelope postmarked Kensington 4 December 1941: 'I am bored stiff, being now isolated in sand to all intents and purposes – although we live in a village full of most delectable cafés (of the continental type) where the troops are allowed to disport themselves, our kindly and (you can bet) beloved Colonel has forbidden officers to go there. The man could perhaps be forgiven for being an unimaginative fool in matters of that sort, if he were any use on the military side. But any of the 2nd Lieutenants knows four times as much as any Major in the regiment, twice as much as a sergeant, twice as much as a trooper, and 10 times (as a moderate estimate) as much as the colonel.'[4] Lindsay gives a much more sympathetic account of Kellett, remembering him for instance declaiming some Edward Lear 'with passionate enjoyment'.[5] Douglas's commander, Stanley Christopherson, was, according to James Holland: 'bright, well travelled and charming. [He] made friends easily and was a gifted sportsman, as well as being socially smooth as glass.'[6]

On 18 November 1941 the Allied troops started their advance across the Egyptian frontier and took very severe casualties as they encountered German commander Rommel's main forces. Tobruk was relieved, however, and Benghazi recaptured as British troops advanced towards Agheila. According to Lindsay: 'the British were left in a tricky position, stretched out and thin on the ground, and the supply position perilously weak until Benghazi could be got going as a major supply base.'[7] A few days before that Douglas had taken his men for a weekend tour through Syria in a two-ton lorry. 'It was much enjoyed by all,' he told Jean Turner:

> We didn't see many signs of the Syrian campaign – a few shrapnel splashes, burnt out vehicles, and blown bridges, round which we had to make detours.

The mountain views are better than any description could be. We came up the coast road (if you have a map) through Haifa, over the Libanese border up to Beyrouth, through 'the village that men still call Tyre' where I was delighted to observe some old ships like swans asleep, though perhaps not so colourful as Flecker's. Beyrouth was disappointing – an early blackout and the fact that everything closes early as a precaution against Australian orgies, made sightseeing difficult. We climbed out of Beyrouth and camped the first night sleeping round the lorry on the first hilltop we came to, or rather in a little dip beside it … [The next] day we climbed almost all day to Zable, a little village where we shopped, buying potatoes and Turkish delight. From Zable we went to Rayak, hoping to get through to the 2000 year old ruins at Baalbek, but a bridge was blown and we couldn't get through. So we came back to Zable and took the main road to Damascus, which began to descend in a breathtaking spiral. We were getting a bit behindhand, so I took over from the driver, and got the lorry into Damascus about ½ an hour before dark, by dint of driving which left everyone, including myself, rather shaky. On the way we passed the burnt out remains of someone who had been less lucky and gone straight over the edge. (Burnt out remains of a lorry, not a person). Damascus also wasn't very thrilling, and we camped outside on a very cold windswept plain. Then we set out for Tiberias and the Sea of Galilee.[8]

The Sea of Galilee was very warm and 'a lovely sight and lovely to bathe in, being fresh water and very clean'. His squadron commander was indulgent if, perhaps, a little naive, especially as far as the driving was concerned. Stanley Christopherson wrote in his diary entry of Friday, 14 November 1941: 'Douglas, a new officer who has just joined the squadron, took his troop away to Syria for the weekend. It really is an excellent idea, leaving Friday morning and returning Sunday night. They take rations, bedding, etc., and go where the spirit moves them, camping where they like. This time they are going to Haifa, Beirut, Damascus, Baalbek. It's a great change for them to get away from camp, and a good chance of driving instruction.'[9]

The early days of Douglas's war in the desert saw the Sherwood Rangers somewhat demoralized: 'In November and December the Regiment boasted a total of three tanks. The training went on. We fired the Browning guns on the ranges … Visitors with first-hand accounts of the fighting in Africa told us that the new American "Grant" tanks were mechanically most reliable, but the German anti-tank guns had a nasty habit of penetrating the thickest armour.'[10] The war news generally wasn't promising: the *Prince of Wales* and the *Repulse* had been lost off Singapore and the *Barham* had been sunk in the Mediterranean. The war in the desert wasn't going well either: 'on the 21st of January', Lindsay reported, 'Rommel attacked strongly on a narrow front, seized a lot of British petrol and stores and cut off some of our forces in the Benghazi area. We had managed to keep our heads, and our troops formed a solid front south of Gazala. But the Germans re-took Benghazi.'[11]

Douglas wrote to his mother on 16 February 1942 to tell her that he'd been in trouble with the authorities: 'I had the misfortune to kill an Arab who ran out from behind a lorry into a truck I was driving.'[12] He doesn't say anything about the misfortune of the dead Arab but he gave Blunden a few more details in a letter of 1 March 1942: 'I had an accident last time I was in Cairo and killed an Arab – he did the usual chicken-crossing-the road stunt, at the double, from behind a stationary vehicle. I was exonerated but somewhat shaken. It is curious how doll-like a broken up body looks, in spite of blood. A pity it's not so odourless as a doll.'[13] He had already told his mother about the accident:

> I am sorry there will have been such a gap in letters by the time this arrives – that is largely due to my encounter with another member of the Douglas family, one Major Sholto Douglas, Royal Scots. I duly went to a Godforsaken spot near Cairo for a month's camouflage course, and got there by driving 400 miles across the Sinai desert … We used the truck I had brought to take us the 26 miles to Cairo each evening, but one morning about midday I was driving in to collect some I. A. pay for Frank [Stoakes of Merton College] when an Arab ran out from behind a stationary lorry. He ran right across me, so without braking fully I swung in towards his starting point to give him more room. Unfortunately he had seen the truck too late & tried to run back. I hit him with one mudguard and broke his left foot more or less clean off under one wheel. He had burst some small artery in his stomach & vomited blood all over everyone but we got him off to hospital within five minutes & made out an accident report. Unfortunately this had to go before Major Douglas, who threatened to have me court-martialled for using a W. D. vehicle for personal use. I replied (later having given him time to cool off) that the truck was under my charge, and that I had authorised the journey, which constituted it a matter of duty, whatever he thought. This he had to admit, & instead, rather than give in, he said some officers had told him I'd been a leading light in complaining about the mess. To this I replied in polite but meaning phrases that I still thought the messing filthy & that I should be glad to know who the officers were & to have their accusations made to me in his (Major Douglas') office. However he wouldn't tell me their names so gave

in & instead announced his intention of taking over the truck which although he wasn't entitled to, I couldn't stop him doing.[14]

He continued the story in another letter:

… not long after that, I was made Orderly Officer, without the customary days notice, and that evening I had tickets to go to a concert in Cairo by the Palestine Orchestra. The tickets were 75 piastres (15/-) each, & although I hadn't paid for them, it seemed a bit hard to waste even someone else's money. There was no chance to telephone, so I got someone else to do Orderly Officer for me. This was quite in order, and I went along to the orderly room & said I'd got someone else, & what was I to do? They replied that all I need do was give them my deputy's name & Room number. This I did, & departed to my rendezvous in Cairo. But my deputy 'thought it would be all right' if he didn't mount the guard. He knew the Orderly Sergeant would be there & do it for him. But not only the Orderly Sergeant, but also Major Douglas was present at Guard mounting, purely by chance, & I believe the only time during the whole month. He sent for the Orderly Officer in terrific wrath. My deputy appeared & said I had never told him he had to mount the Guard. This was a lie, in any case. But it was no excuse, since if he accepted the responsibility, it was his job to find out its extent. However, the use of my name as a red rag diverted the bull's attention, & I was sent for the next morning. After being kept waiting ¾ of an hour, I was told the Commandant did not wish to see me, but that he had awarded me a week's Orderly Officer (equivalent of a week's C. B. for a trooper) & was writing a report about me to Middle East. The adjutant read me the report, which mentioned the truck & the accident, very carefully but not very truthfully worded, & continued to say that I had no sense of discipline & had no right to be an officer. The adjutant added in a whisper (the Commandants' [sic] office being next door) that he didn't think the letter would be sent, but was intended to put the wind up me. So I waited, doing Orderly Officer, for 2 days & then counter-attacked by applying for weekend leave, inventing 2 more fabulously expensive concert tickets & a fiancée in Cairo. At the same time I put in a most formal report beginning Sir, I have the honour to submit the following, with reference to etc. etc … saying that it was not my fault if my deputy failed, when I had provided him & informed orderly room, & even if I was technically responsible for his actions during my absence, giving me 7 days Orderly Officer & writing a report to M. E. would do no one any good. Furthermore, I added, perhaps he (Major Douglas) was not aware of the fact that my truck, when he had (illegally, I pointed out) taken it over, had made its first journey under his authorization, at exactly the same time of day to collect pay for exactly the same officer. Since he had threatened to Courtmartial me for authorizing such a journey, this would sound a little odd, if I had to report it to my Colonel. My Colonel, moreover, did not like to hear of his officers being harshly punished without even being interviewed & asked for an explanation of their actions, and would not be particularly pleased with Major Douglas for taking over a Sherwood Rangers truck & using it for his own purposes. In any case was it fair to keep me in camp when my fiancée, who lived in Cairo & could not see me at any other time of the year, was thus being more punished than I? And if, as he had twice told me, I had failed the course, not through lack of knowledge of the subject, but for not finding a proper deputy orderly officer, & for complaining about a filthy mess in a book specifically provided for complaints, he had better send me back to my regiment straight away, but must be prepared to explain why to my Colonel, who (I mentioned casually) was an M.P. The desired result was obtained. I was immediately taken off Orderly Officer, and as I had already squared the Transport Corporal, there was no need to take back custody of the truck.[15]

We are right back in the headmaster's office at Christ's Hospital. The same arrogance, the same obsession with 'fairness', the same dislike of authority figures. Authority figures still didn't like him either. As Graham says:

Kellett, the Colonel, was a natural focus for Douglas's dissatisfaction. A man who carried an aura of pomade wherever he went and whose fastidiousness in dress extended to making the bows of his shoe-laces fall in loops of identical length, Kellett might simply have passed Douglas off as scruffy; but in addition to finding him untidy he found him a nuisance. For during his first weeks with the regiment Douglas insisted on bringing to the notice of his colonel every shortcoming he found and each thought for its improvement: to the amusement of his new comrades a steady correspondence developed between them. The ambitious and immensely self-confident Kellett was the last person to tolerate the criticisms of a newly arrived subaltern. Meeting on equal terms, two such powerful characters could hardly have co-existed happily – one fellow-officer thought Kellett and Douglas shared a 'feline' quality – but the gulf which Kellett understandably saw between himself and his junior officer, made their exchanges unwelcome to him.[16]

Douglas knew that Kellett didn't like him. He wrote to his mother: 'The Colonel evidently intended to get rid of me for one reason or another, because he (The Colonel) told me he would see the General & arrange for my return & when I left shook hands with me & said he had seen the General and fixed everything & I should soon be back. When I interviewed the General

I found the Colonel hadn't said anything at all to him. Meanwhile I shall try [to] escape to the front line somewhere, by myself.'[17] Kellett sent Douglas to a camouflage course near Cairo at the end of December 1941. Douglas wanted nothing to do with the course.

In February 1942 Douglas was posted to Division HQ in Palestine as Camouflage Staff Officer, having been on the camouflaging course that he didn't want to attend. He wrote to his mother in March that he had 'arbitrarily' been made a Camouflage Staff Officer:

> This doesn't mean any promotion, although I believe I get extra pay. It's not even anything to do with the result of my course and its happened just when I particularly wanted to stay with the Regiment. As with everything in the Army, I arrived here to find no one knew what I was supposed to do, there is no office for me and the car and driver I'm supposed to have don't exist. I've been here 3 days and seem to be completely ignored. What I want is an interview with the General to tell him I don't want the job. My Colonel saw him before I came here, and he was alleged to have said he'd see me as soon as I arrived, but it seems to have slipped his memory. So I have had nothing to do for 3 days but write letters, and it looks as though this may continue indefinitely. If nothing happens in another two days I shall ask for an interview, and if I can't get away I shall threaten to resign my commission. This usually has the desired effect as they are short of officers & don't want to lose any ... This place is very similar to the last I was in, and there is nothing whatever to do with all the spare time I've got. I've seen G. S. O.'s [sic] 1 and 2, a Colonel and a Major, who obviously have no idea what I'm here for, but are determined not to let me get away, their line being 'It says in black and white that you ought to be here, and you've done a Camouflage course, so obviously you've got to stay'. This is the intelligent principle which is of course responsible for our armies [sic] notable successes & the extreme elasticity of its organisation.[18]

He had added sarcasm to his formidable armoury of complaining rhetoric. He wrote to Blunden at about the same time: 'I was fed up with sitting in camp doing nothing. Now I'm 10 times fedder up with being an elegant little staff officer with quite a lot to do, and no chance of getting back to the regiment.'[19] He flew often from Palestine to Cairo, although he was prey to airsickness. He wrote to his mother that he was 'leading a luxurious life and don't seem to have much hope of escaping to something more active. Meanwhile I'm taking advantage of it, as seems only sensible. I've been over and met the local Air Force and can fly (on duty) more or less

Douglas in Cairo with a friend

whenever I like.'[20] In Cairo he visited the Mani family. He had been visiting them since January 1942 and they were kind to him. 'When I left them,' he wrote to his mother, 'I wrote a bread and butter letter in very bad French to old Madame Mani, who was apparently ... so touched that she wept. I have never had to kiss so many people at once ... Mother and five sisters, all on both cheeks.'[21] The Manis were a family of French Egyptian Jews who he had got to know during his camouflage course. 'They took me', he wrote to Margaret Stanley-Wrench, 'among other places to a Jewish Wedding which was a fantastic sort of musical comedy but had impressive moments, and the singing was lovely.'[22] Generally Douglas had a reactionary attitude to Jews. 'The Jews en masse are horrible', he wrote to his mother, 'and I can sympathise with anyone who feels an urge to exterminate them. They are like rabbits but not so pretty. Every other rabbit characteristic, promiscuous breeding, dirtiness, lousiness, cowardice, they have in abundance. They are filthy sullen slovenly swine, and I can't be more accurate than that ... If the Jews are educated they only learn how to profit from people.'[23] While this is unacceptable now it was less so in 1942. Anti-semitism was intellectually, morally, socially and philosophically defensible, even attractive, at that time. As Gertrude Himmelfarb observed, 'passive, social anti-Semitism was "the prerogative of English gentlemen".'[24] Not many of the fashionable elite would go so far as Douglas however and his sympathy with an extermination programme. Anti-semitism notwithstanding he could get on with individual Jews. He told Jean Turner in a letter that he had 'just had a hectic month in Cairo, and escaped another engagement by the skin of my teeth. She was a French Jewess (and in fact still is, and is following me to Palestine in due course). She is very charming (of course) but I don't think I want as one Stoakes of Merton, now out here, put it, "a lot of little Solomon Douglasses".'[25] The girl was Renée Mani. 'What a family', he wrote to Jean Turner, 'of five sisters and 3 brothers, one brother died, another sister had a brick dropped on her head which finished her career (she was a ballet dancer), and two have had fiancés killed in air smashes. The atmosphere of gloom is not so noticeable as you might expect, and they are all most generous and amicable, but naturally subject, individually to fits of utter depression which make my own efforts in that direction look very amateur.'[26] He was in fact ambivalent about Jews and wrote to Jean Turner in the same letter that he had been shown over a Jewish communal development and was impressed by the 'paradise for children who live together away from their parents, grouped according to age. They go to visit their parents for about 2 hours at weekends and all day on Saturdays. The parents work like stink. No one has any money of his or her own. But they all seem pretty happy, particularly the kids.'[27] He wrote to girlfriend Olga Meiersons in October 1942 that 'I don't like, almost I hate & fear, many Jews – yet I feel more & more that in the end it will be a Jewess I marry. Probably from constantly suffering real or fancied injustice, I have acquired something of a Jewish mentality myself.'[28] His social life in Cairo was better. John Waller writes of Douglas's 'retiring nature' which is only strictly true if it is applied to literary acquaintances.[29]

When he wasn't with the Manis 'I stay with rather an Oxonian collection of people', he told Jean Turner, 'David Hicks, once of Worcester and the fiancé of Betty Sze's (Mrs Betty Carey's, by the way) best friend, also Bernard Spencer a minor poet who once edited things with Spender – but to do him justice, has forgotten it, and a gentleman of most effeminate appearance who rather surprisingly fought in the International Brigade as a machine gunner. Among his booty is Nieves, a very hot (in every sense) Spanish wife. Hamo Sassoon has arrived out here but I haven't met him yet ... Renée, incidentally, is succeeded by Olga (Latvian, Palestinian Area, Fortunée, Reman, Marcelle, Pilar, (Cairo area, Iraqui, Turk, Turk, Spanish). So the situation is well in hand.'[30] Olga was the subject of some rather heavy-handed lovemaking. He wrote to her in ponderous sub-Wildean tones the day after they met: 'If we meet again (and I shall try very hard to arrange that we do), expect nothing of me except that I shall interest you. If you are ever bored with me, it will be because I am bored with you, and I don't think I shall ever be bored with you. I shall never ask you to do anything for me that I wouldn't do for you ... although I'm disillusioned, I'm not cynical. Most of all I am never cynical about making love. If I tell you between two kisses that I love you more than anyone in the world – you can believe me. But not for long – love comes in waves, it can't be kept burning at the same pitch for years, or it just burns you up altogether.'[31] This not very romantic letter is all about, as he himself acknowledges, Keith Douglas: 'I have few enough friends to be able to count them. To most of them I don't write more than once a year, and they write back to me less often than that. But I know that if I walk round a corner one day, anywhere in the world, and meet one of them, we shall begin exactly where we left off at our last meeting.' He sent her some of his poems with the letter, and wrote a brief gloss: 'My poems aren't written in thumping dactylic metres like your friend Thomas Hood's, so perhaps you'll not like them. I don't make use of alliteration much either – it's your Germanic instincts which demands such things go. My verse is not particularly regular, but it has a certain amount of meaning, and rhythm as well, though subtler than Hood's, I like to think.' He added a PS that evening after a few drinks: 'I have been reading a book called Valse des Fleurs [by Sacheverell Sitwell], about Imperial Russia in the 19th century. Whenever I read such fantastic descriptions it reminds me that England will never be my home country. I must make my life extend across at least half the world, to be happy. I love people, and I think my only real ambition apart from those ambitions connected with making my living, is to meet more and more people, each different & more fascinating than the last, and to love them all, and to be loved by them.' We don't have Olga's response to this grandiose and self-serving letter but it must have been positive because her reply prompted Douglas to write again in an equally pompous way: 'As ever you are so serious and monitory. Thank you also for the photographs – I tore one up immediately, in which you looked like a rabbit in a silly symphony. No one saw it. The other two, which I think are good, I kept; I think the "bang" of curls on your forehead gives you the appearance of a rather "odd" lady novelist, or else a retired prostitute, but it may be something to do with the lighting. Anyway, that photograph has a worldly, cynical and tragic quality. The other is most like you, but technically a bad photograph. Who took them? All that may sound very carping and critical, but I was very glad to have them.'[32] Douglas never got the hang of innocent flattery.

Douglas was in Cairo and Alexandria for the summer of 1942. He was in an apparently loving relationship with Milena Gutierrez-Pegna, who worked in Alexandria, but the affair ended badly. He wrote to Olga on 7 October 1942:

> I think I told you about the Chinese girl I once nearly (or as I thought then, nearly) married. I don't know if I made it clear that all my life since then has been a kind of recovery from that episode. I had recovered anyway, as far as one ever does. Now I have done exactly the same thing over again. I met in Alexandria a Spanish-Italian girl, I just saw her walk past me on the beach, and went mad about her, without any will to love her. Well, the incredible happened, for a bit. I introduced myself, took her out, and she seemed to fall as much in love with me as I was with her, in the same mad sort of way. But the story went on more incredibly still after she had agreed to marry me, but I knew with doubts in her mind, (about what I could not make out, except that she seemed afraid we could not get on together by temperament) I went to the desert. It happened that my best friend had come to Alex, and I had introduced him to Milena. I have known him 8 years, & we were always together at school & at Oxford. Well, you see what is going to happen. But it sounds too theatrical for real life. I came back by accident, having broken down with a lorry outside Alex. I towed it in, in the dark, & went to her house for the night. She was out with Norman. That seemed pretty natural & I sat down to wait. They came in soon afterwards, and immediately a sort of strain settled on the room. Everything everyone said was forced out. Milena went up to find some blankets for me and I went after her and asked her what was the matter. She told me, partly, but not about Norman – she hadn't even told Norman. That is the worst night I've ever spent, bar one. I'm still feeling somehow how a man might feel who has to walk miles & miles home with a bad wound, dragging his feet, trying to hold himself so as not to feel the wound too much. It has opened the old wound as well. A week before, she was, or seemed, happy with me – now it is absolutely, irrevocably over, & she is as beautiful as ever, & I think, happy, if only I'll leave her alone … Naturally, for me, this alters nothing in the way I feel about you: ours is an understanding, and I think we love each other. One can't stop loving. But there are these women in the world who send me mad. I suppose I shall meet others, and if none of them will marry me, I shall never marry. Perhaps it is better than marriage to have friends like you. Please Olga, never think that anything that happens to me would alter that. Even if I had married a woman

I was mad about, I should keep my friendships, & if it broke my marriage & ruined my greatest happiness, I would still keep them – I can't help myself.[33]

He didn't seem to hold a grudge against Ilett. In telling the same story to Brenda Jones he was generous: 'Do you remember Norman Ilett, of Mid. B, now Sub-Lt RNVR? I introduced him [to Milena], and he cut me out. I must say he looks very nice in his white uniform – he was always a bit brown but out here he has become a sort of golden chocolate – if such a colour exists, and of course is incredibly lean and full of heroic tales.'[34]

In August 1942 Douglas wrote to his mother that he expected to be rejoining the Second Derbyshire Yeomanry, which had arrived in Africa and was stationed a few miles from him: 'But at the moment I am wanted by that and the Colonel of the Sherwood Rangers so it rests with the General to decide. Anyway it seems that I'm rid of camouflage at last, and not before I was heartily sick of the whole subject. But I mustn't count my chickens too soon. I missed being bombed and shelled by one day and went back [to Alexandria] with some trucks to be mended.'[35] In September he wrote to her again: 'It appears to be arranged at last that I am to leave this ridiculous job and return to the SRY. I discovered that Kellett had actually asked for me several times but the people here had told me he had not so as to make me think I had no chance of going and to prevent me from annoying them with applications for transfer.'[36] He told her, quite unsentimentally, that his friend John Masefield (the nephew of the poet) had been killed, thanked her for '15 Poets' and 'some very opportune socks' and reassured her that her letters to him weren't boring. Norman Ilett had expected not to return from 'an unusually stupid expedition': 'He said goodbye fully expecting not to return, and even gave me three pounds as an advance legacy. But he was back in two days demanding the three pounds, which having been entrusted to me were of course, spent.'

Douglas described his wait for action in his memoir of this part of the war, *Alamein to Zem Zem*:

I had to wait until 1942 to go into action. I enlisted in September 1939, and during two years or so of hanging about I never lost the certainty that the experience of battle was something I must have … I had arrived in the Middle East in August 1941. As a result of passing a course on which I was sent by accident, I found myself posted away from my regiment to a Divisional staff. I still wanted to get into action, and probably looked impatiently at my colleagues and superiors on this staff. For eight months I honestly tried hard to make sense of the job I was given – in other words to persuade the staff colonel and major to whose department I was attached to give me some work to do. The situation emerged clearly and simply as the months passed. My job was to give camouflage training. The Staff officers of G staff, under the General, arranged training programmes: they invariably forgot to include camouflage … After eight months of relative inaction, not being at any time a patient person, and having a hatred for wasted time, I tried to get back to my regiment. I could not be released: with the charm and politeness with which everyone on a staff always speaks to everyone else, I was told I was indispensable.[37]

By October 1942 he was some two hours' drive from Alexandria, at Wadi Natrun[38] having rejoined the Sherwood Rangers after their first battle (the battle of Alam El Halfa) amid the preparations for the battle of El Alamein, a small railway junction in Egypt, 70 miles west along the coast from Alexandria. The Sherwood Rangers had been training for the Alamein assault since the middle of September but a stalemate followed. The Sherwood Rangers were hampered by poor equipment. As Lindsay says: 'Many of the 25-pounder guns had no proper towing equipment, so we attempted to tow them with the tanks, which nearly always resulted in tearing off the dumb-iron of the gunners' vehicle and burning out the clutch of the tank. New tanks started to arrive in twos and threes: Grants, Lees, and the new Mark VI Crusader with the 6-pounder gun. We were longing for the new Shermans we had heard so much about – here, at last, was to be the answer to the superior tank design. For in the matter of tanks we had certainly had something to grumble about … The Grant and Lee were elephantine enough … [and] it was a miracle if a Crusader engine functioned for more than about 36 hours without some strange and terrible trouble developing.'[39] The regiment was not strong enough to mount a substantial attack and the German forces were short of petrol and supplies. 'Neither side,' wrote Lindsay, 'had enough reserves to alter the stalemate'. The Sherman tanks arrived and 'at last we had an answer to the German Mark IV Special with its ugly long 75mm gun'. The regiment's strength was now 13 Crusaders, 20 Grants and 11 Shermans.

On the evening of 23 October 1942, the battle of El Alamein began. Lindsay recalled that when 'our barrage for the attack opened … you might have thought the end of the world was coming. The din was unbelievable … The lanes that had been cleared through our own minefields were marked with tape, and we set off with Lieut. Garrett's Crusader troop leading, followed by our navigator, Captain McCraith. Then came [Douglas's] "A"

Squadron with nine Crusaders.'[40] Douglas was largely impressed by the new Crusader, certainly aesthetically. As he wrote in *Alamein to Zem Zem*: 'My own tank was a Mk. III Crusader – then comparatively new to us all. I had once been inside the Mk. II, which had a two-pounder gun and a four-man crew, and was now superseded by this tank with a six-pounder gun and only three men in the crew … This tank is the best looking medium tank I ever saw, whatever its shortcomings of performance. It is low-built, which in desert warfare, and indeed all tank warfare, is a first consideration. This gives it, together with its lines and its suspension on five great wheels a side, the appearance almost of a speedboat. To see these tanks crossing country at speed was a thrill which seemed inexhaustible – many times it encouraged us, and we were very proud of our Crusaders; though we often had cause to curse them.'[41] *Alamein to Zem Zem* is a prose memoir of part of the war, but parts of it have the same effect on readers as some of his desert poems: 'The bodies of some Italian infantry men still lay in their weapon pits, surrounded by pitiable rubbish, picture post-cards of Milan, Rome, Venice, snapshots of their families, chocolate wrappings, and hundreds of cheap cardboard cigarette packets. Amongst this litter, more suggestive of holiday makers than soldiers, there were here and there bayonets and the little tin 'red devil' grenades, bombastic little crackers that will blow a man's hand off and make a noise like the crack of doom. But even these, associated with the rest of the rubbish, only looked like cutlery and cruets. The Italians lay about like trippers taken ill.'[42] As Scannell says, 'there is something chilling about the cold accuracy of his observation but the power and precision of his description is undeniable.'[43] We have the same feeling when we read 'Vergissmeinicht' or 'How to kill'.

Douglas wasn't present at the outset of the battle. He defied orders and reported to the regiment at El Alamein on 28 October. As he wrote to his mother: 'I am still supposed to be with Div HQ, but they forgot about me, & I trotted off when no one was looking. They haven't noticed yet, although they told me they couldn't spare me to return to the regt!'[44] He described the decision in *Alamein to Zem Zem*:

> The offensive loomed very large in rumour, among so many officers living more or less inside the horse's mouth. I decided, if there were no other means of going into action with my regiment, to run away from Divisional Headquarters in my truck, and report to my Colonel. I thought vaguely that this might be straightened out later. To plan this was the natural result of

having the sort of little-boy mentality I still have. A little earlier, I might have wanted to run away and be a pirate. But it was surprising how easily the plan was realized and justified. For eight months I had done no mechanized training, my regiment was equipped with tanks, guns and wireless sets which I had never handled, scarcely seen, in my life; and it seemed possible, and even likely, that my Colonel who had applied for me before the battle, would not want an untrained officer to join him during action and endanger everyone's life while learning the job. If he refused me I was determined not to come back to Division but to drive away down the coast road to Alexandria, and from there through Cairo and Ismalia and across the Sinai desert to Palestine, to amuse myself until I was caught and court-martialled.[45]

Douglas was welcomed back[46] and he was happy: 'I am back,' he wrote to Jean Turner, 'and thank heaven for it, with the regiment, and life is pretty mobile and interesting. I have a camera and a permit to use it, being a camouflage king.'[47] Christopherson wrote on 26 October 1942 that 'Keith Douglas came back from Division, where he had been acting as camouflage officer, and joined the squadron again. At that time A Squadron was very short of officers, so the CO accepted his return with alacrity. He had left them at Division without saying a word to a soul, after having had a row.'[48]

Douglas might have been happy to be seeing some action but it was a chaotic landscape that he described in *Alamein to Zem Zem*: 'lorries appeared like ships, plunging their bows into drifts of dust and rearing up suddenly over crests like waves. Their wheels were continually hidden in dustclouds: the ordinary sand being pulverized by so much traffic into a substance almost liquid, sticky to the touch, into which the feet of men walking sank to the knee. Every man had a white mask of dust in which, if he wore no goggles, his eyes showed like a clown's eyes. Some did wear goggles, many more the celluloid eyeshields from their anti-gas equipments. Trucks and their loads became a uniform dust colour before they had travelled twenty yards: even with a handkerchief tied like a cowboy's over nose and mouth, it was difficult to breathe.'[49] As Lindsay put it: 'Our feelings about the battle of Alamein were politely summed up by the infantry private who said respectfully to Lieut. Keith Douglas, "I'll be glad when this is over, won't you, Sir?"'[50] Douglas described the battle of El Alamein to Olga Meiersons:

> I have had a busy time since I saw you last – the regiment has been filmed and the C. C. of our Brigade has broadcast. Churchill, it appears has mentioned

us (naming no names) in a speech. The first few days, my first in any kind of action, were undeniably sticky, and the Germans undoubtedly fought as long and as well as they could. But when they broke they broke properly, and the pursuit was very like hunting in England, except that instead of killing the fox when we found him, we gave him a tin of bully beef and searched him for souvenirs. My worst day was spent in a tank full of someone else's blood from the day before. The flies were incredible … I spent a whole day broken down by the roadside talking to the crew of a German tank who had given themselves up. One of them had been in Paris and was armed with the usual postcards. My German was more adequate than I thought, although pretty lousy on the whole. One of them had a pretty thick local accent of some kind which puzzled me – I am stone deaf anyway after 2 weeks of gunfire and my ears will go on singing for months yet.[51]

He had acquired a new camp bed and air mattress to accompany his camera, an Italian automatic, three Luger pistols (of which he gave away two and lost the third) and some German novels.

The regiment pushed on towards Mersa, chasing the retreating Axis troops. 'As we moved ahead', wrote Lindsay, 'we could see that the Axis had pulled up sticks and left in a tearing hurry':

> … the loot – more especially in the way of food and drink – was terrific. You could have spent three weeks there picking it up. Lieut. Douglas, longing to salvage some most tempting cases of chianti, with the necks of the flasks peeping lovingly out of the case, was disgusted when his driver ran the tank over them. They turned out to be a booby-trap and blew the track and tyres off his tank. Again the Germans had gone while the going was good and left their Italian allies stranded. Douglas, combing with his troop the ground between the coast road and the sea, passed groups of Italians pointing feverishly to packets of cigarettes and watches as an inducement to capture them. But there was no time for a halt – until later when Douglas wandering out too far among the sandhills broke a track on his tank and was forced to stop and wait for the fitters. This placed him at the mercy of any stray Italians who might be longing for the first step home. By a stroke of luck, the first group to arrive was an Italian concert party. They lined up by the tank and sang until the fitters came. "That's real high-class music, Sir," was the verdict of the crew. Douglas's poetic soul was delighted at this aesthetically sound judgment – the Italians were from Milan Opera.[52]

Douglas described the incident in *Alamein to Zem Zem*:

Tank maintenance in the desert, Douglas is in the foreground standing on the tyres

The next morning we went back to the regiment with orders for a move at 8 o'clock, to take Mersa Matruh. 'A' squadron were strung across the road, my troop combing between the road and the sea. As we approached an Italian position five men came out holding up their hands, with packets of cigarettes in them. One pointed also to his watch, as an inducement to us to take them. This was very different from the German method of surrendering. They climbed on to the tank and we moved on. But the main advance had left us behind and when we broke a track crossing a little ditch, we were stranded out of sight of everyone. The tank was stuck in the ditch, and before we could mend the track would have to be towed off it. By now it was about 9.30 and I set out with one of the crew to walk to the road – the other two members (this was a 4-man tank) staying with the five prisoners. Luckily we had plenty of rations … Already a procession of lorries, nose to tail, some of them bearing the Cairo area sign, and all of them patently from base units – their drivers and crew goggling at everything they passed – were tearing down the road towards Mersa, with supplies of every kind … The new type of pistol had jammed; the moving parts had somehow seized up, and we could not make out how to strip it, so I called to four German soldiers who were walking past. They all lifted their heads in apprehension to endure something more. A corporal walked across to them holding the revolver; he could not make them understand what he wanted. When I crossed over and spoke to them in halting German they smiled in huge relief. Only to tell us how to strip the pistol; they had it in bits in a moment, but advised us to prefer the old type of Luger, which was much more reliable ... In the morning we located the tank, to my relief ... The Italians had apparently been entertaining as well as useful. They were not fighting troops, but the equivalent of an ENSA [the Entertainments National Service Association] concert party, and one of them was a pardre. They were all very young, and one of them, before the war an opera tenor in Milan, had beguiled the night with what my driver and operator considered 'real high-class music'. They washed up after breakfast and mended our track with great cheerfulness.[53]

Christopherson wrote in his diary entry of 3 November 1942: 'Keith Douglas returned with a new tank. I asked him to take charge while Sam [Garrett] and I went out to refuel and took with us John Bethell-Fox, who was wounded in the knee. It was rather a foolish request to Keith to take charge as at that time there was only one other tank besides his own. However, he did get an order from the CO to control the squadron properly and stop them wandering about!'[54] The following day Christopherson added: 'Moved out of leaguer at first light and soon discovered that the enemy had evacuated from the line of the track and telegraph poles. I was left with only three Crusaders, those of Sam Garrett, Keith Douglas and Corporal Truman ... Twelve enemy tanks then appeared, which [Jack Tyrrell] engaged with H[igh]E[xplosive] but left off when Keith Douglas and Corporal Truman engaged with their 6-pounders from the Crusaders. The enemy tanks then withdrew.'[55] On Thursday 5 November 1942 Christopherson wrote: 'Keith Douglas found a German officer and 20 men, as well as a good load of compasses, binoculars and revolvers ... On his way back to us, Keith Douglas, being rather blind at the best of times and having rather lost direction, approached what he thought was our column. He brought his tank alongside a vehicle and much to his amazement and to the utter consternation of the vehicle driver, found it was a German column. When the German driver saw a tank alongside his vehicle, utter confusion broke out and the whole column broke up. Keith tried to fire his Besa [a machine gun], which jammed, then turned to his 6-pounder, which was quite useless against vehicles of that type, so finally resorted to his Tommy gun, which also jammed. He ended up by having a first class row with Davis, his gunner. His wireless also failed to work at the critical moment.'[56] A couple of days later Christopherson wrote about the captured musicians: 'Keith Douglas wandered too far out to the right flank, broke a track, and had a long walk back to the road to get help. However, he captured an Italian concert party all waiting to give themselves up. Until the L[ight] A[id] D[etachment] arrived to help him, they sang to him and the crew, helped him brew up, and even assisted in replacing the track.'[57]

The sudden, and unusual, appearance of rain allowed Rommel's troops to escape at Fuka on 6 November. As Douglas put it in *Alamein to Zem Zem*: 'The first downpour took us by surprise and washed most of the victorious feeling out of us. The landing ground became a marsh, and we dried our clothes on the exhaust, garment by garment, and battened ourselves into the turret, where we sat throughout a miserable afternoon, eating wet biscuits and cheese.'[58] Douglas, who returned to the regiment on 9 November 1943, but, according to his CO 'without a tank',[59] described the horror of war without flinching, but it wasn't all uncivilized. In the evening Douglas was sent in an armoured car to headquarters. 'On the way down the dark road,' he wrote, 'we came upon six Germans plodding along by themselves. I sat them on the outside of the car and very reluctantly got out and sat outside with them in the rain. They were dejected and said they had had nothing to eat for two days. I gave them some tins of bully which I had put in my pocket from my tank's ration box, and some sodden pieces of biscuit … It was difficult to get rid of the prisoners, but I was determined to find them some food and blankets, because the few people in the regiment who had been taken prisoner and recaptured during the first days at Alamein had been well treated by the Germans.'[60] The rain eased up and the Sherwood Rangers entered Mersa Matruh on 8 November, for some rest and refitting. As Lindsay says, it was the only occasion in six months of fighting when the regiment was not at the forefront of the battle.[61] It had suffered some heavy losses at the battle of El Alamein. Lindsay reports that of its twenty-two officers sixteen had been casualties, so the fortnight's rest was welcome. 'We sat just off the coast road', says Lindsay. 'near the outskirts of Matruh; hearing some history for a change instead of making it … We made ourselves as comfortable as might be. Most of us scrounged materials to make lean-tos of some kind, constructed primitive tables and chairs, and made ovens of oil drums. "A" Squadron picked up some enormously chic black tents with talc windows, asbestos flaps for the hot pipe of a stove and blackout blinds.'[62] He wrote that the regiment lived 'well enough on German ham, Danish butter and Italian tinned fruit. Colonel Kellett had long since discovered that my only real use in wartime was an ability to make chocolate soufflé – so Lieut. Douglas was despatched to Cairo and returned with 2,000 eggs from the Nile Cold Storage Company and a load of Mr. Groppi's best chocolate.'[63] Douglas recounted this story in *Alamein to Zem Zem*: 'I was sent back to

Alexandria in a 15-cwt. the next day to have my eyes tested; for I had lost one pair of my glasses and badly cracked another during the battle. I was given £50 of regimental money and a shopping list like a Quartermaster's inventory. We started early in the morning, a driver, sergeant and myself, and began badly by skidding into a three-tonner on the west road.'[64] After an interlude with Milena, he began to shop in earnest:

> We drove the truck into the docks and arranged to fill the spaces under the seats, etc., with orange gin, liqueurs, cigarettes and cigars; sitting on these, we drove out past the sentry and the Egyptian police, congratulating ourselves on getting English gin for 7s. a bottle, and defrauding the Egyptians who had lived upon us so long. In the afternoon we bought some 2,000 eggs from the Nile Cold Storage Company, and a lot of tinned food. The N. A. A. F. I. refused to serve us, because we didn't live in Alexandria, and we finished the day's shopping by ordering 3,000 petits pains to be ready, newly baked at 9.00 the next morning … In the morning we started back, after the counting and loading of 3,000 beautiful scented new loaves in sacks. On the way back we stopped at the bulk N. A. A. F. I. at Burg el Arab, which we reached about five minutes after their closing time. A dirty R. A. S. C. corporal, who was in charge of it, refused to sell us any beer, although he had plenty of it, as we could see. We did not much relieve our feelings by suggesting that if the fighting troops were as finicky about their working hours as the N. A. A. F. I. employees we shouldn't have begun a battle let alone won it.[65]

Douglas seems to have enjoyed himself in Mersa. Christopherson's diary entry for 11 November 1943 notes that a 'football match in the afternoon against the R[oyal]H[orse]A[rtillery] on a very dangerous and hard ground. Sam Garrett and Keith Douglas had some drinks on board a torpedo boat in Mersa harbour. They both came back much the worse for wear!'[66] This episode seems not to have done Douglas's career any harm. On 13 November 1943 Stanley Christopherson reorganized his squadron 'into the following troops: Sam Garrett comes to Squadron HQ as 2i/c, Archie Stockton 3 Troop, Keith Douglas 2 Troop, Sergeant Goodridge 4 Troop, and Sergeant Hardinge, 5 Troop.'[67]

On 14 November Christopherson wrote that two new tanks had arrived for A Squadron, 'making us 14 in all. All tanks have to be painted with division and squadron signs, etc., and all given a name beginning with A. Keith Douglas submitted 'Apple Pie & Apple Face' for his tanks. I squashed this, as something told me that the VCO would not approve!'[68] By this time Division Headquarters had realized that their camouflage officer was missing.

'A thrill which seemed inexhaustible.' Douglas with a tank

Christopherson wrote: 'Having gone through the battle he [Douglas] had quite made up his mind never to return to Division. Having discovered what had happened, the G1 at Division was somewhat narked that Keith had not consulted him, and complained to the CO somewhat bitterly at his actions. The CO made Keith go and apologize, which he did tonight, but returned with a bottle of rye whisky and also a bottle of lime!'[69]

On 24 November the regiment left Mersa to join the advance towards Tripoli. By 5 December Douglas's A Squadron had a full complement of Crusaders, B Squadron had 11 Shermans and three Grants (although it had to give two of the Shermans away) and C Squadron had eight Shermans and six Grants.[70] The next day the regiment made good progress. As Lindsay put it, 'the going under our tracks was good, hard, gravelly soil, but we were held up for a time by having to pass through the positions of the Highland Division. We were coming now into the area of the salt lakes, and these treacherous patches of ground, together with the minefields, tended to restrict the possible lanes of advance. The enemy were moving back slowly, leaving small rearguards, and we leaguered now in open country, mostly in leaguers which had just been evacuated by the enemy.'[71] They were soon in action near Agheila. Douglas's squadron reported wire defences running north and south for many miles and sappers were dispatched to cut a gap in the wire for A Squadron to cross, which they did for 150 yards without striking any mines. Heavy fog prevented the enemy shells from hitting their targets but as the fog lifted, the enemy gunners improved their range and their shells started to drop among the regiment's tanks. The enemy's counter-attack was beaten off but the regiment's progress was impeded by mines. 'From Agheila onwards,' reports Lindsay, 'the area of the coastal road was thick with mines and booby traps of very [sic] description.'[72] Lindsay described these traps:

> There were ordinary minefields, mines wired in series, and mines sown in old vehicle tracks so that the unwary driver would say, 'well, someone else seems to have driven up there, so it ought to be all right for me.' There were booby traps with enough explosive to blow a hand or a leg off; booby traps attached to doors, stairways, furniture, loot, and even branches of trees. There were explosive thermos flasks, fountain pens, and other pretty souvenirs which would blow off part of your anatomy when you picked them up, 'presumably manufactured,' speculated Lieut. Douglas, 'by those firms which in peacetime specialise in joke cigarettes, which squirt ink in your face, and stinkbombs'. We imagined a revision of their usual advertisement: 'Causes howls of pain. Try it on your enemies.'[73]

Christmas was nearly upon the men and the regiment's unhappy supply situation didn't permit further progress. On Christmas Day, after the services, most of the men sat on petrol tins round the cooks' lorries. Each of them, according to Lindsay, had 'turkey, pork, Christmas pudding, iced cake, a bottle of beer and fifty cigarettes. Who said the British always had to muddle through? – this was wonderful organisation considering that we were over 900 miles from Cairo. Two captured enemy tents put together made the dining room, and the officers served the Christmas dinner at mid-day. The officers had their own meal in the evening in an improvised dining room made by fitting canvas over the tops of three-ton lorries. The rocks in the desert round us were full of mica and sparkled with a hard brilliance in the moonlight.'[74] Christopherson wrote that the officers' dinner was excellent: 'We each brought our own drink, which consisted of whisky and rum. We all agreed when we had finished that we had not been so full since being in the desert!'[75] Spirits were high. The regiment had been

'I can … teach anyone else to drive.' Douglas with an army truck

successful. '900 miles from Cairo – and a dozen short weeks before Rommel had been almost battering at the city gates … The shoe-shine boys, fly-whisk vendors and beggars had grown importunate beyond all bounds. The rabble in the bazaars had spat, cursed and hurled stones. Perhaps now that Rommel was nearly a thousand miles away the gallant Egyptian proprietor of the "Rhineland Beer and Spaghetti Bar" might have found the courage to nail up again his old original sign: "Union Jack Café. Winston John-Bull Shakespeare, Proprietor. Welcome, Tommy!"[76] Douglas described Christmas in the desert in a letter of December 1942 to his mother: 'I have been trying cooking with flour and margarine, making sort of jam puffs today, and of course in spite of all precautions have sat in the jam, and temporarily spoilt my new German trousers: but the puffs were a great success … It is very cold before and after sundown, with a bitter wind, but reaches a fair heat at midday; I begin and end the day in 2 pullovers, shirt, trousers, tie, battledress top, silk scarf, and British warm; sometimes with a leather waistcoat thrown in. By midday I am down to shirt and trousers and, perhaps, stripped to the waist. I am quite fat again now, as we've done little but eat for some time.'[77]

The regiment moved on again on 27 December. The rift between the natural beauty of the north African desert and the murderous environment wasn't lost on the men. 'We moved on to Nofilia,' reported Lindsay. 'The ground in places was covered with tiny flowers which gave out a scent so strong you might have been in a Bond Street beauty salon. At four in the afternoon we were held up where a blown viaduct was sown all round with mines and booby traps. We moved on eventually and got as far as Sirte. The little fort there had been well equipped with "S" mines by the departing enemy; the Colonel and the Adjutant examined it, treading gingerly from stone to stone.'[78] Douglas was struck by the flowers[79] and wrote to Margaret Stanley-Wrench on 8 January 1943: 'There are indeed flowers of various indeterminate sorts and colours even on these bits of desert, mostly they are mauve and yellow. Occasional and quite veritable daisies & dandelions.'[80] It wasn't all natural history though. Christopherson's diary entry for 2 January 1943 notes that: 'after lunch, Keith Douglas gave the squadron a lecture on camo usage and showed the squadron some photos taken from the air.'[81]

On 10 January the British forces commander Montgomery held a conference on the 'final phase of the North African campaign'. It was to begin with an attack across the Wadi Zem Zem. Douglas got no further. By 14 January the regiment was within two miles of the Bu Ngem road and started to move the following day, with the Sherwood Rangers on the left. 'As we crossed the Bu Ngem road we were engaged by enemy anti-tank fire. The guns were well hidden and cunningly sited in the Wadi Zem Zem. We were traversing broken ground; but the enemy seemed to have every inch of it well covered.'[82] The Wadi was steep on both sides and Douglas's squadron was positioned on the forward slope. Douglas spotted a Mark IV, and

> … by cunning stalking got to within 150 yards of it. Going in for the kill, his gun jammed. This catastrophe made him think of Lieut. Ken Graves' imaginary report by a tank commander: 'The '75 is jammed. The '37 is firing but is traversed the wrong way. I'm saying: "Driver, reverse" on the radio; and the driver, who can't hear me, is advancing. As I look over the top of the turret and see twelve enemy tanks 50 yards away, someone hands me a cheese sandwich.' He tried to get his gun in order, but failed; so he stayed out there giving valuable information until his tank was knocked out. On the way back from his knocked-out tank a Grant tank blew up twelve yards away from him and a roll of bedding, propelled from the Grant by the explosion, knocked him sideways.[83]

Douglas taking a break in the desert

Douglas was wounded at Wadi Zem Zem on 14 January 1943 and he arrived on 25 January at El Ballah, Palestine, where he was hospitalized for six weeks. According to Christopherson Douglas had started to walk back to get help for his wounded crew but trod on an 'S' mine.[84] Christopherson wrote in his diary on 14 January 1943: 'Keith Douglas's troop had an unpleasant time on the left flank, where the ground was very undulating. He played a game of hide-and-seek with a German tank, which was eventually knocked out by a C Squadron tank … Douglas and White [another officer] both had their tanks knocked out. They started to walk back to get help for their wounded crew but trod on a S mine and were both injured – White seriously so, but Keith not as bad.'[85]

Douglas himself described his wounding flippantly to Brenda Jones in a letter of 25 March 1943:

I was rummaging in the remains of my tank for some cigarettes to give to some wounded in a nearby hole, and emerged from the driver's seat to see a

German Mk III tank about 100 yards away, obligingly scanning the middle distance with field glasses. So I ran like hell, and gave the cigarettes to some equally deserving chaps in a hole about a mile away, where I eventually arrived very puffed, carrying a man with no legs, to speak of, round my neck. I was very thankful when I eventually stepped on a mine, as I already had a number of uncomfortable minor ailments a splinter in my foot, various desert sores (equivalent to boils, more or less) shingles (which I'm told is a nervous disease, but which took the form of an immense blister on my forehead and a headache), and one eye more or less blacked out, also my moustache (a recent acquisition), and my eyebrows and eyelashes burnt off by the shell that hit my tank.[86]

Douglas wrote to his mother from the hospital on 26 January 1943:

I have now arrived, after a most uncomfortable journey of nearly 2000 miles in various forms of transport, where I shall stay put for a week or two. I think there are fewer bits in me than I originally imagined, though there may be something in my left thigh and in my right calf & there's definitely something in my right foot because although I can walk on it & wiggle the toes it is numb, as if it had gone to sleep. Anyway I shall know in a day or two as I was X-rayed yesterday, & you can be sure that by the time you get this whatever it was will have been taken out, and I shall be almost out of here, if not quite. Anyway I've had a very small amount of pain & am quite undisfigured. My temperature is a bit subnormal, but the lowest I can see on my chart is 97, & yesterday evening it was 98, which it probably will be again this evening.[87]

He went on to describe his diet in the desert:

We are fed at all hours of the day with most delectable food, and it seems incredible that in 10 days I could come to this from living entirely on tinned stuff & ½ a gallon of water a day for all purposes, with fresh meat about once a month, oranges about as frequent, & an occasional small amount of oatmeal or flour. Not that we didn't live extremely well on these rations, when we had time to cook. Service biscuits, particularly oatmeal ones, can be powdered with a hammer and mixed with a little water & sugar & condensed milk make very reasonable & realistic porridge, which is filling & hot. Out of biscuits & jam most professional looking cakes were made in petrol-tin ovens, and when flour was available every kind of cake, dumpling, jam roll and pancake was evolved from it. We captured from the enemy a sort of paper strips, which, like Japanese water flowers expanded in water & boiled up into very good sliced cabbage, carrots, swedes etc, with plenty of flavour & goodness left in. At other times I've got hold of scrumptious tinned cherries and some very pleasant Macedonian cigarettes, of which we had several crates in the regiment at one time.

Finally, he described his clothing situation: 'I had all my clothes cut off, but am hoping my batman hasn't lost my other kit, & won't before I can get back. All I retain at present is the large leg-pocket of my battledress, luckily containing my pay book, identity card, & money … I was sorry the doctor cut my leather waistcoat off me so clumsily. What with the blood and the cuts & tears I didn't think it would be worth keeping. But it's a great loss.'

He was disgusted by the lack of correspondence from home and the postal services generally. He wrote to Jean Turner to thank her for an airgraph that he'd received a day or two before he was wounded: 'None of my letters seem to have arrived anywhere for months, so I suppose some censor has taken a dislike to me. I am nearly well again but for my foot which had to be opened up and de-peppered … I've heard nothing of Blunden for a long time now, do you know anything of him? I never get answers from anyone now, very soon I really intend to give up writing.'[88] He might have been feeling a bit unloved by his friends and family at home but his condition was slowly improving. An airgraph to his mother dated 3 February 1943 reports that he was 'getting positively obese with staying in bed and eating so much. I can walk now, and so long as I stay on my toes, without limping. I can't yet put my right heel on the ground bit I don't think it will be long – the M. O. is quite happy about it.'[89] He didn't expect to remain in hospital for more than another month. In an airgraph to his mother dated 7 February 1943 he wrote: 'I am up, and can walk quite well already – all healed except my foot which had to be probed. As soon as this heals I'll be as new, except for (I think) a permanently numb big toe, so I shall be able to tread on drawing pins. Everything, including the toe, moves in all directions, quite as efficiently as ever. So I hope to emerge soon.'[90] But he was still complaining about his foot in an airgraph to Jean Turner dated 24 February 1943: he couldn't 'put a shoe on yet, because of the bulbous dressing on my foot, although I can walk perfectly well, and indeed dance, if there was ever anyone to dance with.'[91]

By March he was indignant that he couldn't get any leave. He complained to his mother that junior officers were not allowed leave even if they had been in action continuously for three months. There was no appeal and some of those who were refused leave had not had any since 1940.[92] He wrote to Jo on 11 March 1943 to complain about the postal services as well as his treatment: 'A few airgraphs are beginning to drift through from you, written not later than 16 February – it's now March 11th, which isn't very good, although I don't see what excuse they can have now, mail ought to be better instead of worse than ever. I don't know how long mine are taking, but they certainly aren't arriving in the order I sent them. I'm now in a convalescent depot with very incompetent doctors and orderlies and no nurses. They have been putting sulphonamide dressings on a perfectly clean open wound, which are meant to draw out pus and so simply draw out blood & keep the wound open and very painful (for the first time). So I'm tearing the dressings off as soon as I come away and putting on dry ones.'[93] But the leave situation was improving: 'The Colonel at the hospital who refused me & others leave, has now changed his mind, I hear, and gave the batch after us a fortnight, which is pretty scandalous, I think. I am getting a week from here & hope to get more from the Base Depot.'[94] He described the effects on his body of life in the desert:

> I shall be a mass of scars when I come home, though not very big ones. When I was in Palestine I had a sort of impetigo, or desert sores on my face which has left little red marks. There are 5 desert sore scars on my right hand and 3 on my left, and heaven knows how many on my legs. A scar under my arm, 3 on my back, one on the inside of my right foot, and inside right calf, & a big one & a little one at the back of my left thigh. Also a scar from shingles over my right eye. But the general effect isn't very noticeable. The only one that will show more than a fleabite is the hole in my thigh, which is really an operation scar, the original hole was very small. The one inside my foot is a long straight cut but being inside won't show. There is still a ball bearing in my right calf, but it hardly left a mark going in, and doesn't hurt or impede me at all, although I can feel a lump there if I press it. Being round it won't do any harm.'[95]

By 27 March, when he wrote to his mother, he was still being refused leave but he was optimistic that he would be granted some by base depot: 'Anyway I'm determined to have some.'[96] On 2 April 1943 he wrote to Olga Meiersons that he was requesting his leave that day: 'I have the misfortune to have had to depend on first a villain and then an aged idiot to get my leave at all ... Leave in Palestine is not allowed without giving 14 days notice, which I can't do. So we shall see what we shall see. I suppose the war will eventually end, but the trouble is that all these idiots live on when one would have thought there was a golden opportunity to liquidate them.'[97] In April

1943 he finally got his leave at Tel Aviv with Olga and at Alexandria with Milena and on 6 May he rejoined his victorious regiment at Enfidaville. 'Don't worry', he wrote to Olga on 16 May, 'although I'm back with the regiment all is well. My silence is due to extreme busyness about the most pacific tasks, such as obtaining wine, sheepstealing, etc. Everyone is most happy that the campaign is over and the amount of prisoners and captured material beggars description. The country people here are very nice to us. Beer and other good things begin to reach us, and it seems we are in for a good time, as far as it can be organised ... I found a wine factory & bought 52 gallons yesterday – considerable noise last night.'[98] Christopherson wrote in his diary of 6 May 1943: 'on 6 May Keith Douglas rejoined the squadron after being in hospital recovering from a wound he received in the battle at Zem Zem. He will take over 5 Troop but in the meantime he has been sent away to try and collect some NAAFI stores for the Regiment.'[99]

Douglas spent May and June 1943 in Tunisia. 'I missed all the fighting in this country', he wrote to his mother on 23 May, 'and have simply been occupied in driving all over Tunisia buying wine for the officers and men – it costs about sixpence a bottle and some of it is very good, notably the 1941 vin rosé.'[100] He was clearly pleased to be back in the thick of things. 'Lieut. Keith Douglas', Lindsay wrote, 'swanning around in his truck in the 1st Army's battle area, passed an elaborately painted sign: "YOU ARE BEING TIMED. DO NOT EXCEED YOUR SPEED LIMIT." His driver glanced at it and remarked: "No wonder they've taken such a muckin' long time."'[101] On 25 May Douglas's unit was the only unit of the Eighth Army remaining in Tunisia. 'We enjoyed three weeks of heavenly bathing', wrote Lindsay, 'with a lifeguard patrol organised for non-swimmers. There were squadron and regimental sports. Lieut. Keith Douglas arranged a dance in Montastir for 100 of our men and 100 girls. The girls made a beeline for the food, R. S. M. Bakewell dealt with a gate-crasher and incurred a black eye and, in short, a good time was had by all.'[102] Douglas loved Tunisia. He wrote to his mother on 23 May that he thought it 'a lovely country and would be nice to live in after the war. I now speak French pretty fluently if not very correctly, and could certainly learn to speak it well if I stayed here.'[103] He was enjoying the victory in Africa. 'It is supposed to be the biggest victory over the Germans,' he wrote to his mother, 'since Napoleon beat the Prussians at Jena. I went up and had a look at the last positions they had vacated in the hope of finding some loot but found nothing but very dead bodies and refuse of every kind. I brought nothing back except about fifty fleas. I actually caught and killed thirty two the day after, and you can imagine how many bites I had. I counted up to two hundred and didn't bother to go on although there were some I didn't count … I don't think I'm likely to see Cairo, or England again for some time. I don't know what I'll do about the stuff I had to leave in Cairo. But I intend to come out here again anyway. I should like to marry and live in Tunisia.'[104] He reported to her on Desert Rat politics: 'I had flown up in a day and arrived in a back area where dances are already being organised for the back-end troops. All these back-end people now sport the 8 Army badge and are regarded universally as heroes – the fighting troops do not wear it; not the ones who did the fighting anyway: having seen the people who do wear it, we are not particularly anxious to. The papers here always included a good many pictures of so-called Desert Rats, who are invariably dirty and half-naked, although actually they are the back-end people who have a chance to keep clean & don't bother to. The fighting troops, even on half a pint of water, kept themselves smart … I never even saw a dead one who hadn't got his stockings properly pulled up & clean red hackles.'[105] He told his mother of some of his exploits:

When I first arrived I was sent back some hundreds of miles … to buy wine. I tried at the French military wine control, who only gave me 2 litres, but threw in a hell of a lunch in which we all ate lots of raw onions and drank far more wine than they would allow us to buy. I took photos of all of them, and my driver, who knew no difference between wine & beer, didn't wake up till long after dark. We went back with 2 fighting French & 2 civilians on the truck, and slept beside the road. They all helped except one who did not care for the food we prepared or the blankets we gave him, so I left him in the middle of the road miles from anywhere to find himself something better. We dropped the soldiers at Sfax after they had helped to buy two sheep which we tied up with belts in the back of the truck. The remaining civilian, who is a boy of about 18, took me home with him when we got to Sousse, and his mother provided us all with supper (mostly by making us concoctions of our own rations, as she had no food over), and iced our wine. We also drank most of their only bottle of vermouth. I slept on an immense oriental divan between clean sheets & the drivers slept on the truck with the sheep, which proved a necessary precaution, as they (the sheep) nearly escaped in the night … Almost immediately on my return I was sent out again to First Army to get some of their canteen food & rations as 8 Army was getting nothing & 1st Army living like kings. I stayed the first night with a Free French regiment and the news came during dinner that Tunis and Bizerte had fallen. The result was that five of us finished 6 bottles of wine, a bottle of cognac, and three bottles of whisky. The Captain ... went down with a wump on the floor & was still drunk when I left the next morning, and a Lieutenant was sick in the tent in the middle of a sentence. I made myself sick outside afterwards, as I had to be fit for duty early the next morning. This created a very good impression as I had drunk as much as anyone and still remained on my feet and coherent (in French, too, as no-one spoke any English). The Captain enquired vaguely on waking the next morning '*Où est notre cher vieux camarade d'la Huitième Armèe*', and complained that I hadn't lasted the evening. But he was assured I had outlasted him and moreover it was added in my favour that, '*Le lieutenant est gentleman — il est allé dehors pour dégueuler.*'[106]

DESERT WRITINGS

On 14 June the regiment began the move into Tripolitania, stopping at La Hencka and inspecting the Roman ruins of El Djem which they had only seen by moonlight on the way up.[107] Their final destination was Homs where they stayed in a large palm grove 'on fine white sand dunes by the sea.'[108] The regiment heard of the unconditional surrender of Italy on 8 August 1943 and left Homs six days later for the Nile delta. Douglas's concern about not seeing Cairo again in a hurry was unfounded as he spent about three months there before the regiment was shipped back to the UK. Meanwhile he was promoted to Captain although, as he complained to his mother, 'it will be a long time before I get the pay through.'[109] He had a course in Palestine in August which he enjoyed interspersed, as he wrote to Blunden, 'with some pleasant week-ends among the modern architecture and other modern amenities of Tel Aviv.'[110] He found Cairo 'very crowded', as he wrote to Milena Gutierrez-Pegna on 29 September 1943[111] but he was having some literary conversations there. It was in Cairo that he encountered the group of poets who were publishing *Personal Landscape*, a literary periodical for the north African forces. It's not certain whether he was more attracted by the eccentricity and individuality of the group or the possibility of publication in the magazine. He wrote to Blunden in October 1943 that he was 'now able to get into Cairo occasionally although I still live in primitive conditions. I see a good deal of poets whose names may have reached you – Bernard Spencer, Terence Tiller, Robin Fedden and occasionally Larry Durrell. In the opposite camp lie (and lie and lie) John Waller whose face is folding upon him, and that dirty, inky little wretch G. S. Fraser who looks anything but New Apocalyptic. I think he grows watercress in his ears, which are always full of rich Nile mud.'[112] Fraser was more generous about Douglas. He wrote in his memoir of Cairo, the poem 'Monologue for a Cairo evening':

> And Keith Douglas's shrewd and rustic eyes
> That had endured 'the entry of a demon':
> His poems spat out shrapnel; and he lies
> Where all night long the Narrow Seas are screaming[113]

Lawrence Durrell wrote: 'Later, when that blonde vagabond, Keith Douglas, strayed into our midst, fresh from a desert battle, with a pocketful of fine poems, he and Bernard [Spencer] made common cause and became great friends. I understood this because they had the same sort of poetic frequency and the same lucid approach to words.'[114]

Durrell recalled some of the eccentricities. He too remembered George Fraser's scruffiness. Visiting him to deliver some poems for *Personal Landscape*, wearing tennis shoes and dirty scarf with his uniform, the trousers of which were tied up with string, Fraser explained that he hadn't been reprimanded for his unconventional attire 'probably because his boss was a writer too'.[115] Durrell also recalled a ridiculous interview with a security guard who wanted to behead the poet John Gawsworth for claiming that Prince Rupprecht of Bavaria was the rightful king of the UK.

Durrell told a story about the origins of *Personal Landscape* which suggest that poetry was important in the Middle East:

> It may have been he [the poet Charles Hepburn] who asked me to go round the the Greek Embassy and teach English to the new President of the Greek Government in exile, Panagiotis Cannellopoulos. He was a fine poet as well as a statesman, and I had met him in Athens. He knew no English and was anxious to learn. When I presented myself he told me that he wished to learn the language, but he had no time to bother with trifles. He wanted to start with Yeats. It seemed hopeless, as he knew no grammar whatsoever. I told him that this could not turn out well and a long discussion ensued, during which I explained our problems over *Personal Landscape*, which was a kind of little chapbook of verse printed among private friends. Robin Fedden had found an old press and some paper and we thought it would be a pleasant act of friendship – it fitted into the general atmosphere of the time – but as for the money … it was quite an expensive production, and while we were all in jobs the cost of the first two numbers was quite a wrench. The Greek ardour of Cannellopoulos blazed up, and as I took my leave of him he said: 'All the funds of the Greek Government in exile are at the disposition of your paper!'[116]

'Words are my instruments but not my servants'[117]

Poetry may have been important but in the world of little magazines money was even more necessary. Jonathan Bolton believes that Douglas's development owed a great deal to his association with the *Personal Landscape* group.[118] As Durrell put it in his tribute to Bernard Spencer they saw themselves 'as a band of intellectual mercenaries, being pushed about all over the globe at the behest of invisible powers, but remaining always united in a curious sort of way – bound together by this war-period and by the fact that we were all case-hardened travellers, in a way displaced persons; too much travel had turned us into professional expatriates, restless for the flavour of foreign cities.'[119] Douglas had told Blunden that after the war he intended to pursue a career with the British Council[120] which, as Bolton says, suggests that he saw a future beyond the war, that his 'death-wish' was limited.[121] Bolton argues that Douglas's poetry 'from the time of his first brush with the Cairo literary scene in May–June 1942 begins to adopt certain general characteristics that were common to the *PL* group – poems bearing place-name titles, a keen interest in the landscape and culture of the Middle East, and a careful avoidance of political ideology, on the one hand, and emotionalism and introspection on the other.'[122] It is difficult to deny that Douglas's poetry was affected by *Personal Landscape*.

Douglas's poetry of the desert is unblinking in its attitude to what the poet observed, from dead soldiers to Cairo streets. Certainly he wrote some of his most celebrated poems in the Middle East.

When he wrote 'Simplify me when I'm dead' Douglas hadn't seen any action and we tend to see that his poetry from the desert campaign takes a more clinical view of bodily decomposition, partly because of the fame of 'Vergissmeinnicht'. He certainly saw plenty of it in the desert but it is a mistake to read Douglas merely as a poet of death, although G. S. Fraser remembered his talk in Cairo as 'all of burning tanks and roasting bodies'.[123] 'The Two Virtues', for instance, dated 'Sarafand 1941', is an almost metaphysical dissection of love. Having announced himself as possessing 'the two virtues of a lover/hot as the Indies, mutable as weather', Douglas exposes love's paradox:

> Then being true to love, I'll be inconstant;
> not to be so, would cheat you of the last
> and most of love, sorrow's violent
> and rich effect. In that lagoon the lost,
> the drowned heart is wonderfully recast
> and made into a marvel by the sea,
> that stone, that jewel tranquillity.[124]

But it is as a poet of death that Douglas will be remembered. The much-anthologized 'Vergissmeinnicht' is worth considering.

> Three weeks gone and the combatants gone,
> returning over the nightmare ground
> we found the place again, and found
> the soldier sprawling in the sun.
>
> The frowning barrel of his gun
> Overshadow him – as we came on
> that day, he hit my tank with one,
> it was like the entry of a demon.
>
> And smiling in the gunpit spoil
> the soiled picture of his girl
> who has written: Steffi, Vergissmeinnicht
> in a copybook gothic script.
>
> We see him, almost with content
> abased, and seeming to have paid
> and mocked at by his own equipment
> that's durable when he's decayed.

But she would weep to see today
how on his skin the swart flies move;
the dust upon the paper eye
and the burst stomach like a cave.

For here the lover and killer are mingled
having one body and one heart;
here death, who had the soldier singled,
has done the lover mortal hurt.[125]

As Edna Longley says: 'By displacing his own feeling into the girl's hypothetical reaction, Douglas combines the intimate ("how on his skin") with the universalised: "lover and killer" (which includes loved and killed) ... [the poem] also exemplifies Douglas's unusual blend of statement and mimesis ... In "Vergissmeinnicht" Douglas not only consonantally imitates the thick intricacy of "a copybook gothic script", or increases horror though dynamic assonance ("the burst stomach like a cave"), but in the "mingled" r, l and t sounds of the last quatrain makes his final statement sensuously and musically incontrovertible.'[126] G. S. Fraser considered 'Vergissmeinnicht' Douglas's most skilful poem. He pointed out in his Chatterton Lecture:

What gives us the effect, for instance, in the first stanza, of the tanks lumbering bumpily and relentlessly on is a kind of wheeling motion in the stanza itself, repetitions and a concealed rhyme:

'Three weeks *gone* and the combatants *gone*,
returning over the nightmare *ground*
we *found* the place again, and *found*
the soldier sprawling in the sun ...'

What saves the stanza about the dead soldier's appearance from being merely repellent is, again, the deliberate formality of the syntax and the choice of a literary adjective – 'the swart flies' not 'the black flies', and an objective precision of statement, without emotional commentary, that gives an effect of icy pity:

'But she would weep to see to-day
how on his skin the swart flies move;
the dust upon the paper eye
and the burst stomach like a cave.'

And in the last stanza the effect of aesthetic distance, of the whole experience being held in control, is clinched by the eighteenth-century antithesis:

'And death who had *the soldier* singled
has done *the lover* mortal hurt.'[127]

I don't agree with Fraser's view of the word 'swart'. It doesn't seem to me that Douglas's lexical choice is one of the high spots of this lyric. The poet's point – that the appearance of the flies is not dependent on the provenance of the dead meat around which they crowd – would be better served by a word that is common to the vocabulary of all readers rather than an archaism.

Douglas's unblinking view of death is on show again in another poem of the war, 'Dead Men', which was published in 1943 in *Citizen*. The corpses of dead soldiers are eaten by wild dogs, 'a casual meal for a dog'. We see it again in 'How to kill':

Under the parabola of a ball,
a child turning into a man,
I looked into the air too long.
The ball fell in my hand, it sang
in the closed fist: *Open Open*
Behold a gift designed to kill.

Now in my dial of glass appears
the soldier who is going to die.
He smiles, and moves about in ways
his mother knows, habits of his.
The wires touch his face: I cry
NOW. Death, like a familiar, hears

and look, has made a man of dust
of a man of flesh. This sorcery
I do. Being damned, I am amused
to see the centre of love diffused
and the waves of love travel into vacancy.
How easy it is to make a ghost.

The weightless mosquito touches
her tiny shadow on the stone,
and with how like, how infinite
a likeness, man and shadow meet.
They fuse. A shadow is a man
when the mosquito death approaches.[128]

The poem has an ABCCBA rhyme structure, but it is the half-rhymes, 'dust' and 'ghost', 'stone' and 'man', and the contradictions, the ball as a child's toy used as an image of adult war, the 'gift' of death, that carry the poignancy of the enemy soldier's sudden eclipse. The 'dial of glass', that is the telescopic sight on the rifle the poet is using, puts a distance between the killer and the killed. As William Scammell noted,[129] it is a familiar trope in Douglas's poetry – the 'house ... of glass' in 'The House', the lens of 'time's wrong-way telescope' in 'Simplify me when I'm dead', the 'separative glass cloak of strangeness' in 'Syria', the 'powerful enlarging glass' of the fish's eye in 'The Marvel' and 'with a crash I'll split the glass' in 'On a return from Egypt'. The rifle's lens is a way of objectifying the victim, of imposing some detachment on the scene. This distance is persuasively attributed to the influence of the Cairo poets by Jonathan Bolton in *Personal Landscapes: British Poets in Egypt during the Second World War*. Bolton quotes Douglas's poem 'Syria' and comments:

In Douglas's metaphor, the glass cloak of the self is a somewhat unnecessary shield against the amiable intentions of the Syrians, an aspect of the self that protects one against friends but leaves one vulnerable to the enemy, which induces a hatred for the Other. Later, Douglas would recognize the need to shed this glass cloak of strangeness, the cultural conventions of his upbringing, and to accept differences in both the Orient and in himself. He succeeded in this endeavour to some extent, discovering an aspect his Other that he designated '*Bête Noire*' – 'my particular monster.' Like Durrell's 'autre,' Douglas's beast represents a sort of demonic presence inhabiting both interior and exterior spaces, and he described it variously as 'A medieval animal with a dog's face,' 'a toad or worm curled inside the belly,' 'a persuasive gentleman,' and 'a beast on my back.' Such disparate and varied representations of the Other suggests, as Douglas put it, 'how amorphous and powerful' are those elements of the self that have not been incorporated into one's personality. Much of the poetry Douglas wrote during his tour of duty in the Middle East represents an attempt to articulate his sense of personal fragmentation and the loss of will inaugurated by his consciousness of the Other.[130]

As Scammell says, 'The detachment is psychologically truthful and … tactically essential to survival – though what survives is not much more than a "ghost".'[131]

But Douglas's eye was not only cast unflinchingly on dead bodies. 'Enfidaville', for instance, is a masterpiece which is barely a war poem at all, although it recounts the devastation of a town as a consequence of war:

> In the church, fallen like dancers
> lie the Virgin and St Thérèse
> on little pillows of dust.
> The detonations of the last few days
> tore down the ornamental plasters,
> shivered the hands of Christ.
>
> The men and women who moved like candles
> in and out of the houses and the streets
> are all gone. The white houses are bare
> black cages; no one is left to greet
> the ghosts tugging at doorhandles,
> opening doors that are not there.
>
> Now the daylight coming in from the fields
> like a labourer, tired and sad,
> is peering about among the wreckage, goes
> past some corners as though with averted head,
> not looking at the pain this town holds
> seeing no one move behind the windows.
>
> But they are coming back; they begin to search
> like ants among their débris, finding in it
> a bed or a piano, and carrying it out.
> Who would not love them at this minute?
> I seem again to meet
> the blue eyes of the images in the church.[132]

As Scammell says, this is the most 'directly tender' of Douglas's poems.[133] It concerns the devastation of Enfidaville while he was recuperating from injury and is about war in the wider sense, the consequences for a community rather than an individual. It is difficult not to respond emotionally to the 'ghosts tugging', the 'tired and sad' daylight, the re-crucified Christ. Who indeed would not love the town's reluctant victims?

'Desert Flowers' is just as carefully observed as 'Enfidaville', and nor does it rely on a dead supporting cast:

1

Perched on a great fall of air
a pilot or angel looking down
on some eccentric chart, the plain
dotted with the useless furniture
discerns dying on the sand vehicles;
squashed dead or still entire, stunned
like beetles: scattered wingcases and
legs, heads, appear when the dust settles.

But you who like Thomas come
to poke fingers in the wounds
find monuments and metal posies.
On each disordered tomb
the steel is torn into fronds
by the lunatic explosive.

2

On sand and scrub the dead men wriggle
in their dowdy clothes. They are mimes
who express silence and futile aims
enacting this prone and motionless struggle
at a queer angle to the scenery,
crawling on the boards of the stage like walls,
deaf to the one who opens his mouth and calls
silently. The decor is a horrible tracery
of iron. The eye and mouth of each figure
bear the cosmetic blood and the hectic
colours death has the only list of.

A yard more, and my little finger
could trace the maquillage of these stony actors:
I am the figure writhing on the backcloth.

3
Living in a wide landscape are the flowers –
Rosenberg, I only repeat what you were saying –
the shell and the hawk every hour
are slaying men and jerboas, slaying
the mind. But the body can fill
the hungry flowers and the dogs who cry words
at nights, the most hostile things of all.

But that is not new. Each time the night discards
draperies on the eyes and leaves the mind awake
I look each side of the door of sleep
for the little coin it will take
to buy the secret I shall not keep.

I see men as trees suffering
or confound the detail and the horizon.
Lay the coin on my tongue and I will sing
of what the others never set eyes on.[134]

Here death is a natural part of life. The jerboas are killed by the hawk just as men are killed by shells. But the aside to Isaac Rosenberg is a knowing reference to the fact that it had all been done before. In 'Break of day in the trenches' Rosenberg had written of the danger of war to the 'poppies whose roots are in man's veins.'

Two other Cairo poems, 'Cairo Jag' and 'Behaviour of fish in an Egyptian Tea Garden', are deservedly well-known. 'Cairo Jag' is a colourful account of sleazy Cairo life but it isn't condescending, nor does it attempt the demotic even when Douglas describes Marcelle's 'shrieks in Arabic about the fare'. The poem is, as Scammell says,

> … an evocation of the city and its fantastical inhabitants, partly a meditation on the marvels of this particular war, in which soldiers are metamorphosed into tourists and tourists into corpses … it is all one whether you eat cake, indulge in casual sex or dedicate yourself to 'dull dead' love, like Marcelle, shriek or beg, dance or sleep. Tragedy and comedy are interchangeable, like the echoing phrases 'stamped *Décédé*' (deceased) and 'stink of jasmin'. Whichever 'conventions' you choose to read the evidence by, whatever drug you favour – drink or sex, 'fatalism' or 'hashish', love or death – whether you reach for a bundle of letters or of rags, whether you live sleeping ('somnambulist') or

sleep dying 'scattered on the pavement like rags' it all amounts to the same bewildering fate, signed and decreed by 'Holbein's signature', the skull. Just an hour or two away from all this, however, is a 'new world' which parodies both the world of nature ('gun barrels split like celery', 'metal brambles', 'all sorts of manure') and the fleshpots of Cairo. Here the logic of desire has been taken to its ultimate conclusion. There is neither sense nor propriety in this brave new world, in which men trade their lives for 'a packet of chocolate and a souvenir of Tripoli'.[135]

'Behaviour of fish in an Egyptian tea garden', on the other hand, conveys a sense of menace without describing the boisterous sleaze of Cairo life:

As a white stone draws down the fish
she on the seafloor of the afternoon
draws down men's glances and their cruel wish
for love. Slyly her red lip on the spoon

slips-in a morsel of ice-cream; her hands
white as a milky stone, white submarine
fronds, sink with spread fingers, lean
along the table, carmined at the ends.

A cotton magnate, an important fish
with great eyepouches and a golden mouth
through the frail reefs of furniture swims out
and idling, suspended, stays to watch.

A crustacean old man clamped to his chair
sits coldly near her and might see
her charms through fissures where the eyes should be
or else his teeth are parted in a stare.

Captain on leave, a lean dark mackerel
lies in the offing, turns himself and looks
through currents of sound, The flat-eyed flatfish sucks
on a straw, staring from its repose, laxly.

And gallants in shoals swim up and lag,
circling and passing near the white attraction;
sometimes pausing, opening a conversation:
fish pause so to nibble or tug.

Now the ice-cream is finished, is
paid for. The fish swim off on business:
and she sits alone at the table, a white stone
useless except to a collector, a rich man.[136]

'Behaviour of fish in an Egyptian tea garden' does project a sleazy atmosphere but it does so subtly. Its loose ABBA rhyme structure makes use of half-rhymes to evoke a sense of unspoken danger.[137] The men-fish are brilliantly drawn. The magnate with 'great eyepouches and a golden mouth', is the man of the world we all recognize. Scammell asks: 'What could be more evocative of commercial power and the Midas touch?' As he says '"Gold" might have done nearly as well, but "*golden*" picks up "Ma*gn*ate" … The inversion in the next line ("through … frail reefs … swims out") subtly mimes his negotiation of the tables and chairs; "frail reefs", with its hint of paradox, is a marvellous image for the wrought-iron delicacy of the furniture; and the sentence fizzles out in its delayed verbs – what he is is more interesting than what he does. The stanza virtually abandons rhyme, or stretches it to near invisibility ("fish/out", "mouth/watch"), yet it is difficult to see how it could be improved.'[138] The cotton magnate is the epitome of powerful menace. As is the Captain on leave, the 'lean dark mackerel' who 'lies in the offing', though for a different reason. The cotton magnate's power stems from his wealth, the Captain's from recent action. He 'turns himself' and in that moment we sense his malignant power as he 'looks/through currents of sound'. It is a skill that is beyond the average bar room predator. Similarly the old man whose 'teeth are parted in a stare' is instantly recognizable. As Scammell says, he is 'dying or dead, all but his teeth and claws, extremities which relate him to the woman he stares at, who is also characterized by hands and mouth, although they are at an earlier stage in the cycle of appetite.'[139] We are surprised by the fact that his teeth are parted in a stare. Usually we stare with the eyes not the mouth, but this old man is unable to stare normally because there are fissures where his eyes should be. It's hard to imagine a more menacing image drawn in just a four-line stanza. The reader naturally feels protective of the woman with such predatory males around, but she needs no help. We sense that she has been here before. At the end of the poem she sits alone while the men-fish have left to go about their business.

* * *

On 17 November 1943 the Sherwood Rangers embarked for the UK. Their ship sailed to Augusta in Sicily and stayed in the harbour for a week. On 1 December they sailed through the straits of Gibraltar and then, on 9 December, 'a heavenly sight greeted our eyes: the green hills of Scotland and red-tiled roofs of a Clydeside town. The Scots on shore cheered us, and we lined the rail to wave back at them. There were prolonged discussions as to the best way of whipping all the silk stockings, spirits, cigarettes, Turkish delight and other souvenirs through the Customs ... "Any man who has anything to declare, take one step forward." Not a man moved. The Customs inspection was over.'[140]

They reached Chippenham Park, near Newmarket, on 12 December and leave began. Douglas enjoyed three weeks' leave in England, and began the last year of his life.

6

1944

In the new year of 1944 'invasion preparations throbbed into life',[1] but the Allied troops were not over-confident. As Lindsay says, 'the defences of the Atlantic Wall had been developed for years. First the ports had been fortified, then the Pas de Calais as being the narrowest part of the channel and therefore the most likely scene for a British invasion. There were underwater barricades and booby-traps of all types, strongpoints protected by armour-plate and concrete, mines, wire and obstacles of every sort.'[2]

At the beginning of February the Sherwood Rangers went to a firing camp near Kircudbright to prepare for tank warfare in European conditions. Douglas's squadron went back to Chippenham Park to train for waterproofing their vehicles. They were told that they must expect to deal with up to five feet of water on wading ashore.[3] 'A' Squadron was now re-equipped with American Sherman tanks and Douglas became the squadron's second-in-command. Christopherson was impressed by Chippenham Park, 'a most delightful country estate surrounded by a park ... the beauty of which was somewhat spoilt by the erection of Nissen huts and concrete tracks for tracked vehicles.'[4] Christopherson recalled that days at Chippenham Park quickly became hectic. Douglas's squadron was passed over for the amphibious tank training, much to their delight. According to Christopherson they couldn't see 'a Sherman tank waddling in the sea like an overgrown duck under heavy shellfire.'[5]

Douglas began another 12 days' leave in February 1944 but he wasn't enjoying himself. 'I feel so savage about this filthy country', he wrote to Jean Turner, 'and the way it is run that I couldn't say anything entertaining or amusing. I now live in a tin hut and a sea of mud (which freezes every few days) and no laundry arrangements or showers, with about ½ as much food as civilians are eating.'[6]

Douglas didn't write much while he was training in the UK but started again when he went to war. A month after Douglas died *Lilliput* ran his story,

'Death of a Horse', about a wounded horse being put down, presumably based on his experiences at the Army Equitation Centre at Weedon. It showed how he had taken in the sights of the war and could render them graphically, without sentimentality, for the reader:

> Some one said: 'The old hammer type.' Simon stiffened. But he was ready to see the horse stagger, desperately trying to stand, twisting on the ground in its death agony. The orderly's hand fell. He struck the tube and there was a small report. The horse's knees gave way so quickly that it was hardly possible to mark its fall. It lay still, only stiffened and relaxed its legs once; the suddenness of its death was shocking.
>
> 'Now the jugular vein', said the vet. He had a knife, and inserted it about halfway down the horse's neck, so as not to spoil the skin, he said. The blood poured out exactly in the manner of water from a burst drain. The vet stood in blood, with blood running all round him, and blood jetting up over his hand. He held his thumb in the incision and said casually: 'Take particular note of the colour': it was black, and reminded Simon of Homer's adjective. And at this point another man arrived, who wore a curious costume of sacking, already soaked in old blood. This was the knacker, whose business was to cut the horse up and remove it.[7]

Douglas had learned to witness death dispassionately. Another story, 'The Little Red Mouth', was written at Beni Yusef in 1943 but not published until 1970, in *Stand*, describes death with equal detachment. While thinking of a girl in Alexandria, Sylvie (Milena?), he stumbles across an enemy corpse:

> It was like a carefully posed waxwork. He lay propped against one end of the pit, with his neck stretched back, mouth open, dust on his tongue. Eyes open, dulled with dust; and the face, yellowish with dust, a doll's or an effigy's. He had a woollen cap on his head. The blood on his shirt was brown, hardened until the cloth was cardboard: he had opened his haversack and taken out towels to wrap round his legs against the flies. But the blood had soaked through the towels and the flies had defeated him. A crowd of flies covered him: there were black congregations of them wherever the patches of blood were, and they were crawling on his face in ones and twos. His left hand was raised, supported in the air apparently by rigor mortis, the fingers crooked as though taking hold. It was this seeming to be arrested in motion, which made the pose so vivid. The right hand clutched together a corner of the towel, as if he had seized it at that moment, when a wave of pain washed over him. Pain, a climax or orgasm of pain, was expressed in his face and attitude as I

would not have believed a motionless body and countenance could express it. It is not too much to say his position was a cry of pain.[8]

Another story, 'Giuseppe', about an Italian parachutist in the desert, remained unpublished. It is equally unemotional in its depiction of desert fighting:

> Looking up, he saw the mountain tower against the rosy dawn sky. He heard a scream from somewhere high above him, a human scream approaching rapidly like the scream of a shell; and saw the body of a man fly out, black against the sky for a moment, making the motions of a swimmer, and screaming. The man fell with a short noise of impact on the hard ground, doubled up in an impossible position. Now the bodies of live men began to hurtle down, one after another. Most of them screamed. After a quarter of an hour, the falling of men stopped as a hailstorm stops, suddenly. In the early morning sunlight of a Tunisian winter day, Giuseppe saw the single figure of a Maori standing high up, outlined against the sky. He was shouting down a message to the dead men. 'That's what you bastards get for machine gunning our wounded,' he yelled, in a voice cracked with fury and exhaustion.[9]

But Douglas's most significant prose work was, of course, *Alamein to Zem Zem*, his memoir of the desert war, or the part that he had played in it anyway. He found a publisher in Meary James Thurairajah Tambimuttu, a Sri Lankan (before the days of Sri Lanka) poet who founded and edited *Poetry* (London), which became perhaps the most respected poetry periodical in the UK, certainly the best-known. In July 1943 Tambimuttu started a book-publishing business, Editions Poetry London, which published Elizabeth Smart's *By Grand Central Station I Sat Down and Wept*, David Gascoyne's *Poems 1937–1942*, Lawrence Durrell's *Cefalu*, Henry Miller's *The Cosmological Eye* and *Sunday After the War*, Vladimir Nabokov's *The Real Life of Sebastian Knight*, Cleanth Brooks's *Modern Poetry and the Tradition* as well as Douglas's *Alamein to Zem Zem*. *Alamein to Zem Zem* is a thinly disguised account of desert warfare in the Sherwood Yeomanry. The names of the main characters are changed but it is not difficult to work out who is who.

Tambimuttu had written to Douglas's mother in July 1942 saying that he had been trying to contact Douglas with a view to publishing his poetry in *Poetry* (London) 'and the two yearly anthologies that I collect for Messrs Faber and Faber'.[10] Douglas wrote to his mother on 13 August 1942 instructing her to submit 'A Storm', 'Soissons 1940', 'Song: Do I venture away too far',

'The Marvel' and 'Absence' and any other poems she liked.[11] The sonnet 'A Storm' is dated 1936 and was published in *Bolero* (Oxford) in Spring 1939.[12] 'Soissons 1940' is a beautiful lyric. Its Nietzschean final stanza is a new note in Douglas's poetry:

> You who believe you have a kind creator
> are with your sire crowding into twilight,
> as using excellent smooth instruments
> material man makes himself immense.
> Oh you may try, but can't deny he's right
> and what he does and destroys makes him greater.[13]

'Song' is dated Cairo, 12 September 1941. It repeats two lines at the end of every stanza: 'for the poisonous sea and a cruel star/the one by day and one at night have charmed me.' It is another example of Douglas's anticipated death. While it celebrates the 'hot coast of your love' the poet himself is charmed by sea and star and is not long for this world:

> So I believe I'm doomed my dear
> That I have jilted myself and you
> and when the sea's embalmed me
> I'll fade into the deceitful blue ...[14]

'The Marvel', also dated 1941 ('Linney Head, Wales [May] 1941'), has a less personally elegiac tone but is a masterpiece of realism:

> A baron of the sea, the great tropic
> swordfish, spreadeagled on the thirsty deck
> where sailors killed him, in the bright Pacific.
>
> Yielded to the sharp enquiring blade
> the eye which guided him and found his prey
> in the dim country where he was a lord.
>
> Which is an instrument forged in semi-darkness;
> yet taken from the corpse of this strong traveller
> becomes a powerful enlarging glass
>
> reflecting the unusual sun's heat.
> With it a sailor writes on the hot wood
> The name of a harlot in his last port.

For it is one most curious device
of many, kept by the interesting waves,
which I suppose the querulous soft voice

of mariners who rotted into ghosts
digested by the gluttonous tides
could recount many. Let them be your hosts

and take you where their forgotten ships lie
with fishes going over the tall masts –
all this emerges from the burning eye.

And to engrave that word the sun goes through
with the power of the sea
writing her name and a marvel too.'[15]

William Scammell writes that this poem is a 'marvel of Hughesian power and delicacy, leavened by a detached yet wholly engaging wit.'[16] Scammell has Ted Hughes's selection of Douglas's poetry in mind but the use of nature to enquire about creation is a Hughesian trope generally. 'Absence', originally 'The Garden', is dated 1940 and conjures a rather Yeatsian scene:

The long curtained French-windows conceal
the company at dinner by candlelight.
I am the solitary person on the lawn,
dressed up silver by the moon.
The bush on my left sleeps, the tree on my right
is awake but stays motionless to feel …'[17]

Tambimuttu's negotiating tactics were beginning to annoy Douglas, who wrote to Tambimuttu's assistant Betty Jesse on 10 October 1944: 'About Tambi, is it any good my saying will he either make up his mind or send it [*Alamein to Zem Zem*] back because someone else wants it? I am writing a letter to this effect & I'll put it in this one. If you think it's a good thing, give it to him. If not, tear it up. Needless to say I don't want it (the book) back & no one else wants it.'[18] The letter of the same day to Tambimuttu survives in the British Library: 'I don't know if you want the Diary to publish or not. But will you make up your mind by the 24th of March, & let me know by then, because if you don't want it or if I don't hear by that date I shall submit it to someone else on the 24th, who seems interested in it. I can't afford to wait because of military engagements which may be the end of me – so that date is final.'[19] Tambimuttu had agreed to publish a collection of Douglas's poems and his diary of his part in the desert campaign and he wrote to Tambimuttu again in March:

> I don't agree about the £10 for various reasons. I've signed my part of the 2nd agreement & Dorothy Sauter has signed yours, and you have, therefore agreed to publish two books. Now if you could use the majority of my poems in the War Diary, I wouldn't mind you amalgamating the two – although I still don't see why I should be punished, by a fine of £10, because you have changed you mind … you are paying me only for my MS and you are using a lot of illustrations. That's OK. I submitted them with the MS, as part of it. But the fact remains that if you had got anyone else to illustrate it you'd have had to pay him extra, above the advance royalties you're paying me. So it seems a bit hard to deduct £10, doesn't it? … So I suggest –
>
> That deducting £10 is not very fair – Betty agrees with me, I believe.
>
> That you don't deduct it.
>
> That you publish the diary first & wait a bit and then
>
> Publish *Bête Noire* [the poems] – by which time I can let you have about 20 more poems – I already have 5 or 6.
>
> After all – you have signed agreements to publish two separate MSS – & I think in the end you'll be glad if you do publish both.[20]

Douglas was concerned that a combination of military censors and libel lawyers would emasculate *Alamein to Zem Zem* but he recognized the need to have it read. His Colonel (Spence) had read it and Douglas wrote to Betty Jesse about his response: 'Keith, I have read and enjoyed the ms. Now I am not quite sure what is expected of me. I assume I don't have anything to do with the security angle, which seems OK. From the Regimental angle it seems a pity to go for Black Michael ['Sweeney Todd' in *Alamein to Zem Zem*] to such a tune, if in the final form he is to be easily identifiable. Some of your remarks about Flash [Piccadilly Jim in *Alamein to Zem Zem*] will raise a storm, but I suppose it's a free country and you can write what you like within the limits of the law.'[21] The widow of Colonel 'Flash' Kellett had seen it,[22] and his commanding officer, Stanley Christopherson, had read it but Douglas knew that he was treading a fine line in *Alamein to Zem Zem*. His letter to Tambimuttu of March 1944 contains an instruction to him to let *Poetry* (London)'s solicitors look it over regarding possible libel.[23] He wrote again to Betty Jesse on 26 March 1944: 'A Censor may raise objections to the detailed description of wireless procedure during battle – giving away code names, etc. It might be as well – since Censors are not only ignorant but dimwitted and in a hell of a hurry, to mention that this procedure has been completely cancelled and is never used – and anyway the enemy knew all about it, because we captured an interception officer who explained all our own codes to us.'[24] Tambimuttu published it in 1946, with sixteen poems printed as an appendix, two years after Douglas's death. The last letter we have of Douglas's is a long justification of *Alamein to Zem Zem* to Jocelyn Barber. She had read the proofs and reviewed them carefully: 'Perhaps you will get to like it … We'll see.'[25] Tambimuttu recalled Douglas in his memoir in *Poetry London*: 'I can say without any hesitation that Douglas's view of life and his actions were the most sound and realistic that any man of our generation can come to. He accepted the greatest gifts of this life and lived with passionate sincerity. His conclusions about life in action are the most mature any poet has arrived at in this war.'[26]

Douglas spent Sunday 2 April 1944 with Betty Jesse. He wrote to her the following Tuesday: 'Sunday was a wonderful day. These haywire occasions are what make people friends – and lovers, sometimes. In a sense everything couldn't have gone wronger, but in hundreds of other ways that was made up. If I never see you again, it's not a bad time to remember as the last day of a short and peculiar friendship, which has made me happier – and of course unhappier – than I have been for a long time.'[27] He went on to suggest a weekend together at an hotel in London.

Douglas told her a story of army life in the UK in this long letter:

> I've been on another long drive, to a small place on the coast where there is a tank range. In the evening we split up (7 officers) and 4, me included, went to see Charles Laughton in *The Man from Down Under* – lowest form of modern melodrama, about the worst film of the last five years. The other 3 went to a pub. When we came out of the flicks we hunted everywhere for the missing three for about an hour, and were at last going home, about 12.00, when we met John (the irresistible Frenchman), in the street. He said 'Frightfully sorry, we forgot the time. The others are playing billiards in a pub about 100 yards up across the crossroads'. I raised a tremendous display of authoritative wrath and said he, and they, could bloody well stay and play billiards for the rest of

the night, and we'd send a truck for them at 5.0 in the morning. The rest of us then drove off, turned right at the crossroads, switched off the engine and lights and shoved the truck up an alley. We were then going to creep back and surprise them all as John was telling them the bad news. But unfortunately we couldn't find the bloody pub anywhere and didn't find it, until we had staggered round for an hour, having several adventures with canned black Yanks and knocking at every door where a chink of light showed. At last we rang a bell somewhere and a most presentable girl answered the door. We said; 'Have you got 3 Sherwood Rangers officers inside?' she replied: 'Yes. Are you Keith? We got in and found the three of them drinking gin, in a horrible cold alcoholic rage. We hadn't meant them to be under the strain for an hour, but it had certainly shaken them. However, all was amicably settled at last and apart from losing the way and landing up with the front wheels of the truck in the sea, we got home without incident.

Betty predictably rejected his proposal that they spend a weekend together at an hotel and Douglas wrote to her again on 10 April to say that he understood why she didn't want 'to sneak about in & out of hotels' but to suggest an evening together nearer to where he was: 'In any case I don't think London will see me again for some time: I don't think they'll let us far out of here.'[28] He did get to London again, however, and saw Betty once more before he was shipped out to fight again. He wrote to her on Monday 24 April to describe his adventurous journey back to the camp: 'I got back at 3.30 a.m., & John [Bethell-Fox] went on by train & did his 4 mile walk. I did my 4 mile walk, too; and slept a bit & then ran 2 miles at 7.30, pretty energetically, to my surprise. Then I went on a TEWT – tactical exercise without troops, i.e., wandering across country in a lot of jeeps eating cheese sandwiches and maintaining military arguments.'[29] He told her another story which only serves to illustrate his lack of gallantry: 'I went (by order) to a Brigade HQ cocktail party with the Colonel and some other stooges. I met a god awful land girl with some titled relations and a moustache, who writes short stories and poems so I drank about 4 gins and took her in the garden. After a bit I took her glasses off – to see if she looked better without them, but she didn't. I didn't want to be nasty so I said: "You want to keep your face moving, then you'll be all right". Thinking this over I didn't think it sounded so nice after all, so I tried to improve it by saying she had a nice dress anyway: but unfortunately about then I spilt a pint of gin down the front of her so I had to walk her round the garden to get her dry. She seemed to be incorrigibly wet ...' One wonders what the incorrigibly wet and probably bewildered girl made of Douglas's no doubt well-meant attention. Douglas clearly loved Betty deeply, as attested by the rest of this letter, but it is doubtful that he ever saw her again. Douglas justified his adventure in London in a letter to Jocelyn Baber: 'I'm not allowed a night in London any more, but I got there for an experimental day last Sunday travelling all night and arriving 0420, whereupon I went to sleep on a sofa (and subsequently in a bath at Nuffield House [a residential club for military officers]). I left London 9.54 and arrived in my bedroom (I live in some style now, during the fattening process) at 03.30. Sleep at 03.30½. This was barely legal, as I didn't leave until after midnight on Saturday (i.e. on Sunday morning) and considered 03.30, on the other hand as Sunday night. Anyway, I said goodnight to the Colonel on Saturday night and good morning to him on Monday at breakfast, so he had no cause to complain.'[30] Douglas's chop logic doesn't seem to have got him into any trouble. Douglas's mother wrote to John Waller and G. S. Fraser about Douglas's planning that 'on his return to England he had ceased to see a future. The futility of making plans overwhelmed him. He saw no future after "D" Day. Not that he was morbid about it. He made the best of the last of his leave.'[31]

At the end of April 1944 his squadron moved to Sway, a top-security camp in the New Forest, where they enjoyed what Lindsay called 'comfortable billets'.[32] Douglas certainly liked it. He wrote to Jocelyn Baber, his mother's employer, from the camp: 'This neighbourhood is delightful and flowers and sunshine attend us all the time however oily and mechanical our duties are. I get up (not from choice) and go for a swim at 7.30 every morning, though I can't say it seems to make me any fitter.'[33] There was a huge amount of planning as the Normandy landings were a massive Allied initiative. All leave was cancelled and the Sherwood Rangers were 'put into Purdah and wired in'. As Lindsay said, the cancellation of leave caused much resentment among the troops affected, but 'it was difficult for the planners to know what else to do; the stoppage of leave, the control over diplomatic mail bags and the sudden disappearance of well-known war reporters was bound to cause comment.'[34] The squadron left Sway in the middle of May for Hursley Park, near Winchester, their assembly area preparatory to the invasion.

On 2 June they left for Southampton Docks. As Lindsay records, the journey was 'flawlessly organised, and civilians en route were wonderfully kind and dashed out at halts to give us tea and buns – to the great disgust of the Military Police who had (quite rightly) been ordered to keep us in Purdah till the bitter end.'[35] The weather was good when they embarked that evening but broke on the evening of 3 June, when the operation was postponed for 24 hours. The weather was still bad on the following day, when the troops moved off from the quay and anchored outside Southampton Water. At midnight on 5 June 1944 the armada set sail for France. Lindsay described the voyage: 'There were heavy seas with waves five or six feet high. Our craft were open to the skies, and the green seas came washing over. There was much preparation to be done en route; we were wet through and got no sleep. All were, or felt, sick. But one good thing about the voyage was the absence of attentions from the Luftwaffe or enemy craft. The bad weather had driven the enemy's surface patrols into port, and our heavy bombing had temporarily upset the working of the German radar system.'[36]

Lindsay quotes from Douglas's friend Lieutenant Stuart Hills's account of the landings:

> By the time that 'A' [Squadron] arrived, 90 minutes later, to support the Devons, there was already great congestion on the beaches. Small wonder – for on the first three tides the armies had to land a total of 130,000 men and 20,000 vehicles. One check point inland counted 18,836 vehicles passing in one day – one vehicle every four seconds for 24 hours ... Major Stanley Christopherson was to contact the Essex Regiment, but the road was fiercely congested, and he had no vehicle other than his tank. Luckily he spotted a police horse, already saddled. He hopped out of his tank, commandeered the police horse, and in his overalls, carrying his tin hat and map-case, rode three miles to find the Essex Colonel.

> Well – here we were, landed in France, with not too much damage done. When the Führer heard of it, he boasted 'they won't stay more than nine hours'; he sent an order to Runstedt [commander of German forces in France] that 'the enemy must be annihilated by the evening of today' – the 6th of June ... 'A' Squadron and the Essex Regiment leaguered that night just short of Bayeux.[37]

The Sherwood Rangers were, according to Lindsay, the first troops to enter Bayeux.[38] Keith Douglas survived in Normandy for about 48 more hours. Lindsay described the circumstances of Douglas's death:

> That night, Lieut. Keith Douglas and Lieut. John Bethell-Fox went on a foot patrol into the village of St. Pierre. The inhabitants were all cowering in the cellars and afraid to talk, but at least one citizen was found who revealed that there were twenty Germans in the village. Turning a corner, Douglas and

Bethell-Fox suddenly came face to face with a German patrol of an officer and eight men; both patrols beat it hastily in wild surprise.

On the 9th we managed to hold on to Point 103 [high ground which overlooked the villages of St. Pierre and Fontenay] although there was heavy anti-tank fire and 14 enemy tanks were reported round our positions. The country was close and awkward and it seemed impossible to find a good 'hull-down' position from which to attack the enemy tanks.

Lieut. Keith Douglas and Lieut. John Bethell-Fox, out on another patrol, came to a stream which was defended by a strong enemy group. They got out of their tanks to compete the reconnaissance on foot. As Keith Douglas was running along a ditch he was killed by a mortar shell.[39]

Captain Keith Douglas, killed in action on 9 June 1944, was mentioned in despatches.[40] John Bethell-Fox described his last few hours with Douglas in his unpublished memoir, *Green Beaches*:

Keith and I were sent down on a reconnaissance on the right to see if we could get close under cover of an orchard, and find out what was really going on.

We trundled down the slope, and smashed our way into this orchard, driving along the parallel lines of trees. I pulled off another piece of aerial in this orchard. Eventually we reached the end of the orchard and there, in front of us, was the river. Another fifty yards on was a small church, and a road with vehicles churning up and down. We both got out of our tanks, took a few grenades and a German sub-machine gun; Keith had collected that somewhere, and crawled out of the orchard to the river. We waded across and started crawling towards the church; we had hardly moved a few yards when a burst of machine gun fire came flying over us, cutting the branches, and making the leaves flutter down gently on our heads. With a common accord we turned round, sprinted and dived in the river, with bullets flying after us. Until then we had been lucky; we now had to get back to our tanks across an open field. Keith thought the best would be to swim up stream for a hundred yards, then climb out and make a dash for the orchard. The Jerries would not be expecting us to come up then and we might get across without trouble. Once in the orchard it was only a matter of seconds before we had jumped down our turrets, started and away! We rolled back quietly to our Squadron; we knew what we wanted to know. Jerry was there and he could not come this way with tanks because of the river, which although not very deep, had very sharp and high banks which would not be negotiable in a tank.

When I reached the top end of the orchard I saw tracer flying over Keith's tank which was two hundred yards ahead of mine. Those tanks I had seen earlier on in the low ground must have opened up, defilading the open we had to cross before rejoining our squadron. Those shells followed Keith all the way; by that time I was half way across the open, and when they decided to fire at me, I was going too fast even for their guns. The squadron was lining the hedgerows along the top of this crest, these hedgerows formed a square, and per force the squadron was in the formation of a square. I drove inside the square through a gap in the trees, swung sharp right and directed my tank alongside the Colonel's. I saw Keith's tank on the left, with Keith climbing out at the turret and running along the hedgerow towards Stanley's. Two tanks were moving up on the right, but for some reason, instead of being inside the hedge, they were driving *outside*, in full view of the enemy guns. The next minute both were hit, and I remember vividly that picture of surprised pale men, diving to the ground, or struggling to get out of their tanks.[41]

Bethell-Fox tended to some injured men in a ditch and then again reported to Christopherson:

The Colonel looked worried. He turned round when I arrived, and looked at me in the manner of a child telling a doubtful story, 'John,' he said 'I have bad news for you.' I did not answer, just felt a little puzzled and waited for what was to follow. The Colonel then said 'Keith has been killed.' I simply stared at him and felt hot tears running down my cheek, Keith my only real friend and he who had been through the whole African business, of all people, Keith had to be killed after three days in France … I managed to go and see Keith later on, in company with the Padre. We said a short prayer over his grave and I said my last goodbye to him.

Letters to the poet's mother after his death show that Keith Douglas was a lovable character. Admittedly, letters of condolence to a dead soldier's mother are not the place for realism but there is genuine affection in them. One such came from the Sherwood Rangers' chaplain, Leslie Skinner, who buried Douglas:

He was a lovable boy and made a splendid officer. His warm hearted friendliness, his brave unselfishness, his talents with words and in drawing, and perhaps above all his eager joy of living are very vivid in our memories. He was loved and greatly respected by all, and is much missed in his Squadron and indeed throughout the whole Regiment. Because of these things – and many more – he meant much to us, and we can therefore to some extent at least, understand how keenly you must miss him, to whom he meant so much more. Keith will always live in our minds as one of those happy folk who never tired of sharing his happiness or in passing on his zest for living and appreciating the loveliness of things around him ... I laid him to rest under a shadow of a tree on the hill mentioned [near Andrieu in Normandy], overlooking the valley running down to St. Pierre and Tilly, and his grave is marked with a temporary wooden cross I made, until such time that he can be re-interred in an official War Cemetery.[42]

Tony Rudd recorded that his aunt had not been surprised by the poet's death. 'She had always regarded him as somebody who courted danger. Indeed, his stories of his role in the Syrian campaign confirmed that he had as usual been taking every kind of risk. She had always felt that he was somehow doomed; somehow fated to find life difficult; destined to be in frequent awkward collision with events or people. She had always felt uncomfortable in his company. She had deplored the times when, in my compliant fashion, I had copied Billy's noisy way of eating soup and swallowing it from the front of the spoon instead of the side ... poor Billy killed, we learned later, by a single shell splinter in the head.'[43] Christopherson, too, wrote to Jo: 'I knew Keith so well ... He was one of the bravest people that I have ever met, and simply didn't know the meaning of the word fear; and I don't say that because he was your son ... We shall miss him most terribly.'[44]

John Waller remembered that he knew Douglas 'both in Oxford where he struck me as slightly sombre and reserved, though with dark expressive eyes, and again in Cairo, in September 1943, after he had returned from his desert campaigns and was kicking his heels in boredom at a base camp outside the city ... He seemed to me then an unaffected person and a natural poet, modest sometimes to the point of seeming shy, but shrewd in judgment and understanding. Perhaps in those last meetings I felt him also to be a little depressed and cynical.'[45]

POSTSCRIPT, POST-MORTEM

David Roberts (the Christ's Hospital history teacher who greatly admired him) wrote Douglas's obituary in *The Blue*:

> With his death Christ's Hospital has lost one of its most gifted and vivid personalities. No one who knew him even casually is likely to forget him, and to those of us who knew him well his loss is irreparable.

> Friendship with him was liable to be an exacting and exciting adventure, for he expected much of his friends but not more than he himself was prepared to give in return. His generosity was one of his most attractive characteristics. No man or woman could do the generous thing more gracefully and in this respect he was full of the most delightful surprises. People who did not know him well were apt to find him alarming, for he could be ruthlessly outspoken and disconcertingly direct in his criticism. Nothing, however, that he said or did, could in the end hide his essential lovableness ... He became one of the ablest of our History Grecians. Eileen Power, who once saw some of his work, gave this estimate of him. 'This boy has nearly all the gifts; he has a clear incisive mind which is reflected in his prose, and when a subject appeals to him he shows real imagination and understanding. But he will not make a scholar or a historian; he is much more likely to be a painter, a novelist or a poet.' This prophecy came true.[1]

Tambimuttu championed Douglas's work. Editions Poetry London published *Alamein to Zem Zem* in 1946 and Waller and Fraser's edition of Douglas's 'Collected Poems' in 1951; Tambimuttu also published individual poems by Douglas in *Poetry London* before and after the poet was killed. 'Pas de trois' and 'Stars' were published in the October–November 1942 edition; 'The Prisoner' in the November–December 1942 edition; 'The Offensive' was published in the following issue; 'The Hand', 'John Anderson' and

'Leukothea' appeared in the September–October 1947 edition; 'Words', 'Song' ('Do I venture away too far …'), 'The Knife' and 'Leukothea' (again) were published in the November–December 1947 issue; 'Adams' and 'I Experiment' were in the June–July 1948 edition; 'Poem: I listen to the desert wind', 'Egypt', 'The House' and 'Negative Information' were published in the November–December 1948 edition; 'Absence', 'Gallantry' and 'The Prisoner' appeared in the May 1949 edition; and 'Actors waiting in the wings of Europe', 'Farewell poem' and 'I watch with interest, for they are ghosts' were in the November 1950 edition.

Tambimuttu was fired from *Poetry London* on 31 March 1949 and his diligence was not rewarded well. Waller and Fraser's edition of Douglas's *Collected Poems* contained a barely concealed reference to Tambimuttu's apparent interference: 'Certain posthumously published poems were printed from the earlier instead of the obvious later revised versions. But worse – whole poems were found to have been altered and emended by other hands than the author's and this frequently to their detriment.'[2] As A. T. Tolley said in *The Poetry of the Forties*, Tambimuttu's 'decided achievements deserve to be disengaged from the legends that have come to surround him.'[3] They now have. The *Poetry London* archive has been discovered and deposited at the British Library[4] and it is clear that, as Chris Beckett says, 'the repetition over time of colourful anecdote has substituted for serious consideration of his achievements, and unsubstantiated innuendo has littered partisan histories and memoirs of the period.'[5] Tambimuttu has now been exonerated. The widely held view that he was a charlatan is exposed as a myth: his catholicity of selection is now perceived as a strength. As Beckett says, 'Tambimuttu published, quite deliberately side-by-side, the out-moded but still widely-read Georgian poetry of Walter de la Mare, European poetry in translation (Hölderlin and Rilke), and work from young poets whose work impressed (Keith Douglas, Charles Causley, R. S. Thomas, Alan Ross); he championed the virtues of minor poetry, published Americans abroad (Henry Miller and Anaïs Nin) and welcomed English surrealism (Philip O'Connor and David Gascoyne). Above all, Tambimuttu welcomed modernity, even if for some readers the poetry of W. S. Graham proved to be quite incomprehensible.'[6] The tone of Waller and Fraser's criticism was picked up by reviewers of Douglas's collected poems.[7]

'What does the archive tell us about the matter?' Chris Beckett asks, before going on to answer his own question:

It tells us that March [the new owner of *Poetry London*] decided to proceed with a collected edition shortly after Tambimuttu was dismissed (2 April 1949). Several letters from Tambimuttu to March written in the months immediately following show him anxious to edit the volume: 'Have you written to Keith Douglas's mother? I should like to edit the book (as I arranged with Keith) & possibly Blunden could supply a foreword & I hope I will be given a fee for the work.' Returning from Paris in May ... Tambimuttu found himself barred from the office and released from all editorial responsibilities, including the editing of Douglas's poems. An angry letter to March followed: 'You have no right to edit the Keith Douglas since you don't know the history and scope of his work. I found very valuable Keith things scattered & strewn in odd corners & you will never recognize them. You or no one else could ever say whether anything was missing.' By June, Tambimuttu was resigned to March's decision: 'OK about K. Douglas but for accuracy's sake you'd better let me see a final draft of the book since many of the poems have a case history & Keith left the editing of particular lines to me [...] Keith also gave me final instructions as to their publication & I must see that everything is in order. I would hate it if anything went wrong.'[8]

Beckett gives just one example which makes the demonization of Tambimuttu very clear:

A particularly pointed remark in the notes supplied by Waller and Fraser concerns the poem 'The House' (composed in 1941): 'This is the poem as Douglas wrote it,' the editors unequivocally declare: 'The version published in *Poetry London* contains unwarranted alterations made in the MS text in some foreign hand.'[9] The inference of the note – wrapped within the term 'foreign hand' – is that the alterations were made by Tambimuttu. Here, perhaps, we may think, is an instance of a whole poem being 'emended', as the 'Editors' Preface' had forewarned. A careful comparison of the text of the poem as it first appeared in *Poetry London* and as it was subsequently printed in *Collected Poems* reveals that Waller and Fraser made several textual changes. And yet, if we turn to the more recently published definitive text in Desmond Graham's scholarly edition of Douglas's poems, we find that Graham's text of 'The House' agrees exactly with the text published by Tambimuttu (with the exception of the placement of two commas, and a palaeographical preference for 'suspicious' over 'suspicions'). In his letter to March, Fraser borrowed the diction of war from Douglas to suggest, extremely, that *mutilation* had occurred: 'There is very definite and real evidence of altering of some of the poems in handwriting – and for that matter of their being printed in a mutilated state'.

On Graham's authority, the revisions of 'The House' are in Douglas's hand. Yet Fraser's private letter to March is unambiguous in its accusation that the hand of alteration – the mutilating hand – was Tambimuttu's, and the choice of the term 'foreign hand' over 'unidentified hand' in the note to the poem seems to reflect this conviction: since the handwriting had been putatively identified by Waller and Fraser as Tambimuttu's, the latter term, arguably the more common expression, is shunned in favour of a term that has the advantage of suggesting the guilty (and 'foreign') editor in all but name. Significantly, in the subsequent edition of the poems (published, ironically, by Faber and Faber in 1966), in which Waller and Fraser's texts were maintained, the note to 'The House' is trimmed to a less provocative statement, although the editors are still assertive of their judgement: 'Another version appeared in *Poetry London*, but the present version is the correct one'.[10]

One consequence of all this 'animosity and … innuendo, the disproportionate accusation and the readiness to discredit in public'[11] was that Douglas's poetry was ignored for several years, although as Beckett admits, it was 'at odds with the hesitant self-regard and ironical tone of the Movement poetry of the 1950s'.[12] Douglas's next prominent outing was Fraser's British Academy lecture in 1956, in which Fraser again referred to the 'inaccurate texts' which he and Waller had corrected. Ian Hamilton's damning review of the republished editions of *Poetry London* in the *Times Literary Supplement* of 19 February 1971 repeated the familiar criticisms of Tambimuttu's interference[13] but by then Geoffrey Hill had reviewed Ted Hughes's selection of Douglas's poetry in *Stand*. Hill's verdict was that Douglas 'must count as one of the finest British poets of the last 40 years'[14] and that should have been enough to ensure the poet's reputation, but he was soon forgotten and in spite of Desmond Graham's pioneering work[15] Keith Douglas remains largely ignored.

NOTES

ABBREVIATIONS

The following abbreviations have been adopted for frequently recurring publications, names and places. Otherwise, for printed sources the usual convention has been adopted of a full citation in the first instance, followed by a recognizable shortened form.

AZZ   Keith Douglas, *Alamein to Zem Zem* (1946).

BL   British Library ADD MS.

Christopherson   James Holland (ed.), *An Englishman at War: The Wartime Diaries of Stanley Chistopherson DSO MC TD 1939–45* (2014).

CP   Desmond Graham (ed.), *Keith Douglas Complete Poems*, third edition (2000).

Graham   Desmond Graham, *Keith Douglas 1920–1944: A Biography* (1974).

LET   Desmond Graham (ed.), *Keith Douglas: The Letters* (2000).

PM   Desmond Graham (ed.), *Keith Douglas: A Prose Miscellany* (1985).

INTRODUCTION

1. James Holland, *Normandy '44: D-Day and the Battle for France* (2019), 249.
2. Christopherson, 390–1.
3. Christopherson, 390–2.
4. Vernon Scannell, *Not without Glory: Poets of the Second World War* (1976), 38.
5. Alan Seeger, *Poems* (1917), 144.
6. *Poetry Review*, Vol. 31, 211.
7. Graham, 79.
8. Based on the dates in CP.
9. *Keith Douglas: Poems Selected by Ted Hughes* (1964), ix.
10. Ibid., 12–14. Hughes's analysis owes much to G. S. Fraser's pioneering Chatterton Lecture, delivered to the British Academy in 1956.
11. Robin Fedden . (eds), *Personal Landscape: An Anthology of Exile* (1945), 14.

12. Declan Ryan, 'The battle against Bullshit', *Times Literary Supplement*, 7 June 2019, 10.
13. G. S. Fraser, *Keith Douglas, A Poet of the Second World War*, Chatterton Lecture, British Academy (1956), 108.
14. Keith Douglas, 'Poets in this war', *Times Literary Supplement*, 23 April 1971, 478.
15. Lorrie Goldensohn, *Dismantling Glory: Twentieth-Century Soldier Poetry* (2003), 102.
16. 'Nach Auschwitz ein Gedicht zu schreiben, ist barbarisch'. See https://www.marcuse.org/herbert/people/adorno/AdornoPoetryAuschwitzQuote.htm
17. Scannell, 17.
18. Scannell, 22.
19. LET, 328.
20. R. Caddell and A. Flowers, *Basil Bunting: A Northern Life* (1997), 41.
21. Robert Graves, 'The Poets of World War II', *The common asphodel* (1949), 310–11, 312. Graves also blamed the professionalization of the armed forces since the First World War.
22. See C. Reilly, *English Poetry of the First World War* (1986), xix.
23. Jon Stallworthy (ed.), *The New Oxford Book of War Poetry* (2014), xl.
24. Victor Selwyn (ed.), *Return to Oasis: War Poems and Recollections from the Middle East 1940–1946* (1980), xii.
25. Selwyn, xiii.
26. Selwyn, xxiv. Douglas's poems were not included in the original *Oasis* but he was generously represented in the 1980 reissue.
27. Scannell, 20.
28. Selwyn, xviii.
29. Keith Douglas, *Collected Poems*, edited by John Waller and G. S. Fraser (1951), xix–xx. See also Norman Ilett in *The Christ's Hospital Book*, 294.
30. Fraser, Chatterton Lecture, 93–4.
31. Letter to Maurice Wollman quoted in Keith Douglas, *Collected Poems*, edited by John Waller, G. S. Fraser and J. C. Hall with an introduction by Edmund Blunden (1966), 15.
32. *The Blue*, January 1966, 64–5.
33. *The Blue*, September 1966, 249–50.
34. *The Blue*, September 1966, 250–1.
35. *The Blue*, January 1967, 45–6. This anecdote may be opaque for those who are not familiar with rugby. The Scottish national team plays in navy jumpers and white shorts. Morpurgo argues that Douglas convinced the opposition that both were international players.
36. Waller, Fraser and Hall, 18.

CHAPTER I:
CHILDHOOD

1. See Philipp Blom, *Fracture: Life and Culture in the West 1918–1938* (2015), 31–3.
2. A. J. P. Taylor, *English History 1914–1945* (1967), 139. This section draws heavily on Martin Pugh's *We Danced all Night: A Social History of Britain between the Wars* (2009).

3. W. B. Yeats's friend, Constance Markievicz, was the first female MP but she had refused to take the seat she won for Sinn Fein.
4. Blom, 11.
5. Douglas's birth certificate records that he was born at 6 Garden Road. His father's occupation was given as Civil Engineer.
6. From over 14 per cent in 1900 to just over 8 per cent in 1920 (Pugh, 44). Douglas was originally vaccinated in February 1920. Medical Interrogatory, 17 September 1931, Christ's Hospital archive.
7. *The Times*, 24 January 1920, 16.
8. *Tunbridge Wells Advertiser*, 30 January 1920, 16.
9. See Graham, 3–5.
10. National Archives J 77/2738/4904.
11. See Graham, 2.
12. Christopher Budgen, *Cranleigh: A History* (2008), 1.
13. Michael Miller, *Around Cranleigh* (2005), 42, 86–7.
14. Graham, 1.
15. Graham, 5.
16. See Graham, 5.
17. BL 56359L
18. BL 59833, folio 40.
19. Keith Douglas, *Collected Poems*, edited by John Waller and G. S. Fraser (1951), xx.
20. Graham, 9.
21. BL 59833, folio 2.
22. BL 59833, folio 1.
23. BL 59833, folio 2.
24. Brotherton Library, Leeds, Special Collection, BL 20c Douglas/1.
25. PM, 13.
26. Brotherton Library, Leeds, Special Collection, BL 20c Douglas/1/Box E/A.
27. Brotherton Library, Leeds, Special Collection, BL 20c Douglas/1 (a) 1.
28. Graham, 24.
29. Pugh, 49.
30. PM, 15–16.
31. Graham, 10.
32. Brotherton Library, Leeds, Special Collection, BL 20c Douglas/1/Box I (a) I.
33. *Edgeborough Guildford 1913–1929*, a list of boys and teaching staff by term. KD first appears on page 262.
34. Presentation to Mr and Mrs A. H. James on their retirement from the school 28 July 1934, Edgeborough School archive.
35. BL 56355, folio 7.
36. BL 59833, folio 5.
37. Waller and Fraser, xv.
38. BL 56355, folio 8 and BL 59833, folio 6.
39. BL 56355, folio 21.
40. BL 59833, folio 14. Douglas's Edgeborough reports are in the Brotherton Library, Leeds.

41. Brotherton Library, Leeds, Special Collection, BL 20c Douglas/1/Box I (a) I.
42. BL 56355, folio 19.
43. Graham, 13, 263. Report in Brotherton Library, Leeds.
44. BL 59833, folio 15.
45. Brotherton Library, Leeds, Special Collection, 20c Douglas (a) A.
46. Edgeborough School Magazine, April 1927, 25.
47. BL 56355, folio 66.
48. *Edgeborough Guildford 1913–1929*.
49. Edgeborough School Magazine, April 1927.
50. BL 56355, folio 29.
51. Brotherton Library, Leeds, Special Collection, BL 20c Douglas/1/Box I (a) I.
    'Boundaries' in cricket are the result of batsmen being aggressive and hitting to
    the edge of the pitch for four or six runs. It is a typical piece of childish bravado.
52. BL 56355, folio 27.
53. BL 56355, folio 29.
54. BL 56355, folios 64–5.
55. BL 56355, folio 65.
56. Brotherton Library, Leeds, Special Collection, 20c (a) A.
57. See BL 59833, folio 7.
58. Brotherton Library, Leeds, Special Collection, 20c (a) A.
59. BL 56355, folios 79–81. Douglas had a real taste for sweets and requests for them
    pepper his letters to his mother.
60. Brotherton Library, Leeds, Special Collection, 20 c (a) A.
61. BL 56355, folios 71–4.
62. Graham, 16.
63. BL 56355, folios 76–8.
64. Brotherton Library, Leeds, Special Collection, BL 20c Douglas/1/Box I.
65. Brotherton Library, Leeds, Special Collection, 20c Douglas/1/Box I (a) A.
66. Edgeborough School Magazine, August 1929, 45.
67. Edgeborough School Magazine, August 1929, 49.
68. Edgeborough School Magazine, December 1929, 12.
69. Brotherton Library, Leeds, Special Collection, BL 20c Douglas/1/Box I (a) I.
70. *Edgeborough Guildford 1913–1929*.
71. Edgeborough School Magazine, December 1929, 2.
72. BL 56355, folio 39.
73. BL 56355, folio 31.
74. Brotherton Library, Leeds, Special Collection, 20c(a) A.
75. BL 56355, folios 35–6.
76. BL 56355, folio 38.
77. BL 56355, folios 71–4.
78. The manuscript of this poem is in BL 56355, folios 71–2.
79. Graham, 15.
80. National Archives J 77/2738/4904.
81. Letter 11 February 1931. BL 56355, folios 43–7.

82. BL 56355, folios 68 and 83.
83. Brotherton Library, Leeds, Special Collection, 20c (a) A.
84. Brotherton Library, Leeds, Special Collection, BL 20c Douglas/1/Box A-J.
85. Edgeborough School Magazine, July 1930, 42.
86. Graham, 18–19.
87. Brotherton Library, Leeds, Special Collection, 20c (a) A.
88. Brotherton Library, Leeds, Special Collection, 20c (a) A.
89. Brotherton Library, Leeds, Special Collection, 20c (a) A.

CHAPTER 2:
HAPPINESS SEEMS JUST TO HAVE STARTED

1. A line from the poem, 'On leaving school'.
2. Keith Douglas, *Collected Poems*, edited by John Waller and G. S. Fraser (1951), xv.
3. George Gissing, *New Grub Street* (1891, 2016), 28.
4. Waller and Fraser, xv–xvii.
5. Ilett, N. (ed.), *The Christ's Hospital Book* (1953), 292–3.
6. *The Blue*, March 1993, 61.
7. He was moved to Middleton B later.
8. Letter of 3 February 1931 from A. H. James, Christ's Hospital archive.
9. Letter and nomination form at Christ's Hospital archive.
10. Letter from M. J. Douglas, 29 April 1931 to the clerk to Christ's Hospital, Christ's Hospital archive.
11. Letter from A. H. James, 28 April 1931, Christ's Hospital archive.
12. Letter from M. J. Douglas 29 April 1931 to the clerk to Christ's Hospital, Christ's Hospital archive.
13. Undated letter from M. J. Douglas (but late June 1931) to the clerk to Christ's Hospital, Christ's Hospital archive.
14. Letter of 30 June 1931, Christ's Hospital archive.
15. Documents in Christ's Hospital archive.
16. Letter of 5 August 1931 from M. J. Douglas to the clerk to Christ's Hospital, Christ's Hospital archive.
17. Document in Christ's Hospital archive.
18. Medical Interrogatory, 17 September 1931, Christ's Hospital archive. His paternal grandfather had suffered badly from asthma.
19. Medical Interrogatory, 17 September 1931, Christ's Hospital archive.
20. BL 56355, folio 89.
21. BL 56355, folio 90.
22. BL 56355, folio 105.
23. BL 56355, folio 94.
24. BL 56355, folio 92. A Grecian is a sixth-former.
25. BL 56355, folio 94.
26. BL 56355, folios 96–8.

27. BL 56355, folios 100–1.
28. BL 56355, folio 103.
29. BL 56355, folio 107.
30. Graham, 22–3.
31. CP, 126–8.
32. CP, 129–30. See BL 53773, folios 132–5.
33. *The Blue,* January 1966, 62–8.
34. LET, 89.
35. LET, 123–4.
36. G. S. Fraser, *Keith Douglas, A Poet of the Second World War* (1956), 98–9.
37. *The Outlook,* July 1933, 20, December 1933, 6 and 8.
38. *The Outlook,* April 1935, 5 and 16.
39. Graham, 19. Tony Rudd was born in Wandsworth on 24 April 1924.
40. Anthony Rudd, *One Boy's War* (1990), 103.
41. BL 53773, folio 1. Douglas visited the ancient Roman town of Aquileia during his visit to Gorizia. It is about 34 kilometres southwest of Gorizia, in north-eastern Italy.
42. BL 59834, folio 48.
43. BL 59834, folios 52–3.
44. Graham, 45–6.
45. See below, p. 80.
46. CP, 7.
47. Rudd, 102–3.
48. Quoted in Graham, 23.
49. Graham, 56.
50. See Graham, 263.
51. *The Outlook,* March 1932 (no. 33), 6–7. This essay is not collected in PM.
52. *The Outlook,* December 1934 (no. 41), 8. I have retained the typographical error in line 6.
53. *The Outlook,* December 1934 (no. 41), 14. Although the title is a well-known quotation from Catullus this isn't a translation of the Latin poet's elegy to his brother.
54. Graham, 23.
55. William Scammell, *Keith Douglas: A Study* (1988), 63.
56. *The Outlook,* April 1935 (no. 42), 4.
57. *The Outlook,* April 1935 (no. 42), 5.
58. *The Outlook,* July 1935 (no. 43), 10. A draft of this story is in the BL 56358, folios 4–5.
59. *The Outlook,* July 1935 (no. 43), 14.
60. Brotherton Library, Leeds, Special Collection, 20c (a) K.
61. Graham writes that a contemporary of Douglas's couldn't recall the names of Stephen Spender, T. S. Eliot, W. H. Auden or Cecil Day Lewis being mentioned in class (Graham, 28).
62. *The Outlook,* December 1935 (no. 44), 3. I have followed the orthography of the original published version.

63. Graham, 27. His assertion that Douglas's poem also draws on Edith Sitwell's *Façade* sequence seems a little fanciful but more plausible than the suggestion that 'The Alchymist' is an 'imitation' of Pound's poem.

64. *The Outlook*, December 1935 (no. 44), 4–5. 'Si quis mala viderit pabula terrae' is a quotation from Ovid's 'Remedia Amoris'. 'Tu operans sis secretus horum' is a quotation from 'Secretum secretorum', a 10th century Arabic work of astrology.

65. See, e.g., Guerney's translation, published in 1931, 95–102.

66. *The Outlook*, December 1935 (no. 44), 15.

67. *The Outlook*, December 1935 (no. 44), 14.

68. *The Blue*, June 1935, 213.

69. Mark Thompson, *The White War: Life and Death on the Italian Front 1915–1919* (2008), 133.

70. BL 59834, folio 31.

71. BL 56355, folios 108–9.

72. He once said that the boys in the school were the machine and that he was the oil.

73. Flecker was wounded in 1916 and invalided out of the Army in 1917.

74. BL 56355, folio 110.

75. *The Outlook*, April 1936 (no. 45), 4.

76. Although T. S. Eliot used the archaism 'sempiternal' in line 2 of 'Little Gidding'.

77. *The Outlook*, April 1936 (no. 45), 7. I have used the original punctuation and retained the 1936 wording.

78. BL 59834, folios 57–9.

79. BL 59834. Henry Williamson's *The Star-Born* (1933) is a mystical novel, essentially about the second coming of Christ. It has something in common with T. F. Powys's *Mr. Weston's Good Wine*, published six years before Williamson's novel.

80. Scammell, 6.

81. Williamson, 181.

82. *The Outlook*, April 1936 (no. 45), 12. I have again used the original punctuation. The .303 cartridge was adapted for use with machine guns after the First World War.

83. Cecil Day Lewis and Edmund Blunden (eds), *Collected Poems of Wilfred Owen* (1963), 55.

84. Graham, 38. Douglas's OTC Certificate 'A', awarded on 10 March 1936, is in the Brotherton Library, Leeds.

85. Noel Burdett, cited in Graham, 40.

86. *The Blue*, July 1937, 232.

87. Graham, 51.

88. *The Outlook*, April 1936 (no. 45), 13.

89. Graham, 28. Although the murals, depicting incidents in the history of the Christian church, were painted between 1913 and 1923 and are not particularly pre-Raphaelite.

90. Graham, 28.

91. BL 56360, folios 3–6.

92. Graham, 41.

93. Keith Douglas, *Collected Poems*, edited by John Waller, G. S. Fraser and J. C. Hall with an introduction by Edmund Blunden (1966), 18–19.
94. BL 56356, folio 2.
95. BL 56356, folio 3.
96. *The Outlook*, spring 1980. Douglas's poem, 'Dejection', was accepted in 1938.
97. Scammell, 62.
98. In line 3 'intricate patterned' becomes 'delicate-patterned'. The accompanying linocut is unattributed but given the Japanese theme it is reasonable to suppose it is Douglas's.
99. *The Outlook*, July 1936 (no. 46), 8.
100. *Keith Douglas: Poems selected by Ted Hughes* (1964), ix.
101. Scammell, 68.
102. *Keith Douglas: Poems selected by Ted Hughes*, ix.
103. *The Outlook*, December 1936 (no. 47), 14.
104. Although the final four lines are included in the notes as a variant.
105. BL 56357, folio 68.
106. Although Scammell thinks this rhyme 'enhances meaning', Scammell, 63.
107. *The Outlook*, December 1936 (no. 47), 18.
108. Some may also hear an echo of 'Ode to a Nightingale' in the 'winking cups'.
109. Scammell, 63.
110. Scammell, 63–4.
111. Vernon Scannell, *Not without Glory: Poets of the Second World War* (1976), 32.
112. BL 56355.
113. BL 59834, folio 72.
114. *The Blue*, June 1936, 229.
115. *The Blue*, June 1937, 193.
116. *The Blue*, June 1938, 199.
117. Graham, 30.
118. BL 56357, folio 71.
119. Graham, 51.
120. BL 56359. Desmond Graham takes the opposite view of it (Graham, 39) but the drawing in 'Book Diary', folio 20, of an obviously Jewish figure gesturing at a tall, short-haired worker with a spanner seems to show where Douglas's heart lies.
121. BL 56359.
122. Graham records one of Christ's Hospital's Latin teachers, D. S. Macnutt, saying that Douglas was always near the top of the class 'with no great effort on his part', and another Latin teacher, A. H. Buck, recalled that 'you could sense his boredom with you and the grammar you were trying to pump into him: in some cases it amounted to a (doubtless deserved) contempt.' His English teacher remembered him as 'antagonistic' and 'intolerant'. Graham, 29.
123. Graham, 52–3.
124. There are notes on Eliot's *Selected Essays* (1932) in Douglas's 'Book Diary', BL 56360.
125. BL 56360, folios 21–2.

126. He was mentioned with credit for both sports in *The Blue* (November 1936, 9–11; 19 December 1936, 66; February 1937, 110; July 1937, 235).
127. Graham, 37.
128. *The Blue*, March 1937, 165.
129. *The Blue*, December 1936, 70.
130. There was no provision for English as a sixth form subject.
131. Graham, 48.
132. Hornsby's recollections are recorded in Graham, 49.
133. Brotherton Library, Leeds, Special Collection, BL 20c Douglas/1/Box I.
134. Brotherton Library, Leeds, Special Collection, BL 20c Douglas/1/Box I.
135. According to *The Blue*, December 1937, 77, he was awarded school rugby colours, on 6 November 1937, for the match against St John's School, Leatherhead. He was characterized in *The Blue* of March 1938 (111) as a 'front-row forward who improved a lot and was chiefly effective in the tight scrums, where his packing was admirable and his front-row tactics disconcerting to opponents. A fair tackler, but unable to get off his feet when dribbling fast. Bad hands.'
136. Brotherton Library, Leeds, Special Collection, BL 20c Douglas/1/Box I. Graham (54) contradicts her.
137. The editorial notes that accompany the cover designs do have a ring of Douglas passive-aggressiveness: 'Editorial (compulsory). The Editor is overwhelmed; hardly could he sit down to a quiet smoke in his study without hordes and hordes of people trooping in with reams of reams of printable stuff. His only regret is that certain things were crowded out which would normally have been printed. A less cynical Editor might almost begin to have to have a suspicion that one or two people are beginning to think that the "Outlook" is worth while.' (From the March 1937 edition.) And, from the July 1938 edition, 'If the Editor must write an Editorial, he would like to point out what a pity it is that some otherwise quite intelligent people have really good essays and poems and linocuts lying about in corners, instead of sending them in to grace the pages of the "Outlook". That is all. He now leaves it to more fluent pens to give you, perhaps, a hint of the Summer Term.' These are very different from the editorials that precede and follow them.
138. Blunt's poem appears in Sir Algernon Methuen's *An Anthology of Modern Verse*, a popular edition in schools. See Graham, 24.
139. He used the Bernard Guilbert Guerney translation but, it seems, from memory as there are some discrepancies.
140. *The Outlook*, March 1937 (no. 48), 12.
141. BL 56359. This piece is misquoted in PM.
142. *The Outlook*, July 1937 (no. 49), 12–13.
143. *The Outlook*, July 1937 (no. 49), 23.
144. Graham, 49.
145. *The Outlook*, July 1937 (no. 49), 25.
146. Scammell, 65–6.
147. *The Outlook*, December 1937, 7.

148. Scannell, 33.
149. BL 56355.
150. LET, 48–9.
151. LET, 52–3.
152. Carol Z. Rothkopf and Barry Webb (eds), *More than a Brother: Correspondence between Edmund Blunden and Hector Buck 1917–1967* (1996), 106. The Earl of Douglas was referred to as 'the Douglas' in Shakespeare's *Henry IV, Part I*.
153. PM, 36. Douglas was awarded an Open Exhibition by Merton College in October 1938.
154. *The Outlook*, April 1938 (no. 51), 9–11.
155. *The Outlook*, April 1938 (no. 51), 22–3.
156. *The Outlook*, April 1938 (no. 51), 16.
157. *The Outlook*, April 1938 (no. 51), 13. This poem, with minor variations, is titled 'On leaving school' in CP. I have quoted the original.
158. *The Outlook*, July 1938 (no. 52), 11.
159. CP, 17.
160. BL 56355, folios 163–7. The poem, 'Dejection', appeared in the March 1938 issue of *New Verse*. G. S. Fraser, in his Chatterton Lecture, said that the poem 'says nothing very much, but says it very agreeably'.
161. BL 56355, folio 163–4.
162. BL 56355, folios 166–7.
163. BL 56355, folio 167.
164. Notably 'Caravan', 'Images', 'Famous Men', 'A Storm' and 'Pleasures', variants of some of which were published while Douglas was at Oxford University.
165. *The Cherwell*, 27 April 1940, 8.
166. Scammell, 66–7.
167. *The Blue*, November 1937, 9.
168. *The Blue*, July 1938, 231.
169. It appeared between a long poem by Frederic Prokosch and a sonnet by Stephen Spender.
170. Graham, 61.
171. *Keith Douglas: Poems Selected by Ted Hughes* (1964), xi.
172. Scammell, 96.
173. See *The Christ's Hospital Book*, 292.
174. Owen Sheers: *Battlefield Poet: Keith Douglas*, BBC4 programme, 2010, www.owensheers.co.uk/works/other-projects/presenting/.
175. BL 56355, folio 111.
176. Cunningham wrote to Douglas's mother in December 1945 to tell her that his son was to be named Keith Douglas Cunningham, and to let her know how proud he was of his friendship with her son. Brotherton Library, Leeds, Special Collection, BL 20c Douglas/1/Box I.
177. BL 56355, folios 170–1.
178. Graham, 62.
179. BL 56360, folios 38–9.

180. Brotherton Library Leeds, Special Collection 20c (a), I. The Lord Kitchener National Memorial Fund provided scholarships for the children of combatants.

181. Brotherton Library, Leeds, Special Collection, BL MS 20c Douglas/1/Box I (a) G.

182. Brotherton Library, Leeds, Special Collection, BL MS 20c Douglas/1/Box I (a) G.

183. *The Blue*, July 1937, 247.

184. Graham, 64.

185. *The Blue*, December 1938, 86.

CHAPTER 3:
THIS CITY EXPERIENCES A DIFFICULT TIME

1. From the poem 'An exercise against impatience'.

2. BL 57977, folio 1.

3. LET 61. Margaret Stanley-Wrench died on 10 January 1974 according to a notice in *The Times* of 12 January 1974. The obituary, by Robert Gittings, that appeared in *The Times* three days later described her as a 'poet and writer of distinction'. She for the most part abandoned poetry after *News Reel and Other Poems* for novels and books for children.

4. Quoted in Graham, 67.

5. It was to be over 20 years until her next collection, *A Tale for the Fall of the Year*, which 'showed her delicate and varied gifts at their best', according to Gittings.

6. Graham, 67.

7. *Poetry Review*, Vol. 31, 127. Waller pointed out that since the First World War Oxford had produced several famous poets, not one of whom had won the Newdigate Prize, and that of the 21 winners of that prize since the previous war none had become a celebrated poet. To be fair to Stanley-Wrench, Waller put his finger on one of her problems. 'She made the mistake of including as many as seventy-five poems, which meant that the twenty-five or so really good ones were swamped.' Twenty-five is certainly overstating the number of good poems but 'They have no memorial', for instance, about the Spanish Civil War, is outstanding.

8. Keith Douglas and Alec Hardie (eds), *Augury: An Oxford Miscellany* (1940), xiv. Douglas wrote to Stanley-Wrench in March 1940 begging her to send some poems for the anthology. BL 57977, folio 7.

9. By the poems 'Heredity' and 'Before midnight'. Douglas selected six of his own poems in *Augury* and his short essay on poetry.

10. LET, 136.

11. *Augury*, 35.

12. *Oxford Magazine*, 25 April 1940.

13. Graham, 85.

14. Graham, 85.

15. BL 57977, folio 3.
16. LET, 66.
17. Merton College Register, 1938. Sassoon's army career started as a non-commissioned officer in the Royal Army Ordnance Corps. He was made 2nd Lieutenant 1941 to 1943, and Lieutenant in the Royal Armoured Corps from 1943 to 1946. Sassoon was stationed at the British Security Mission, Syria, from 1943 to 1944.
18. Carol Z. Rothkopf and Barry Webb (eds), *More than a Brother: Correspondence between Edmund Blunden and Hector Buck 1917–1967* (1966), 109. By 'round turn' Buck presumably meant the full encirclement of an object with a rope.
19. BL 56355, folio 112.
20. Graham, 74.
21. PM, 39.
22. LET, 75.
23. LET, 93.
24. LET, 95.
25. Graham, 76.
26. Rothkopf and Webb, 125–6. Although as his contemporary the poet J. C. Hall recalled 'he was a restless and difficult person in many ways … he didn't mix all that much with what you might call the literary set. He preferred to be on the fringe of it and go out and do more masculine things so to speak.' Owen Sheers, *Battlefield Poet: Keith Douglas*, BBC4 programme, 2010, www.owensheers.co.uk/works/other-projects/presenting/.
27. Rothkopf and Webb, 126–7.
28. *The Blue*, November–December 1944, 22–3.
29. BL 56356, folio 8.
30. LET, 113–14. Abu Taylor was a Nigerian law student at Merton.
31. LET, 121.
32. LET, 140.
33. *The Gazette* reported on page 67 of the 17 February 1940 issue, that readers should not believe 'those knowing people who have been spreading a rumour that THE CHERWELL is (a) losing money, (b) about to leave the scene. In the first place, we would remind tattlers that to spread such a rumour is slander, and in the second place, we have been sold out at the leading newsagents on the second day of publication for every week this term, and our circulation has increased considerably. It is admittedly hard for an undergraduate paper to keep alive, not because of lack of talent or support, but because of the scarcity of advertisements.'
34. LET, 126.
35. *The Cherwell*, 17 February 1940, 78.
36. *The Cherwell*, 2 March 1940, 101.
37. *The Cherwell*, 24 February 1940, 94.
38. *The Cherwell*, 2 March 1940, 106.
39. *The Cherwell*, 9 March 1940.

40. Graham, 99.
41. *The Cherwell*, 27 April 1940, 3–4
42. *The Cherwell*, 27 April 1940, 3.
43. *The Cherwell*, 27 April 1940, 6.
44. *The Cherwell*, 27 April 1940, 7–8.
45. *The Cherwell*, 27 April 1940, 14–15.
46. William Scammell, *Keith Douglas: A Study* (1988), 77.
47. *The Cherwell*, 4 May 1940, 19.
48. *The Cherwell*, 4 May 1940, 19.
49. *The Cherwell*, 4 May 1940, 20.
50. *The Cherwell*, 4 May 1940, 17.
51. See p. 121. The 'John Oligarch' piece is included by Desmond Graham in PM, 63–5. 'Sin' is not.
52. *The Cherwell*, 4 May 1940, 20.
53. *The Cherwell*, 4 May 1940, 21.
54. *The Cherwell*, 4 May 1940, 24.
55. *The Cherwell*, 15 June 1940, 128.
56. Michael Meyer, *Not Prince Hamlet: Literary and Theatrical Memoirs* (1989), 29.
57. Meyer's poem appeared in the issue of 25 May 1940.
58. Meyer, 29.
59. *The Cherwell*, 4 May 1940, 32.
60. *The Cherwell*, 4 May 1940, 32. Douglas was not sympathetic to producers generally. In the 15 June issue he (as 'J. O.') took the producer of Eliot's *Murder in the Cathedral* to task for an unimaginative setting.
61. Max Beerbohm, *Zuleika Dobson* (1911), 319. Beerbohm's only novel is referred to in *The Cherwell* of 11 May 1940, 37.
62. *The Cherwell*, 11 May 1940, 35. The same issue carries a piece by 'W. Douglas', 'The Undergraduate prefers Van Gogh'. Keith Douglas had written about van Gogh at school (BL 56260) and in *The Cherwell*, 27 April, 1940, 7–8. The 11 May issue also carried Douglas's positive review of Herbert Farjeon's play *The Two Bouquets*, at the Playhouse.
63. *The Cherwell*, 11 May 1940, 36.
64. *The Cherwell*, 11 May 1940, 36.
65. BL 59834, folios 94–6.
66. *The Cherwell*, 18 May 1940, 51.
67. *Sunday Chronicle*, 2 June 1940, 2.
68. *The Cherwell*, 8 June 1940, 99.
69. *The Cherwell*, 8 June 1940, 99–100.
70. *The Cherwell*, 8 June 1940, 101.
71. *The Cherwell*, 8 June 1940, 112.
72. *The Cherwell*, 15 June 1940, 119.
73. *The Cherwell*, 8 June 1940, 110.
74. *The Cherwell*, 18 May 1940, 59.
75. *The Cherwell*, 25 May 1940, 67.

76. Mostly positive, the theatre reviews were attributed to 'J.O.', the film review to 'K'.

77. *The Cherwell*, 25 May 1940, 76.

78. Scammell, 78.

79. *The Cherwell*, 1 June 1940, 83.

80. *The Cherwell*, 1 June 1940, 84–5. 'J.O.' (John Oligarch perhaps, so Keith Douglas) contributed a review of *Destry Rides Again*, starring James Stewart and Marlene Dietrich, which he found 'untidy', to the 1 June issue.

81. *The Cherwell*, 15 June 1940, 115.

82. *The Cherwell*, 15 June 1940, 116–17.

83. *The Cherwell*, 18 May 1940, 52.

84. *The Cherwell*, 25 May 1940, 74.

85. *The Cherwell*, 1 June 1940, 89.

86. *The Cherwell*, 25 May 1940, 78.

87. *The Cherwell*, 1 June 1940, 91. Rampton refences Douglas's article, 'The undergraduate fallen from his high estate', in the 2 March issue. Walter Douglas was at the Ruskin School of Drawing.

88. *The Cherwell*, 18 May 1940, inside back cover.

89. *Merton College 1939–1945* (1947), 5–21.

90. BL 57977, folio 6.

91. Robin Darwall-Smith, *A History of University College, Oxford* (2008), 469.

92. Darwall-Smith, 471.

93. Joshua Levine, *The Secret History of the Blitz* (2015), 22.

94. Darwall-Smith, 470–1.

95. Levine, 24–5. The story is told in a more lurid version in Douglas Grant's memoir, *The Fuel of the Fire* (1950), 21: 'A pacifist stole a sniper's rifle from an armoury and lay in wait at the top of the college tower. He fired three times. And I turned round at the first shot to see a friend clutching his belly as the blood gushed through his fingers on to the path. He fell dead on the spot, and two other men were wounded.'

96. Graham, 98.

97. LET, 64–5.

98. *The Cherwell*, 27 April 1940, 3–4.

99. Graham, 86.

100. Graham, 86.

101. *Keith Douglas, Collected Poems*, edited by John Waller, G. S. Fraser and J. C. Hall with an introduction by Edmund Blunden (1966), 18.

102. *The Cherwell*, 27 April 1940, 8.

103. LET, 70.

104. LET, 73.

105. Graham, 71.

106. LET, 88. In a later letter to Toni Beckett Douglas acknowledged that the one thing Betty realized was that he was 'trying to have confidence in myself in the face of a conviction that I'm no use' (LET, 91).

107. Graham, 76.

108. Graham, 78.
109. BL 57977, folio 6.
110. LET, 80.
111. LET, 101.
112. LET, 81. *Un Carnet de Bal* is an iconic French film released in 1937.
113. LET, 81–2.
114. LET, 82.
115. LET, 85.
116. LET, 86.
117. LET, 87.
118. *Times Literary Supplement,* 7 June 2019, 10.
119. Graham, 91.
120. Graham, 84.
121. LET, 92.
122. LET, 93.
123. LET, 96.
124. BL 9833, folios 21–2.
125. LET, 99.
126. LET, 102.
127. LET, 102–3.
128. LET, 107.
129. LET, 112.
130. Although Douglas did recognize that his letter was 'maudlin and ridiculous' (LET, 114).
131. LET, 113.
132. LET, 118.
133. LET, 118–19.
134. LET, 119–20.
135. LET, 121.
136. LET, 119.
137. LET, 122.
138. See Douglas's letter to Toni, LET, 126–8.
139. LET, 132.
140. LET, 135.
141. LET 141–2.
142. Graham, 97.
143. Meyer, 29–30.
144. LET, 142–3. Douglas had enlisted in the 3rd Cavalry Training Regiment of the Warwickshire Yeomanry at Manor Road, Oxford, on 7 September 1939. He gave his permanent address as The Rectory at Withyham in Sussex and declared that he had been Sergeant and in charge of the Demonstration Platoon of the Junior Division of Christ's Hospital OTC from 1934 to 1938 and a member of the Oxford University OTC Cadet Horsed Cavalry Squadron from 1938 to 1939. He was passed as medically fit for service in the Cavalry of the Line the following day and transferred

to the Army Reserve. At that time he was 5 foot 10 inches tall and weighed 153
pounds. He had a 'fresh' complexion, blue eyes and medium brown hair.
145. LET, 144.
146. LET, 152.

CHAPTER 4:
THE FILTHIEST SCRUFFY HOLE I'VE EVER FALLEN IN

1. BL 56355, folio 115. The date of enlistment on his Service and Casualty Form is
   18 July 1940.
2. BL 56356, folio 8.
3. LET, 145.
4. Weedon was closed after Douglas's group had departed.
5. Graham, 107.
6. BL 56355, folios 117–19.
7. LET, 151–2.
8. Brian Gardner (ed.), *The Terrible Rain: The War Poets 1939–1945* (1987), 130. The
   'Budolph Hotel' is the Randolph Hotel.
9. Graham, 109.
10. Gardner, 125.
11. Gardner, 126.
12. LET, 153.
13. LET, 153–4.
14. LET, 154–5. Natasha Litvin was later Stephen Spender's wife, Deirdre Newstubb
    was a student at Slade School of Fine Art.
15. LET 155.
16. LET, 158.
17. LET, 159–60.
18. LET, 160.
19. A. J. Jones, *The Second Derbyshire Yeomanry: An Account of the Regiment during the World
    War 1939–45* (1949), 17.
20. LET, 162.
21. LET, 163.
22. LET, 165.
23. BL 56355, folio 121.
24. BL 56355, folio 122.
25. Colonel Barnes who had long been medically unfit was replaced in
    Gloucestershire by Major J. B. Browne. According to A. J. Jones, Barnes had
    done 'a grand job of work in raising the Regiment from a puny infant into its
    lusty youth. A fine spirit emanated all ranks, who had completely absorbed the
    Yeomanry traditions and had established a very strong *esprit de corps*' (18). Major-
    General Richard McCreery commanded the 8th Armoured Division.
26. BL 56356, folio 12.
27. LET, 165.

28. LET, 172.
29. LET, 171.
30. LET, 171.
31. LET, 170.
32. LET, 175.
33. Jones, 18. Douglas told Jean Turner that he was going from Wickwar to 'somewhere between Horley and Dorking' (Letters, 179), i.e. Charlwood.
34. Jones, 18.
35. LET, 179–80.
36. LET, 207–8. He told Jean in March 1942 that Diana was being 'a good deal too devoted for my conscience' (Letters, 219). He thought he would marry Diana eventually but hoped that someone would teach her how to dress before he did.
37. BL 56355, folio 124. This letter is postmarked 17 July 1941.
38. LET, 183–4.
39. LET, 185.
40. Although he told his mother that he had had 'a pleasant and interesting voyage out' (BL 56355, folio 128).
41. LET, 185.
42. BL 56355, folio 126.
43. BL 56355, folio 128.
44. BL 56355, folio 126.
45. BL 56355, folio 127.
46. On Douglas's Army Form B199A.
47. BL 56355, folio 127.
48. Mary Benson, *A Far Cry: The Making of a South African* (1990), 23.
49. LET, 190–1. Veganin is a painkiller. The Regiment that Douglas was posted to was the Nottinghamshire Sherwood Rangers Yeomanry. His Army record shows that he was posted on 14 September 1941. He told Brenda Jones that he 'loathed' Cairo (LET, 198).
50. LET, 197.
51. LET, 198.
52. LET, 198–9.
53. BL 56355, folio 129.
54. LET, 202.
55. BL 60585, folio 141.
56. William Scammell, *Keith Douglas: A Study* (1988), 98. We know from his 'Book Diary' at Christ's Hospital that Douglas was familiar with the works of Christina Rossetti (BL 56360, folio 8).
57. Vernon Scannell, *Not Without Glory: Poets of the Second World War* (1976), 39.
58. 'Article Title', *New Review*, August 1974, 73.

CHAPTER 5:
THE DESERT

1. Brian Gardner (ed.), *The Terrible Rain: The War Poets 1939–1945* (1987), 100. On 26 June 1944, two or three weeks after Douglas's death, Jarmain was killed in the village of St Honorine-la-Chardonorette in Normandy by a fragment of mortar shell.
2. Gardner, 98.
3. T. M. Lindsay, *Sherwood Rangers* (1952), 27.
4. LET, 205.
5. Lindsay, 54.
6. James Holland, *Normandy '44: D-Day and the Battle for France* (2019), 60.
7. Lindsay, 27.
8. LET, 206–7. He toned down the risk in his letter to his mother, although he told her that his troops 'looked a bit green' (BL 56355, folio 130). He added that the 'other drivers are nuts, Syrians & Australians, are undoubtedly the world's worst, & *will not* get out of the crown of the road.'
9. Christopherson, 222.
10. Lindsay, 27.
11. Lindsay, 27.
12. BL 56355, folio 131.
13. LET, 217–18.
14. BL 56355, folio 132.
15. BL 56355, folio 133.
16. Graham, 137–8.
17. BL 56355, folio 136.
18. BL 56355, folio 135. The postmark is Staines 28 March 1942.
19. LET, 217.
20. BL 56355, folio 136.
21. BL 56355, folio 131.
22. BL 57977, folio 9.
23. BL 56355, folio 134. He liked the rabbit analogy and used it in a letter of 1 March 1942 to Blunden (LET, 217).
24. See T. G. Otte, *The Foreign Office Mind: The Making of British Foreign Policy 1865–1914* (2011), 328.
25. LET, 223.
26. LET, 225.
27. LET, 226.
28. BL 59833, folios 32–3.
29. 'Oxford poetry and disillusionment: II', *Poetry Review*, Vol. 31, 211.
30. LET, 226–7.
31. BL 56355, folios 174–6.
32. BL 59833, folios 30–1. Douglas was unimpressed by England to the end. He wrote to Blunden a couple of months before he was killed that he was 'not much perturbed at the thought of never seeing England again, because a country which

can allow her army to be used to the last gasp and paid like skivvies isn't worth fighting for. For me, it is simply a case of fighting *against* the Nazi regime. After that, unless there is a revolution in England, I hope to depart for sunnier and less hypocritical climes' (LET, 328).

33. BL 59833, folios 32–3. Milena's father was from Gibraltar and her mother was Italian.

34. LET, 242–3. Douglas wrote to Hamo Sassoon on 11 February 1943 that he 'managed to say Bless you my children & started grinding teeth. (Milena very beautiful.)' Brotherton Collection, Leeds University, BC MS 20c Douglas/1/Box E.

35. BL 56355, folio 138.

36. BL 56355, folio 139.

37. AZZ, 7–8.

38. BL 53773, folio 47.

39. Lindsay, 34–5.

40. Lindsay, 37.

41. AZZ, 14.

42. AZZ, 44.

43. Vernon Scannell, *Not without Glory: Poets of the Second World War* (1976), 30.

44. BL 56355, folio 140.

45. AZZ, 8–9.

46. His welcome back to the regiment is described in AZZ, 12.

47. LET, 251. He described his mood as 'that feeling of almost unstable lightness which is felt immediately after putting down a heavy weight' (AZZ, 15).

48. Christopherson, 273.

49. AZZ, 9.

50. Lindsay, 43.

51. BL 56355, folios 177–8.

52. Lindsay, 51. Douglas described the booby-trapped Chianti to his mother in a letter: 'The Italians strew behind them as they retreat those decorative bottles in straw jackets. I had a narrow escape when I saw 5 bottles full of wine nestling in a basket in an Italian infantry position. Luckily before I could stop the tank, the driver ran over it, and the mine, or whatever was under it, went up in smoke & blew the track off the tank.' BL 56355, folio 142.

53. AZZ, 67–71.

54. Christopherson, 276–7.

55. Christopherson, 278.

56. Christopherson, 281–2.

57. Christopherson, 285.

58. AZZ, 58.

59. Christopherson, 287.

60. AZZ, 58.

61. Lindsay, 52.

62. Lindsay, 52–3.

63. Lindsay, 53.

64. AZZ, 65–6.
65. AZZ, 67–8.
66. Christopherson, 288.
67. Christopherson, 290.
68. Christopherson, 291.
69. Christopherson, 292.
70. Lindsay, 55.
71. Lindsay, 55–6.
72. Lindsay, 58.
73. Lindsay, 58.
74. Lindsay, 59.
75. Christopherson, 298.
76. Lindsay, 59.
77. BL 56355, folio 141.
78. Lindsay, 60.
79. As was Christopherson. See Christopherson, 298–9.
80. BL 57977, folios 10–11. He wrote to Hamo Sassoon on 11 February 1943 that it 'took Div HQ 2 weeks to find out their indispensable cam. king was gone. Were they mad. We fixed them' (Brotherton Collection, Leeds University, BC MS 20c Douglas/1/Box E).
81. Christopherson, 300.
82. Lindsay, 61.
83. Lindsay, 61.
84. Christopherson, 303.
85. Christopherson, 303.
86. LET, 271.
87. BL 56355, folio 144.
88. LET, 260–1.
89. BL 56355, folio 146.
90. BL 56355, folio 147.
91. LET, 266.
92. BL 56355, folio 149.
93. BL 56355, folio 150.
94. BL 56355, folio 150.
95. BL 56355, folio 150.
96. BL 56355, folio 151.
97. BL 56355, folio 179.
98. BL 56355, folios 180–1.
99. Christopherson, 357.
100. BL 56355, folio 153.
101. Lindsay, 90.
102. Lindsay, 92.
103. BL 56355, folio 154.
104. BL 56355, folio 154.

105. BL 56355, folio 155.
106. BL 56355, folio 155.
107. Lindsay, 93.
108. Lindsay, 94.
109. BL 56355, folio 156.
110. LET, 297.
111. LET, 301.
112. LET, 307.
113. Ian Fletcher and John Lucas (ed.), *Poems of G. S. Fraser* (1981), 112. 'The entry of a demon' is a quote from Douglas's poem 'Vergissmeinnicht'.
114. 'Bernard Spencer', *London Magazine*, January 1964, 43.
115. Victor Selwyn, Erik de Mauny, Ian Fletcher, G. S. Fraser and John Waller (eds), *Return to Oasis: War Poems and Recollections from the Middle East 1940–1946* (1980), xxv.
116. Selwyn et al., xxvi.
117. *Poetry (London)*, November–December 1947, 3
118. J. Bolton, *Personal Landscapes: British Poets in Egypt during the Second World War* (1997), 126.
119. 'Bernard Spencer', *London Magazine*, January 1964, 46.
120. PM, 132.
121. Bolton, 127.
122. Bolton, 127.
123. BL 56356, folio 180.
124. CP, 80.
125. BL 53773, folio 65. In this manuscript version the poem is called 'The Lover'.
126. Edna Longley, *Poetry in the Wars* (1986), 109–10.
127. G. S. Fraser, *Keith Douglas, A Poet of the Second World War*, Chatterton Lecture, British Academy 1956, 107.
128. AZZ, vi.
129. William Scammell, *Keith Douglas: A Study* (1988), 178.
130. Bolton, 54–6.
131. Scammell, 179.
132. AZZ, xiv.
133. Scammell, 164.
134. AZZ, vi–vii. This is the poem as published in Tambimuttu's *Alamein to Zem Zem* rather than the version in CP, in which parts 1 and 2 are published as 'Landscape with figures 1' and 'Landscape with figures 2'.
135. Scammell, 142.
136. BL 60585, folio 21.
137. The first stanza is ABAB with no half-rhyme.
138. Scammell, 188–9.
139. Scammell, 189.
140. Lindsay, 96.

CHAPTER 6:
1944

1. T. M. Lindsay, *Sherwood Rangers* (1952), 97.
2. Lindsay, 97.
3. Lindsay, 97–8.
4. Christopherson, 370.
5. Christopherson, 374.
6. LET, 317.
7. *Lilliput*, July 1944, 51–2. This story had previously been published in *Citadel*, Cairo, in July 1942. I have quoted the version in the Brotherton Library Special Collection in Leeds. Douglas wrote to Betty Jesse on 10 March 1944 that *Lilliput* was to pay him six guineas for his description of a horse being dissected: 'that's much too little isn't it?' (BL 59835, folio 5). Betty Jesse was Tambimuttu's assistant as well as Douglas's lover.
8. *Stand*, 11: 2 (1970), 10.
9. BL 56357, folios 93–4.
10. BL 56356, folio 38.
11. BL 60585, folio 15.
12. CP, 143.
13. CP, 48.
14. *Poetry (London)*, November–December 1947, 4.
15. *The Cherwell*, 19 June 1941, 122.
16. William Scammell, *Keith Douglas: A Study* (1988), 101. Scammell makes some excoriating comments on T. S. Eliot's remarks on this poem, finding them 'a little dim'. It's hard to disagree with Scammell on this.
17. *Poetry (London)*, September 1949, 4. I have in mind Yeats's 'In Memory of Eva Gore-Booth and Con Markievicz' and 'To Dorothy Wellesley'.
18. BL 59835, folio 5.
19. BL 60587, folio 27.
20. BL 60587, folios 30–1.
21. BL 59835, folio 3
22. BL 56355, folios 169 and 184.
23. BL 60587, folio 31.
24. BL 60587, folio 36.
25. LET, 343.
26. *Poetry London* 10, December 1944, 5–6.
27. BL 59835, folio 6.
28. BL 59835, folio 9.
29. BL 59835, folio 12.
30. LET, 340.
31. Keith Douglas, *Collected Poems*, edited by John Waller and G. S. Fraser (1951), xx.
32. Lindsay, 98.
33. LET, 340–1.

34. Lindsay, 100.
35. Lindsay, 100.
36. Lindsay, 102.
37. Lindsay, 104–5. Christopherson's encounter with the police horse is told by Christopherson himself in Christopherson, 384.
38. Lindsay, 106.
39. Lindsay, 106.
40. Lindsay, 173.
41. Although *Green Beaches* was not published, Tambimuttu quoted this section of the manuscript in *Poetry London*, 10, 4–5.
42. Brotherton Collection, Leeds University, 20c/1 (a) H.
43. Anthony Rudd, *One Boy's War* (1990), 103.
44. Brotherton Collection, Leeds University, 20c/1 (a) H.
45. Waller and Fraser, xxi.

POSTSCRIPT, POST-MORTEM

1. *The Blue*, November–December 1944, 22–3.
2. Keith Douglas, *Collected Poems*, edited by John Waller and G. S. Fraser (1951), v.
3. A. T. Tolley, *The Poetry of the Forties* (1985), 122. It's not surprising that Tambimuttu's reputation was damaged. He doesn't come out of Julian Maclaren-Ross's memoirs very well – see J. Maclaren-Ross, *Collected Memoirs*, 298–312 and Maclaren-Ross's article in *Punch* magazine, 'The Man from Madagascar', 25 May 1955, 637–9.
4. BL 88907 and BL 88908.
5. Chris Beckett, 'Tambimuttu and the *Poetry London* Papers at the British Library: Reputation and Evidence', *British Library Journal* (article 9, 2009), 1.
6. Beckett, 14.
7. Notably by Wrey Gardiner in 'The Poetry of Keith Douglas', *Poetry* (Autumn 1951).
8. Beckett, 18.
9. Waller and Fraser, 145. Tambimuttu himself recorded in his essay, 'Last lunch with Keith Douglas', that 'I feel quite sure that this statement is correct since as he hovered, tall over my shoulder at the desk, making suggestions for alternative readings, deletion of entire passages, the welding of several poems into one unit … I had taken the unusual precaution of initialling each suggestion Keith made, after making a note of it. There was a sense of hurry and urgency and after a recital of the names of people who had read his poems, Keith said … "You are the only editor I can trust."' (Victor Selwyn, Erik de Mauny, Ian Fletcher, G. S. Fraser and John Waller (eds), *Return to Oasis: War Poems and Recollections from the Middle East 1940–1946* (1980), 204).
10. Beckett, 19.
11. Beckett, 20.

12. Beckett, 20.
13. *Times Literary Supplement*, 19 February 1971, 206. Hamilton remarked on 'the vapid and sublimely self-confident anti-intellectualism' of Tambimuttu's editorial position.
14. *Stand*, 6: 4, 6.
15. Graham published the first full biography of Douglas in 1974, *Keith Douglas Complete Poems* in 1978, *Keith Douglas: A Prose Miscellany* in 1985 and *Keith Douglas: The Letters* in 2000.

ACKNOWLEDGEMENTS

At Edgeborough School I'm grateful for the generous help of Gill Dixon and Dan Thornburn.

At Christ's Hospital Laura Kidner and her colleagues Tom Hopkins, Mike Barford, Ken Mansell and Clifford Jones were very helpful. I am grateful for permission to use extracts from Marie Douglas's correspondence with the school, for permission to reproduce some of Keith Douglas's linocuts from *The Outlook* and *The Blue*, and to quote from the magazine.

The British Library for reproducing a manuscript of 'Simplify me when I'm dead' for use in the endpapers of this book.

The Brotherton Collection at the University of Leeds for reproducing the photographs used in this book (including the cover image).

Carcanet Press for permission to quote from *Keith Douglas: The Letters* and *Keith Douglas: A Prose Miscellany*.

Oxford University Press for permission to quote from Desmond Graham's *Keith Douglas 1920–1944*.

Faber & Faber for permission to quote from *Keith Douglas Complete Poems* (edited by Desmond Graham).

I am grateful too for the generous help of David Christopherson and James Holland.

INDEX

Note: Numbers in brackets after a page number refer to the note on that page.

Remember me when

and simply for me

So as the processes
Strip off the colour
removing ~~the~~ brown

leave~~ssss~~ me more no
When harvest & came
~~First~~ ~~little~~
— ~~they~~ the moon